The Elementary Math Teacher's BOOK OF LISTS

With Ready-to-Use Patterns and Worksheets

Sonia M. Helton • Stephen J. Micklo

THE CENTER FOR APPLIED
RESEARCH IN EDUCATION
West Nyack, New York 10995

Library of Congress Cataloging-in-Publication Data

Helton, Sonia M.,
    The elementary math teacher's book of lists : with ready-to-use
patterns and worksheets / Sonia M. Helton, Stephen J. Micklo.
      p. cm.
    Includes bibliographical references.
    ISBN 0-87628-289-3 (spiral).— ISBN 0-87628-131-5 (pbk.)
    1. Mathematics—Study and teaching (Elementary)   I. Micklo,
Stephen J.   II. Title.
QA135.5.H438   1997
372.7'044—dc21   96-40268
                                       CIP

Curriculum Standards for Grades K-4 and 5-8, and Changes in Content and Emphasis for Grades K-4 and 5-8 is used with permission from National Council of Teachers of Mathematics (Lists 1, 2, and 3).

Printed in the United States of America

10 9 8 7 6 5 4

ISBN 0-87628-289-3 (spiral)   ISBN 0-87628-131-5 (pbk.)

Clip art courtesy of Dover Clip Art Series and Dover Pictorial Archive Series, Dover Publications, Inc., Mineola, New York.

ATTENTION: CORPORATIONS AND SCHOOLS

Prentice Hall books are available at quantity discounts with bulk purchase for educational, business, or sales promotional use. For information, please write to: Prentice Hall Career & Personal Development Special Sales, 240 Frisch Court, Paramus, NJ 07652. Please supply: title of book, ISBN number, quantity, how the book will be used, date needed.

**THE CENTER FOR APPLIED RESEARCH
IN EDUCATION**
West Nyack, NY 10994
A Simon & Schuster Company

On the World Wide Web at http://www.phdirect.com

Prentice Hall International (UK) Limited, *London*
Prentice Hall of Australia Pty. Limited, *Sydney*
Prentice Hall Canada, Inc., *Toronto*
Prentice Hall Hispanoamericana, S.A., *Mexico*
Prentice Hall of India Private Limited, *New Delhi*
Prentice Hall of Japan, Inc., *Tokyo*
Simon & Schuster Asia Pte. Ltd., *Singapore*
Editora Prentice Hall do Brasil, Ltda., *Rio de Janeiro*

About the Authors

Sonia M. Helton, Ph.D., is professor of Childhood Education at the University of South Florida at St. Petersburg. She currently teaches methods courses in language arts and elementary mathematics and did her doctoral work at the University of Minnesota on the use of the visual arts and the natural creative ability of teachers and children to enhance the mathematics curriculum.

In addition to writing articles for many professional journals in elementary mathematics and language arts, Dr. Helton is the co-author of units in the MINNEMAST project (University of Minnesota, 1964–1970). She is the author of *Ready-to-Use Math Activities for Primary Children* (C.A.R.E., 1993), *Math Activities for Every Month of the School Year* (C.A.R.E., 1990), *Classroom Bulletin Board Activities Kit* (Prentice Hall, 1987), *Creative Math/Art Activities for the Primary Grades* (Prentice Hall, 1984), and co-author of the *E-Z Microcomputer Handbook for Elementary and Middle School Teachers* (Prentice Hall, 1986). She is the senior author for the 1988 Harcourt Brace Elementary Mathematics Curriculum series.

Stephen J. Micklo, Ph.D., is a professor of Childhood Education at the University of South Florida, St. Petersburg. He currently teaches early childhood courses and elementary mathematics methods courses, and did his doctoral work at The Florida State University.

Dr. Micklo has taught young children from prekindergarten through the primary grades and was an elementary school principal. He has written several articles dealing with mathematics for young children for leading professional journals. This is his first book which he was pleased to co-author with Sonia Helton.

How to Use This Book

The Elementary Math Teacher's Book of Lists is designed to help any elementary teacher find the resources needed to implement a sound and professional mathematics program in the classroom. The book is organized into 14 sections with each focusing on a mathematical topic or reference. The lists within each section are assembled for easy reading and reference.

Each section-opening page is followed by a reproducible worksheet which is related to the content of the chapter. Students can work on these activities individually, in small groups, or as an entire class.

Many of the lists include suggested activities, activities books, and manipulatives useful in the classroom. Addresses of resources are supplied for quick reference. Algorithms, which are normally taught in the elementary grades, are also included for a quick teacher reference.

A unique feature of this particular book of lists includes information on pre-algebra activities and technology. Section 11 presents basic information on pre-algebra concepts you will find useful in developing activities for children in grades 3 and up. The information on vectors was developed by Zoltan Dienes and the Minnesota Mathematics and Science Teaching staff (MINNEMAST). These ideas have been modified in this book.

In Section 13 there are lists for using the World Wide Web. Since the field is expanding and constantly changing, the starter lists provided here can be added to as you seek out new information on the World Wide Web or other sources.

The last section includes over 75 patterns normally used in the elementary classroom. Many of the patterns can be used as worksheets, or record sheets for use during cooperative group work, or for individual recording.

We hope you will add to these lists and welcome any suggestions for enhancing future lists.

Sonia M. Helton
Stephen J. Micklo

Acknowledgments

The authors wish to thank the people from the University of South Florida, St. Petersburg Campus who helped assemble the lists and contribute to the book. The authors are grateful for their willingness to share their ideas and contributions.

- *Dr. Denisse Thompson,* Assistant Professor of Mathematics Education, for contributing a list of literature books from her personal library used to teach elementary mathematics methods and algebra for the child.
- *Dr. James Fellows,* Professor of Accounting, College of Business Administration, who helped make accounting easier for elementary teachers by writing the lists on taxes, profit, and interest.
- *Ms. Donna Dicus,* Instructor of Computer Education, who shared her information on technology by designing and assembling the lists in Chapter 13: Technology.
- *Ms. Renee Hoffman,* secretary, whose agile fingers typed much of the manuscript and whose cheerful encouragement kept the authors producing content, when class schedules and advisees were demanding their time.
- *Ms. Jennifer Withrow,* student assistant, who spent many hours classifying resources and activity books.
- *Ms. Elizabeth Hanahan,* student assistant, who spent many hours at the copying machine.
- *Mr. Wayne P. Helton,* whose support was dauntless.

The authors also wish to thank Dr. Winifred Mallam of Texas Woman's University (Denton, TX) for her careful and insightful review of the manuscript for this book.

Contents

Section 1

STANDARDS AND METHODOLOGIES

Name _____

Reproduce the figure on the three nonstandard grids.

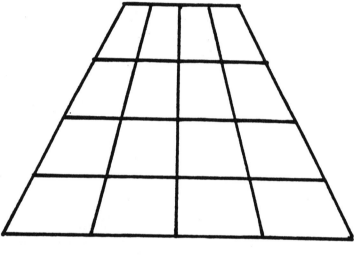
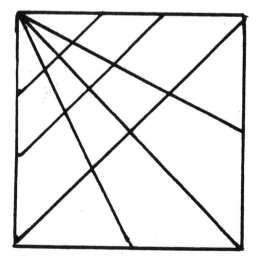
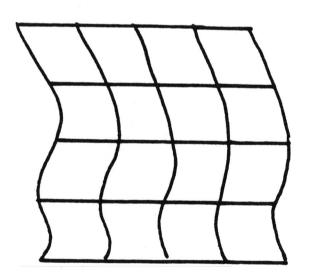

1: National Council of Teachers of Mathematics

Address:

National Council of Teachers of Mathematics, Inc.
1906 Association Drive
Reston, Virginia 22091
Phone: (703) 620-9840
Fax: (703) 476-2970
Internet: nctm@nctm.org

Standards' Publications

Curriculum and Evaluation Standards for School Mathematics
National Council of Teachers of Mathematics
Reston, VA: 1989.
ISBN: 0-87353-273-2

Professional Standards for Teaching Mathematics
National Council of Teachers of Mathematics
Reston, VA: 1991.
ISBN: 0-87353-307-0

Assessment Standards for School Mathematics
National Council of Teachers of Mathematics
Reston, VA: 1995.

Goals for Functioning in Today's Society

1. Mathematically literate workers:

   Expectations:

   - The ability to set up problems with the appropriate operations.
   - Knowledge of a variety of techniques to approach and work on problems.
   - The ability to work with others on problems.
   - The ability to see the applicability of mathematical ideas to common and complex problems.
   - Preparation for open problem situations, since most real problems are not well formulated.
   - Belief in the utility and value of mathematics.

2. Lifelong learning
3. Opportunity for all

3

(continued)

4. Informed electorate

Goals for Students:

1. Learning to value mathematics.
2. Becoming confident in one's own ability.
3. Becoming a mathematical problem solver.
4. Learning to communicate mathematically.
5. Learning to reason mathematically.

2: NCTM Curriculum Standards for Grades K-4

Assumptions for Shaping K-4 Standards:

The K-4 curriculum should:

1. be conceptually oriented.
2. actively involve children doing mathematics.
3. emphasize the development of children's mathematical thinking and reasoning abilities.
4. emphasize the application of mathematics.
5. include a broad range of content.
6. make appropriate and ongoing use of calculators and computers.

Standard 1: Mathematics as Problem Solving

- Use problem-solving approaches to investigate and understand mathematical content.
- Formulate problems from everyday and mathematical situations.
- Develop and apply strategies to solve a wide variety of problems.
- Verify and interpret results with respect to the original problem.
- Acquire confidence in using mathematics meaningfully.

Standard 2: Mathematics as Communication

- Relate physical materials, pictures, and diagrams to mathematical ideas.
- Reflect on and clarify their thinking about mathematical ideas and situations.
- Relate their everyday language to mathematical language and symbols.
- Realize that representing, discussing, reading, writing, and listening to mathematics are a vital part of learning and using mathematics.

Standard 3: Mathematics as Reasoning

- Draw logical conclusions about mathematics.
- Use models, known facts, properties, and relationships to explaining their thinking.
- Justify their answers and solution processes.
- Use patterns and relationships to analyze mathematical situations.
- Believe that mathematics makes sense.

Standard 4: Mathematical Connections

- Link conceptual and procedural knowledge.
- Relate various representations of concepts or procedures to one another.

(continued)

- Recognize relationships among different topics in mathematics.
- Use mathematics in other curriculum areas.
- Use mathematics in their daily lives.

Standard 5: Estimation

- Explore estimation strategies.
- Recognize when an estimate is appropriate.
- Determine the reasonableness of results.
- Apply estimation in working with quantities, measurement, computation, and problem solving.

Standard 6: Number Sense and Numeration

- Construct number meanings through real-world experiences and the use of physical materials.
- Understand our numeration system by relating counting, grouping, and place-value concepts.
- Develop number sense.
- Iinterpret the multiple uses of numbers encountered in the real world.

Standard 7: Concepts of Whole Number Operations

- Develop meaning for the operations by modeling and discussing a rich variety of problem situations.
- Relate the mathematical language and symbolism of operations to problem situations and informal language.
- Recognize that a wide variety of problem structures can be represented by a single operation.
- Develop operation sense.

Standard 8: Whole Number Computation

- Model, explain, and develop reasonable proficiency with basic facts and algorithms.
- Use a variety of mental computation and estimation techniques.
- Use calculators in appropriate computational situations.
- Select and use computation techniques appropriate to specific problems and determine whether the results are reasonable.

Standard 9: Geometry and Spatial Sense

- Describe, model, draw, and classify shapes.

(continued)

- Investigate and predict the results of combining, subdividing, and changing shapes.
- Develop spatial sense.
- Relate geometric ideas to number and measurement ideas.
- Recognize and appreciate geometry in their world.

Standard 10: Measurement

- Understand the attributes of length, capacity, weight, area, volume, time, temperature, and angles.
- Develop the process of measuring and concepts related to units of measurement.
- Make and use estimates of measurement.
- Make and use measurements in problem and everyday situations.

Standard 11: Statistics and Probability

- Collect, organize, and describe data.
- Construct, read, and interpret displays of data.
- Formulate and solve problems that involve collecting and analyzing data.
- Explore concepts of chance.

Standard 12: Fractions and Decimals

- Develop concepts of fractions, mixed numbers, and decimals.
- Develop number sense for fractions and decimals.
- Use models to relate fractions to decimals and to find equivalent fractions.
- Use models to explore operations on fractions and decimals.
- Apply fractions and decimals to problem situations.

Standard 13. Patterns and Relationships

- Recognize, describe, extend, and create a wide variety of patterns.
- Represent and describe mathematical relationships.
- Explore the use of variables and open sentences to express relationships.

(continued)

Summary of Changes in Content and Emphasis in K-4 Mathematics

INCREASED ATTENTION   DECREASED ATTENTION

Number

Number sense
Place-value concepts
Meaning of fractions and decimals
Estimation of quantities

Early attention to reading,
  writing, and ordering
  numbers symbolically

Operations and Computation

Meaning of operations
Operation sense
Mental computation
Estimation and the
  reasonableness of answers
Selection of an appropriate
  computational method
Use of calculators for computation
Thinking strategies for basic facts

Complex paper-and-
  pencil computations
Isolated treatment of paper-and-
  pencil computations
Addition and subtraction
  without renaming
Isolated treatment of division
  facts
Long division
Long division without remainders
Paper-and-pencil fraction computation
Use of rounding to estimate

Geometry and Measurement

Properties of geometric figures
Geometric relationships
Spatial sense
Process of measuring
Concepts related to
  units of measurement
Actual measuring
Estimation of measurements
Use of measurement and geometry
  ideas throughout the curriculum

Primary focus on naming
  geometric figures
Memorization of equivalencies
  between units of
  measurement

Probability and Statistics

Collection and organization of data
Exploration of chance

Patterns and Relationships

Word problems with a variety of structures
Use of everyday problems
Applications
Study of patterns and relationships

(continued)

Problem-solving strategies

Problem Solving

Word problems with a variety
  of structures
Use of everyday problems
Applications
Study of patterns and relationships
Problem-solving strategies

Use of clue words to
  determine which
  operation to use

Instructional Practices

Use of manipulative materials
Cooperative work
Discussion of mathematics
Questioning
Justification of thinking
Writing about mathematics
Problem-solving approach
  to instruction
Content integration
Use of calculators and
  computers

Rote practice
Rote memorization of
  rules
One answer and one
  method
Use of worksheets
Written practice
Teaching by telling

3: NCTM Curriculum Standards for Grades 5-8

Standard 1: Mathematics as Problem Solving

- Use problem-solving approaches to investigate and understand mathematical content.
- Formulate problems from situations within and outside mathematics.
- Develop and apply a variety of strategies to solve problems, with emphasis on multi-step and nonroutine problems.
- Verify and interpret results with respect to the original problem situation.
- Generalize solutions and strategies to new problem situations.
- Acquire confidence in using mathematics meaningfully.

Standard 2: Mathematics as Communication

- Model situations using oral, written, concrete, pictorial, graphical, and algebraic methods.
- Reflect on and clarify their own thinking about mathematical ideas and situations.
- Develop common understanding of mathematical ideas, including the role of definitions.
- Use the skills of reading, listening, and viewing to interpret and evaluate mathematical ideas.
- Discuss mathematical ideas and make conjectures and convincing arguments.
- Appreciate the value of mathematical notation and its role in the development of mathematical ideas.

Standard 3: Mathematics as Reasoning

- Recognize and apply deductive and inductive reasoning.
- Understand and apply reasoning processes, with special attention to spatial reasoning and reasoning with proportions and graphs.
- Make and evaluate mathematical conjectures and arguments to validate their own thinking.
- Appreciate the pervasive use and power of reasoning as part of mathematics.

Standard 4: Mathematical Connections

- See mathematics as an integrated whole.
- Explore problems and describe results using graphical, numerical, physical, algebraic, and verbal mathematical models or representations.
- Use a mathematical idea to further their understanding of other mathematical ideas.
- Apply mathematical thinking and modeling to solve problems that arise in other disciplines, such as art, music, psychology, science, and business.

(continued)

- Value the role of mathematics in our culture and society.

Standard 5: Number and Number Relationships

- Understand, represent, and use numbers in a variety of equivalent forms (integer, fraction, decimal, percent, exponential, and scientific notation) in real-world and mathematical problem situations.
- Develop number sense for whole numbers, fractions, decimals, integers, and rational numbers.
- Understand and apply rations, proportions, and percents in a wide variety of situations.
- Investigate relationships among fractions, decimals, and percents.
- Represent numerical relationships in one- and two-dimensional graphs.

Standard 6: Number Systems and Number Theory

- Understand and appreciate the need for numbers beyond the whole numbers.
- Develop and use order relations for whole numbers, fractions, decimals, integers, and rational numbers.
- Extend their understanding of whole number operations to fractions, decimals, integers, and rational numbers.
- Understand how the basic arithmetic operations are related to one another.
- Develop and apply number theory concepts (e.g., primes, factors, and multiples) in real-world and mathematical problem situations.

Standard 7: Computation and Estimation

- Compute with whole numbers, fractions, decimals, integers, and rational numbers.
- Develop, analyze, and explain procedures for computation and techniques for estimation.
- Develop, analyze, and explain methods for solving proportions.
- Select and use an appropriate method for computing from among mental arithmetic, paper-and-pencil, calculator, and computer.
- Use computation, estimation, and proportions to solve problems
- Use estimation to check the reasonableness of results.

Standard 8: Patterns and Functions

- Describe, extend, analyze, and create a wide variety of patterns.
- Describe and represent relationships with tables, graphs, and rules.
- Analyze functional relationships to explain how a change in one quantity results in a change in another.

(continued)

- Use patterns and functions to represent and solve problems.

Standard 9: Algebra

- Understand the concepts of variable, expression, and equations.
- Represent situations and number patterns with tables, graphs, verbal rules, and equations, and explore the interrelationships of these representations.
- Analyze tables and graphs to identify properties and relationships.
- Develop confidence in solving linear equations using concrete, informal, and formal methods.
- Investigate inequalities and nonlinear equations informally.
- Apply algebraic methods to solve a variety of real-world and mathematical problems.

Standard 10: Statistics

- Systematically collect, organize, and describe data.
- Construct, read, and interpret tables, charts, and graphs.
- Make inferences and convincing arguments that are based on data analysis.
- Evaluate arguments that are based on data analysis.
- Develop an appreciation for statistical methods as powerful means for decision making.

Standard 11: Probability

- Model situations by devising and carrying out experiments or simulations to determine probabilities.
- Model situations by constructing a sample space to determine probabilities.
- Appreciate the power of using a probability model by comparing experimental results with mathematical expectations.
- Make predictions that are based on experimental or theoretical probabilities.
- Develop an appreciation for the pervasive use of probability in the real world.

Standard 12: Geometry

- Identify, describe, compare, and classify geometric figures.
- Visualize and represent geometric figures with special attention to developing spatial sense.
- Explore transformations of geometric figures.
- Represent and solve problems using geometric models.
- Understand and apply geometric properties and relationships.

(continued)

- Develop an appreciation of geometry as a means of describing the physical world.

Standard 13: Measurement

- Extend their understanding of the process of measurements.
- Estimate, make, and use measurements to describe and compare phenomena.
- Select appropriate units and tools to measure to the degree of accuracy required in a particular situation.
- Understand the structure and use of systems of measurements.
- Extend their understanding of the concepts of perimeter, area, volume, angle measure, capacity, and weight and mass.
- Develop the concepts of rates and other derived and indirect measurements.
- Develop formulas and procedures for determining measures to solve problems.

Summary of Changes in Content and Emphasis in 5-8 Mathematics

Increase Attention	*Decrease Attention*
Problem Solving	
Pursuing open-ended problems and extend problem-solving projects	Practicing routine one-step problems
Investigating and formulating questions from problem situations	Practicing problems categorized by types (e.g., coin problems, age problems)
Representing situations verbally, numerically, graphically, geometrically, or symbolically	
Communication	
Discussing writing, reading, and listening to mathematical ideas	Doing fill-in-the-blank worksheets Answering questions that require only yes, no, or a number as responses
Reasoning	
Reasoning in spatial contexts Reasoning with proportions Reasoning from graphs Reasoning inductively and deductively	Relying on outside authority (teacher as answer key)

(continued)

Connections

Connecting mathematics to other subjects and to the world outside	Learning isolated topics
	Developing skills out of context
Connecting topics within mathematics	
Applying mathematics	

Number/Operations/Computation

Developing number sense	Memorizing rules and algorithms
Developing operation sense	
Creating algorithms and procedures	Practicing tedious paper-and-pencil computations
Using estimation both in solving problems and in checking the reasonableness of results	
Exploring relationships among representations of, and operations on whole numbers, fractions, decimals, integers, and rational numbers	Memorizing procedures, such as cross-multiplication, without understanding
Developing an understanding of ratio, proportion, and percent	Practicing rounding numbers out of context

Patterns and Functions

Identifying and using functional relationships	Topics seldom in the current curriculum
Developing and using tables, graphs, and rules to describe situations	
Interpreting among different mathematical representations	

Algebra

Developing an understanding of variables, expressions, and equations	Manipulating symbols
Using a variety of methods to solve linear equations and informally investigate inequalities and nonlinear equations	Memorizing procedures and drilling on equation solving

Statistics

Using statistical methods to describe, analyze, evaluate, and make decisions	Memorizing formulas

(continued)

Probability

| Creating experimental and theoretical models of situations involving probabilities | Memorizing formulas |

Geometry

Developing an understanding of geometric objects and relationships
Using geometry in solving problems

Memorizing geometric vocabulary
Memorizing facts and relationships

Measurement

Estimating and using measurement to solve problems

Memorizing and manipulating formulas
Converting within and between measurement systems

Instructional Practices

Actively involving students individually and in groups in exploring, conjecturing, analyzing, and applying mathematics in both a mathematical and real-world context
Using appropriate technology for computation and exploration
Using concrete materials
Being a facilitator of learning
Assessing learning as an integral part of instruction

Teaching computations out of context
Drilling on paper-and-pencil algorithms
Stressing memorization
Being the dispenser of knowledge
Testing for the sole purpose of assigning grades

4: Publishers of Instructional Materials in Elementary Mathematics

Publisher	*Curriculum Series*
Addison-Wesley Publishing Co. Inc. 2725 Sand Hill, Suite A201 Menlo Park, CA 94025 (800) 227-1936	Addison-Wesley Mathematics K-8, 1991 edition Addison-Wesley Mathematics K-6 1985 edition
American School Publishers/SRA 11 West 19th Street, 2nd Floor New York, NY 10010 (212) 337-5107	*Scoring High in Math 2-8,* 1986 edition *Scoring High in Math 2-8,* 3rd edition
D. C. Heath and Company 125 Spring Street Lexington, MA 02173 (617) 862-6650	*Heath Mathematics Connections,* 1992 edition
Everyday Learning Corporation 1007 Church Street, Suite 306 Evanston, IL 60201 (708) 866-0702	*UCSMP Everyday Mathematics* 1990-1992 edition
Glencoe/SRA 936 Eastwind Drive Westerville, OH 43081 (800) 848-1567	*The Spectrum of Mathematics* *Series K-8,* 1990 edition
Harcourt Brace 6277 Sea Harbor Drive Orlando, FL 32887 (407) 345-2000	*Mathematics Plus K-8,* 1992 edition *Mathematics Today K-8,* 1985 edition
Houghton Mifflin Company 7055 Amwiler Industrial Drive Atlanta, GA 30360 (404) 449-5881	*Mathworks K-2,* 1992 edition *The Mathematics Experience K-8,* 1992 edition
Macmillan/Mcgraw-Hill School Division 6510 Jimmy Carter Boulevard Norcross, GA 30071 (800) 453-2665	*Mathematics in Action Activity* *Program—I Can K-2,* 1992 edition *Mathematics in Action K-8,* 1992 edition

©1997 by The Center for Applied Research in Education

(continued)

Mimosa Publications
28 Crestwood Drive
Trophy Club, TX 76262
(800) 443-7389

Moving into Math K-2, 1990 edition

Open Court Publishing Company
315 Fifth Street
Peru, IL 61345
(800) 435-6850

Real Math K-8

Saxon Publishing, Inc.
1320 W. Lindsey
Norman, OK 73069
(800) 284-7019

Saxon Math K-8

Scott Foresman and Company
1900 East Lake Avenue
Chicago, IL 60025
(708) 729-3000

Great Beginnings K-2, 1992 edition
Exploring Mathematics 3-8, 1991 edition
Invitation to Mathematics K-8, 1985 edition

Silver Burdett & Ginn, Inc.
250 James Street
Morristown, NJ 07960
(201) 285-7714

Silver Burdett & Ginn Mathematics:
 Exploring Your World K-8,
 1992 edition

Steck-Vaughn
P.O. Box 26015
3520 Executive Center Drive
Austin, TX 78731
(512) 343-8227

Working with Numbers Series,
 1990 edition

5: Vendors for Math Resource Materials

Request Catalogs

ABC School Supply
3312 N. Berkeley Lake Road
P.O. Box 100019
Duluth, GA 30136-9419
1-800-669-4222

ACCU/CUT
P.O. Box 1053
1035 E. Dodge
Freemon, NE 68025
1-800-288-1670

Activity Resources Company, Inc.
P.O. Box 4875
Hayward, CA 94541
1-510-782-1300
Grades K-12

AIT
Agency for Instructional Technology
Box A
Bloomington, IN 47402-0120
1-800-457-4509, ext. 207

AIMS Education Foundation
P.O. Box 8120
Fresno, CA 93747-8120
1-209-255-4094
Grades K-9

Association for Supervision & Curriculum
Development (ASCD)
1250 North Pitt Street
Alexandria, VA 22314
1-703-549-9110
Grakes K-College

Carson-Dellosa Publishing Co., Inc.
Dept. NEW 96
P.O. Box 35665
Greensboro, NC 27425-5665
1-800-321-0943

Center for Innovation in Education
20665 4th Street

Saratoga, CA 95070-5878
1-800-395-6088

Children's Television Workshop
One Lincoln Plaza
New York, NY 10023-7129
1-212-875-6630

Classic School Products
174 Semoran Commerce Place, A106
Apopka, FL 32703
1-800-394-9661

Color Fields
923 N. Street
Fortuna, CA 95540
1-707-725-0586 or 1-888-283-5555

Continental Press
520 E. Bainbridge Street
Elizabethtown, PA 17022
1-800-233-0759
Grades PK-12

Creative Publications Order Department
5623 W. 115th Street
Worth, IL 60485-9931
1-800-642-0822

Creative Teaching Press
10701 Holder Street
Cypress, CA 90630
1-800-229-9929
Grades K-3

Creative Teaching Supplies
923 Lomas Santa Fe Drive
Solana Beach, CA 92075
1-800-750-6871
Grades K-3

Cuisenaire Company of America, Inc.
P.O. Box 5026
White Plains, NY 10602-5026
1-800-237-0338

©1997 by The Center for Applied Research in Education

(continued)

Curriculum Associates, Inc.
P.O. Box 2001
N. Billerica, MA 01862-0901
1-800-225-0248

Dale Seymour Publications
P.O. Box 10888
Palo Alto, CA 94303
1-800-872-1100

D. C. Heath & Company
2700 N. Richard Avenue
P.O. Box 19309
Indianapolis, IN 46219
1-800-334-3284
Grades K-8

D & K Studios
4807 Fobes Road
Everett, WA 98205
1-206-334-6322

Delta Education
P.O. Box 3000
Nashua, NH 03061-3000
1-800-442-5444
Grades K-8

Didax Education Resources
395 Main Street
Rowley, MA 01969-3785
1-800-458-0024

DLM Teaching Resources
One DLM Park
Allen, TX 75002
1-800-527-5030

Education Week
P.O. Box 2083
Marion, OH 43305

Educational Enrichment, Inc.
P.O. Box 1524
Norman, OK 73070
1-800-292-6022
Grades 3-5

Educational Resources
(Educational Software & Technology)
1550 Executive Drive
P.O. Box 1900
Elgin, IL 60121-1900
1-800-624-2926

Educators Outlet
P.O. Box 397
Timnath, CO 80547
1-800-315-2212
Grades K-9

EduStic
3366 Baltimore Street
San Diego, CA 92117
1-800-338-7842

EEI Everything Escher, Inc.
Rock J. Walker
13223 Black Mountain Road
San Diego, CA 92129
1-619-673-9942

ETA
620 Lakeview Parkway
Vernon Hills, IL 60061
1-800-445-5985
Grades K-12

Evan-Moor
18 Lower Ragsdale Drive
Monterey, CA 93940-5746
1-800-777-4362
Grades PreK-6 and Grades 4-8

Everyday Learning Corporation
P.O. Box 812960
Chicago, IL 60681
1-800-382-7670
Grades K-6

Extra Editions
P.O. Box 870
Rantoul, IL 61866-0870
1-800-423-9872
Grades K-6

(continued)

Gifts for Educators
Daryl J. Chausse
Angela Chausse
P.O. Box 2928
Costa Mesa, CA 92628
1-800-60-EDUCATOR or 1-714-646-8717

Good Apple
4350 Equity Drive
P.O. Box 2649
Columbus, OH 43216
1-800-321-3106
Grades PreK-12

Great Source
2700 North Richardt Avenue
P.O. Box 19309
Indianapolis, IN 46219
1-800-334-3284
Grades 1-8

Great Source
95 Hayden Avenue
Lexington, MA 02173
1-617-860-1777
Grades K-12

Hands-On Equations
Borenson & Associates
P.O. Box 3328
Allentown, PA 18106
1-800-993-6284

Houghton Mifflin
13400 Midway Road
Dallas, TX 75244-5165
1-800-733-2828
Grades K-8

Ideal
1-800-845-8149
Grades K-9

J & J's Bookworm
79 Larkhill
Thousand Oaks, CA 91360
1-805-492-4152

Judy/Instructo
4350 Equity Drive
P.O. Box 2649
Columbus, OH 43216
1-800-321-3106

J. Weston Walch, Publisher
321 Valley Street
P.O. Box 658
Portland, MA 04104-0658
1-800-341-6094
Grades 5-12

Kaidy Educational Resources
1323 Columbia Drive #307
Richardson, TX 75081
1-800-365-2439

Keith Distributors, Inc.
Books & Accessories
1055 S. Ballenger Highway
Flint, MI 48532
1-800-373-2366

Key Curriculum Press
2512 Martin Luther King Jr. Way
P.O. Box 2304
Berkeley, CA 94702-0304
1-800-995-MATH
Grades 6-12

Key Publishers, Inc.
6 Sunwood Lane
Sandy, UT 84092
1-800-585-6059
Grades 1-6

Kiwi Kids
451 Communipaw Avenue
Jersey City, NJ 07304
1-800-382-8645

K'Nex Education Division
P.O. Box 700
Hatfield, PA 19440
1-888-ABC-KNEX
Grades K-12

(continued)

Lakeshore Learning Materials
2695 E. Dominquez Street
P.O. Box 6261
Carson, CA 90749
1-800-421-5354
Grades K-3

Learning Materials Workshop
274 North Winooski Avenue
Burlington, VT 05401
1-800-693-7164

Learning Wrap-Ups, Inc.
2122 East 6550 South
Ogden, UT 84405
1-800-992-4966

The Markerboard People
Names Unlimited
2300 Spikes Lane
Lansing, MI 48906
1-800-828-3375

The Math Learning Center
University Center Building
P.O. Box 9278
Portland, OR 97207-9278
1-800-547-8887, ext. 3041

Math Technology
P.O. Box 803274
Houston, TX 77280
1-800-456-8666

Mckel—CSMP
2550 South Parker Road, Suite 500
Aurora, CO 80014
1-303-337-0990
Grades K-6

Mimosa Publications
P.O. Box 26609
San Francisco, CA 94126
1-800-646-6721

MindWare ®
2720 Patton Road

Roseville, MN 55113
1-800-999-0398

MLC Materials
P.O. Box 3226
Salem, OR 97302
1-503-370-8130

Modern Curriculum Press
4350 Equity Drive
P.O. Box 2649
Columbus, OH 43216

National Council of Teachers of
Mathematics
P.O. Box 25405
Richmond, VA 23260-5405

NASCO
901 Janesville Avenue
Fort Atkinson, WI 53538-0901
1-800-558-9595

Nichols Schwartz Publishing
P.O. Box 254
Honesdale, PA 18431-0254
1-800-732-4334

Open Court Publishing Co.
315 Fifth Street
Peru, IL 61354-0599
1-800-435-6850
Grades 2-6

Rema-Bound Books
Vandalia Road
Jacksonville, IL 62650
1-800-637-6581
Grades K-8

Polydron USA, Inc.
2750 S. Harbor Boulevard, Suite C
Santa Ana, CA 92704
1-800-452-9978

Scholastic, Inc.
2931 E. McCarty Street

(continued)

Jefferson City, MO 65101
1-800-724-6527
Grades K-8

Scott Foresman
1900 East Lake Avenue
Glenview, IL 60025
1-800-554-4411
Grades K-8

Silver Burdett & Ginn
4350 Equity Drive
P.O. Box 2649
Columbus, OH 43216
1-800-848-9500
Grades K-8

A Small Woodworking Co.
Jim & Kathy Blodgett
P.O. Box 460
34207 82nd Avenue South
Roy, WA 98580
1-360-458-3370

SRA/McGraw-Hill
220 East Danieldale Road
DeSota, TX 75115-2490
1-800-843-8855

Stamping Till Dawn
8572 Boone Circle
Westminister, CA 92683
1-714-898-9887

Steck-Vaughn Company
P.O. Box 26015
Austin, TX 78755
1-800-531-5015
Grades K-12

Summit Learning
P.O. Box 493
Ft. Collins, CO 80522
1-800-777-8817
Grades K-9

Teacher Created Materials
Westminster, CA 92683
Grades PreK-8

Teacher Magazine
Editorial Projects in Education, Inc.
4301 Connecticut Ave., N.W., Suite 250
Washington, D.C. 20008
1-202-364-4114

Teaching Resource Center
P.O. Box 1509
San Leandro, CA 94577
1-800-833-3389
Grades K-6

Tessellations
2123 S. Priest, Suite 213
Tempe, AZ 85282
1-800-655-5341

Texas Instruments
P.O. Box 6118
Temple, TX 76503-6118
1-800-TI-CARES
Grades K-8

Tricon Publishing
2150 Enterprise Drive
Mt. Pleasant, MI 48858
1-517-772-2811

Ventura Educational Systems
910 Ramona Avenue, Suite E P.O.
Box 425
Grover Beach, CA 93433
1-800-336-1022
Grades K-8

The White Rabbit
Children's Books
7755 Girard Avenue
La Jolla, CA 92037
1-800-920-9000

(continued)

World Teachers Press
395 Main Street
Rowley, MA 01969
1-800-458-0024
Grades K-8

Zometool Marketing
1675 Broadway, Suite 1800
Denver, CO 80202
1-303-534-4756

6: Publishers of Teacher Activity Books and Materials

Addison Wesley Publishing Company
2725 Sand Hill Road
Menlo Park, CA 94025
1-415-854-0300

Allyn & Bacon
Dept. 894
160 Gould Street
Needham Heights, MA 02194-2310
1-800-852-8024

The Center for Applied Research in
  Education
A Division of Simon & Schuster
West Nyack, NY 10995

Delmar Publishers
3 Columbia Circle, Box 15015
Albany, NY 12212
1-800-347-7707
email: info@delmar.com

Harcourt Brace Publishing
6277 Sea Harbor Drive
Orlando, FL 32887

HarperCollins Publishers Inc.
10 East 53rd Street
New York, NY 10022

Heinemann Publishing
3601 Hanover Street
Portsmouth, NH 03801-3912
1-800-541-2086

Longman
10 Bank Street
White Plains, NY 10606

RIGBY
P.O. Box 797
Crystal Lake, IL 60014
1-800-822-8661

Scholastic Book Services
730 Broadway
New York, NY 10003

The Wright Group
1920-120th Ave. N.E.
Bothell, WA 98011
1-800-523-2371

7: Holistic Teaching Methods in Elementary Mathematics

Constructivist's Approach to Teaching Elementary Mathematics

Principle: All knowledge is constructed by the learner; therefore, learning is an intensely personal affair.

We construct knowledge in different, yet similar ways by utilizing our:

past experiences,

existing knowledge structures,

learning styles,

and motivations.

Therefore, constructivism suggests that

1. Direct instruction and large group instruction is inappropriate.
2. Children should engage in topic conversations in the classroom by forming cooperative learning groups that bring out the cognitive knowledge in each individual student.
3. Teacher does not teach as normally defined, but becomes a guide and facilitator for processing knowledge. This implies that **conferencing** with each child is important.
4. A great emphasis is placed on INTEGRATION of content and materials using real-world problems.

Sample Lesson Plan

Preparation:

1. *Select* good literature.

   Select stories from published literature to use for motivation.
2. *Use* manipulatives and objects from the real world.

   Identify the commercially designed manipulatives and real objects that will be used in the lesson.
3. *Document* the process of mathematical thinking through writing.

   Encourage students to document the process of solving a problem by writing both in the spoken language and the language of mathematics.
4. *Prepare* recording activities for cooperative groups.

   Design instruction and record sheets for groups of students to record work.
5. *Integrate* with other subjects.

   Find real-world problems which portray the mathematical content to be taught and can be related to other subjects.

(continued)

Lesson Implementation

1. DISCUSS and talk about the mathematics in the lesson, then read story/story problem.

   Select good literature or use a teacher-created story. Remember the literature will not teach the concept, but it is used to motivate and help students relate the mathematical idea to a life situation.

2. MODEL the logical and mathematical thinking needed through the use of manipulatives.

   Select real objects to use as manipulatives, or select commercial manipulatives that are appropriate for teaching the math concept.

3. READ the written words in the story along with the symbolic language of mathematics.

   Read the story or story problem aloud to students.

4. DEMONSTRATE the mathematical concepts at all learning levels: concrete, representational, and abstract.

   Help students make the connection between the *spoken* language, the *written* language and the *symbolic* language of mathematics. All three need to be coordinated so the student will understand the concept.

EXAMPLE:

Print sentence on cards.

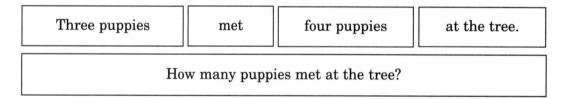

| Three puppies | met | four puppies | at the tree. |

| How many puppies met at the tree? |

Draw picture of problem.

(continued)

Have students *count and tally*.

/ / /　　　　　　/ / / /

Say the number words or math idea.

"three"　　　"four"

Show symbolic representation of math idea.

| 3 |　| 4 |

Show written alphabetical representation (word) of math idea.

| three |　| four |

Write the mathematical sentence in the language of mathematics.

| 3 + 4 = 7 |

Label the answer as a complete thought.

There are seven puppies at the tree.

5. WRITE in the language of mathematics by documenting and recording the process of mathematical thinking on record sheets or in notebooks.

8: Communicating and Writing in Elementary Mathematics

Getting Started:

1. A teacher should keep a journal, learning log and other forms of writing mathematics along with the students.

2. Set the tone for communicating and writing in mathematics:

   a. *Motivate* the students through story problems.

   b. Establish a *sharing* atmosphere.

   c. Encourage students to *explore* different methods to solve and document the process of communicating a mathematical idea (e.g., drawing, acting out, making a table, designing a graph).

   d. Encourage students to *create* original problem situations to solve and communicate to others through writing.

   e. *Conference* with each student about learning mathematics.

Kinds of Writing in Mathematics

1. Developing a problem-solving heuristic

   Document through writing each of the steps in developing a problem-solving heuristic by practicing the skills and applying these skills to different math problems. Follow the heuristic with selected math problems given daily.

   Read the problem.
   Rewrite the problem in your own words.
   Circle the facts.
   Draw a picture or make a graph or table of the problem.
   Write the formula.
   Calculate.
   Verify / Check.

2. Developing solutions to nonroutine problems through the use of creative expression

   Students select techniques and various media to solve a math problem and write about the process of solving the problem. The process might include constructing, building, drawing, acting out, calculating, and random note writing.

3. Documenting analytical thinking in mathematics

   Students document the logical process used to solve a problem by communicating their math ideas using the *symbolic* language of mathematics. This is achieved through the use of standard and nonstandard algorithms, tables, charts, and various models for organizing data. Encourage children to formulate questions, write problems from the questions and solve problems.

4. Evaluating personal experiences in mathematics

   Students write out feelings and perceptions regarding the math experience and answer such questions as:

©1997 by The Center for Applied Research in Education

   a. What I learned today in mathematics class

   b. What I liked about what I learned

   c. What I didn't like about what I learned

   d. What my teacher can do better to help me learn

Conferencing With Students About Mathematics

Techniques for Questioning:

1. What did you like best about this problem?
2. What did you learn from this problem?
3. What do you intend to do in the next problem you have like this one?
4. What surprised you about this problem?
5. What questions do you have to ask me?

Remember to listen to the student first, for it is the *student's* answer to the problem, not yours.

Conference Guidelines

1. Short conferences are more effective than long conferences.
2. Frequent conferences are effective.
3. Limit the student's response and your response to one problem at a time.
4. Encourage the student to expand on his or her problems as much as possible.

Sample 30-Minute Period Conferencing Schedule:

1. First 10 minutes—visit certain students who need special help.
2. Next 15 minutes—have 5 individual conferences for 3 minutes each.
3. Final 5 minutes—Pull class together to share problems orally.

Alternative 30-Minute Period Conferencing Schedule:

1. First 5 minutes—mini skill lesson
2. Next 15 minutes—5 individual conferences for 3 minutes each
3. Final 10 minutes—group sharing

Word Problems to Encourage Communicating and Writing Mathematics

These problems are examples of the kinds of problems students could document by writing and recording the logical process used to solved the problem and showing, using various methods, how they solved the problem.

(continued)

1. Antelope Hill, Buffalo Corner, Coyote Canyon, and Desperado Gulch line along a straight road in the order named. The distance from Antelope Hill to Desperado Gulch is 100 miles. The distance from Buffalo Corner to Coyote Canyon is 30 miles. The distance from Buffalo Corner to Desperado Gulch is 60 miles. How far is it from Antelope Hill to Buffalo Corner?

2. Hassan is giving his comic book collection to his friends. He has 400 comics to give away. He gives Miriam half of his comic books. Then he gives Margaret half of what he has left. Then he gives Wayne half of what he now has left. Finally, he gives Cliff half of what he has left. How many comic books did Hassan give to each friend?

3. Gladys, Jeanette, Jesse, and Steve went fishing. Gladys caught 16 fish, Jeanette caught 13 fish, Jesse caught 17 fish, and Steve caught 14 fish. How many more fish did Jesse and Steve catch than Gladys and Jeanette? *(31 − 29 = 2)*

4. If a giant's foot is 4 times the size of your foot, how tall is the giant compared to you? *(4 × your height)*

5. How many different ways can you add four even whole numbers and get 10 as a sum?

6. In an office, there are two square windows. Each window is 4 feet high, yet one window has an area twice that of the other window. Explain how this could take place.

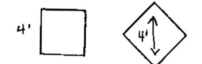

7. I am thinking of two 2-digit numbers. They have the same digits, only reversed. The difference between the numbers is 54, while the sum of the digits of each number is 10. Find the two numbers.

8. Find a book with a large number of pages. Note the number of pages in the book. Place a bookmark anywhere in the book. Have the students look at the bookmark and guess the number of the page it is marking. Try this several times. Have students keep a record in their notebooks or journals of how many times their guesses were within 10 pages of the bookmark.

9. Ask the students to close their eyes and guess how long a minute is. Check them with a clock. See if they can come within 15 seconds, then within 10 seconds, then within 5 seconds. Have them record and write about how close they came each time.

10. A gross of pencils is 144 pencils. If each pencil is 18 centimeters long, how long would the line be if all the pencils in a gross were laid end to end?

11. There are 48 children in two clubs. There are 15 boys in one club. There are 10 boys in the other club. How many girls are there in both clubs?

12. A chicken can lay about 5 eggs each week. How many eggs can you expect 5 chickens to lay in 3 weeks? 1 month? 1 year? 5 years? 10 years?

13. Here is a table showing the runs scored by two teams in three baseball games played against each other. If this scoring pattern continues, what will be the score of the 5th game that they play?

(continued)

Game	1	2	3	4	5
Robins	2	4	6	—	—
Crows	5	6	7	—	—

14. Which of the four numbers in the array doesn't belong? Why not? *(23 because it is not a multiple of 5)*

    23 20

    25 15

15. Find the three consecutive numbers that add up to 24.

    $1 + 2 + 3 = 6$

    $2 + 3 + 4 = 9$

    $3 + 4 + 5 = 12$

    $4 + 5 + 6 = 15$

16. How many 2's must you multiply together to reach a 3-digit number?

17. How many breaths do you take in one 24-hour day?

18. Given the sequence of numbers, *2, 3, 5, 8,* explain why the next number might be 12, or 13, or 2, or 5.

19. What is the greatest number of coins you can use to make 35¢? What is the smallest number of coins you can use? In how many different ways can you make 35¢?

20. What was the final score of the Tigers–Sharks baseball game?

    a. If their scores are added, the sum is 8.

    b. If their scores are multiples, the product is 15.

    c. The Sharks won the game.

21. 3 yuchs = 2 ughs

    4 ughs = 6 wims

    2 yuchs = how many wims?

(continued)

22. I am taking these people to dinner. How many people are going to dinner?

    a. myself

    b. my wife

    c. my 2 sons and their wives

    d. each son's 2 children

23. The 3-digit number 53A is exactly divisible by 6. Find the value of A.

24. Jeremy worked a math problem and got 16 as his answer. However, in the last step, he multiplied by 2 instead of dividing by 2. What should have been the correct answer?

25. During the recent census, a man told the census-taker that he had three children. When asked their ages, he replied, "The product of their ages is 72. The sum of their ages is the same as my house number." The census-taker ran to the door and looked at the house number. "I still can't tell," she complained. The man replied, "Oh, that's right. I forgot to tell you that the oldest one likes chocolate pudding." The census-taker promptly wrote down the ages of the three children. How old are they?

9: Mathematics and Children's Literature: A Bibliography*

These books are used as resources when teaching mathematics pedagogy courses for teachers of the elementary grades.

The key below has been used to categorize the books in the bibliography according to their main areas of mathematical emphasis. For each book, the key is located at the end of the bibliographic reference.

1. Classification
2. Counting, numeration, number sense
3. Operations with whole numbers
4. Operations with fractions
5. Operations with decimals
6. Money
7. Number theory (factors, multiples, etc.)
8. Geometry
9. Measurement
10. Statistics and probability
11. Prealgebra (patterns, etc.)
12. Time
13. Problem solving
14. Multicultural connections
15. Miscellaneous

Aardema, Verna. *Traveling to Tondo: A Tale of the Nkundo of Zaire,* New York: Dragonfly Books, 1991. *(12, 14)*

Adams, Barbara Johnston. *The Go-Around Dollar.* New York: Simon & Schuster Books, 1992. *(6)*

Aker, Sizanne. *What Comes in 2's, 3's, & 4's?* New York: Aladdin Paperbacks, 1990 *(1, 2)*

Allen, Pamela. *Who Sank the Boat?* New York: Coward-McCann, Inc. 1982. *(9, 13)*

Anno, Masaichiro and Mitsumasa Anno. *Anno's Mysterious Multiplying Jar.* New York: Philomel Books, 1983. *(3, 11)*

Anno, Mitsumasa. *Anno's Counting House.* New York: Philomel Books, 1982. *(2)*

Anno, Mitsumasa. *Anno's Magic Seeds.* New York: Philomel Books, 1995. *(3, 11, 13)*

Anno, Mitsumasa. *Socrates and the Three Little Pigs.* New York: Philomel Books, 1995. *(10, 13)*

Atherlay, Sara. *Math in the Bath (and other fun places, too!)* New York: Simon & Schuster Books, 1995. *(15)*

Axelrod, Amy. *Pigs on a Blanket.* New York: Simon & Schuster Books, 1996. *(12, 13)*

Axelrod, Amy. *Pigs Will Be Pigs.* New York: Simon & Schuster Books, 1994. *(5, 6, 13)*

Baker, Ann and Johnny. *Raps and Rhymes in Maths.* Portsmouth, NH: Heinemann Publishers, 1991. *(15)*

Bang, Molly. *Ten, Nine, Eight.* New York: Mulberry Books, 1983. *(2, 14)*

Barry, David. *The Rajah's Rice: A Mathematical Folktale from India.* New York: W. H. Freeman and Company, 1994. *(3, 11, 14)*

---

prepared by Denisse R. Thompson, University of South Florida

(continued)

Birch, David. *The King's Chessboard.* New York: Puffin Pied Piper Books, 1988. *(3, 11, 14)*

Blackstone, Stella. *Grandma Went to Market: A Round-the World Counting Rhyme.* Boston: Houghton Mifflin Company, 1996. *(2, 14)*

Bounton, Sandra. *One, Two, Three.* New York: Workman Publishing, 1993. *(2)*

Brisson, Pat. *Benny's Pennies.* New York: Bantam Doubleday Dell, 1993. *(6, 13)*

Bulloch, Ivan. *Measure.* New York: Thomson Learning, 1994. *(9)*

Bulloch, Ivan. *Shapes.* New York: Thomson Learning, 1994. *(8)*

Burns, Marilyn. *The Greedy Triangle.* New York: Scholastic Inc., 1994. *(8)*

Carle, Eric. *The Grouchy Ladybug.* New York: Harper Trophy, 1977. *(8, 9, 12)*

Carle, Eric. *1, 2, 3, to the Zoo: A Counting Book.* New York: Philomel Books, 1968. *(2)*

Carle, Eric. *Rooster's Off to See the World.* New York: Simon & Schuster, 1972. *(2)*

Carle, Eric. *Pancakes, Pancakes!* New York: Scholastic, Inc., 1990. *(13)*

Carle, Eric. *The Secret Birthday Message.* West Germany: HarperCollins Publishers, 1991. *(8, 13)*

Carle, Eric. *The Very Busy Spider.* New York: Philomel Books, 1984. *(8)*

Carle, Eric. *The Hungry Caterpillar.* New York; Philomel Books, 1969. *(2)*

Carroll, Kathleen Sullivan. *One Red Rooster.* Boston, Houghton Mifflin, 1992. *(2)*

Christelow, Eileen. *Ten Little Monkeys Sitting in a Tree.* New York: Clarion Books, 1991. *(2)*

Chwast, Seymour. *The 12 Circus Rings.* San Diego: Gulliver Books, 1993. *(3, 11)*

Clement, Rod. *Counting on Frank.* Milwaukee: Gareth Stevens Publishing, 1991. *(9, 11, 13)*

Crews, Donald. *Ten Black Dots.* New York: Greenwillow Books, 1968. *(2, 8)*

Dayrell, Elphinstone. *Why the Sun and the Moon Live in the Sky.* Boston: Houghton Mifflin Company, 1968. *(9, 14)*

Dee, Ruby. *Two Ways to Count to Ten.* New York: Henry Holt and Company, 1988. *(2, 11, 13, 14)*

Dr. Seuss. *Ten Apples Up on Top!* New York: Beginner Books, 1961. *(2)*

Dr. Seuss. *The 500 Hats of Bartholomew Cubbins.* New York: Random House, 1938. *(2, 13)*

Edens, Cooper. *How Many Bears?* New York: Atheneum, 1994. *(3, 11, 13)*

Ehlert, Lois. *Color Zoo.* New York: HarperCollins Publishers, 1989. *(8)*

Ehlert, Lois. *Fish Eyes: A Book You Can Count on.* San Diego: Voyager/Harcourt Brace Book, 1990. *(2, 3)*

Ehlert, Lois. *Growing Vegetable Soup.* San Diego: Harcourt Brace and Company, 1987. *(9)*

Ernst, Lisa Campbell. *Sam Johnson and the Blue Ribbon Qiuilt.* New York: Mulberry Books, 1983. *(8, 13)*

(continued)

Ernst, Lisa Campbell. *Up to Ten and Down Again.* New York: Mulberry Books, 1986. *(2)*

Falwell, Cathryn. *Feast for 10.* New York: Clarion Books, 1993. *(2, 14)*

Faulkner, Keith. *My Counting Book.* Bosingstoke, England: Brainwaves Limited, 1993. *(2)*

Feelings, Muriel. *Moja Means One: Swahili Counting Book.* New York: Dial Books, 1971. *(2, 14)*

Flournoy, Valerie. *The Patchwork Quilt.* New York: Dial Books, 1985. *(8, 14)*

Friedman, Aileen. *A Cloak for the Dreamer.* New York: Scholastic, Inc., 1994. *(8, 13)*

Fujikawa, Gyo. *Can You Count?* New York: Sunny Books, 1977. *(2)*

Gag, Wanda. *Millions of Cats.* New York: Coward-McCann, Inc., 1928. *(2, 13)*

Geringer, Laura. *A Three Hat Day.* New York: HarperCollins Publishers, 1985. *(2, 13)*

Giganti, Paul, Jr. *Each Orange Had 8 Slices.* New York: Greenwillow Books, 1992. *(3)*

Goennel, Heidi. *Odds and Evens.* New York: Tambourine Books, 1994. *(2)*

Gordon, Jeffie Ross. *Six Sleepy Sheep.* New York: Puffin Books, 1991. *(2)*

Greenfield, Eloise. *Aaron and Gayla's Counting Book.* New York: Writers and Readers Publishing, Inc., 1993. *(2, 14)*

Grifalconi, Ann. *The Village of Round and Square Houses.* Boston: Little, Brown and Company, 1986. *(8, 9, 14)*

Hajdusieicz, Babs Bell. *Shape Up, Curvy Snake.* Austin, TX: Steck-Vaughn Company, 1991. *(8)*

Hamm, Diane Johnston. *How Many Feet in the Bed?* New York: Aladdin Books, 1991. *(2, 7)*

Harshman, Marc. *Only One.* New York: Dutton/Cobblehill Books, 1993. *(1, 2)*

Heide, Florence Parry. *The Bigness Contest.* Boston: Little, Brown and Company, 1994. *(9)*

Heller, Nicholas. *Ten Old Pails.* New York: Greenwillow Books, 1994. *(2)*

Hill, Eric. *Spot's Big Book of Colors, Shapes, and Numbers.* New York: G.P. Putnam's Sons, 1994. *(2, 8)*

Hindley, Judy. *The Wheeling and Whirling-Around Book.* Cambridge, MA: Candlewick Press, 1994. *(8)*

Hoban, Tana. *Count and See.* New York: Macmillan Books, 1972. *(2)*

Hoban, Tana. *Dots, Spots, Speckles, and Stripes.* New York: Greenwillow Books, 1987. *(8)*

Hoban, Tana. *Is It Larger? Is It Smaller?* New York: Greenwillow Books, 1985. *(8, 9)*

Hoban, Tana. *Round & Round & Round.* New York: Greenwillow Books, 1983. *(8)*

Hoban, Tana. *26 Letters and 99 Cents.* New York: Greenwillow Books, 1987. *(6, 13)*

Hong, Lily Toy. *Two of Everything.* Morton Grove, IL: Albert Whitman & Company, 1993. *(3, 11, 14)*

Hopkinson, Deborah. *Sweet Clara and the Freedom Quilt.* New York: Alfred A. Knopf, 1993. *(8, 14)*

Hort, Lenny. *How Many Stars in the Sky?* New York: Tambourine Books, 1991. *(2, 14)*

(continued)

Howard, Katherine. *I Can count to 100 . . . Can You?* New York: Random House, 1979. *(2)*

Hubbard, Woodleigh. *2 is for Dancing, A 1 2 3 of Actions.* San Francisco: Chronicle Books, 1990. *(2)*

Hudson, Cheryl Willis. *Afro-Bets 1 2 3.* East Orange, NJ: Just Us Books, 1987. *(2, 14)*

Hudson, Wade. *Jamal's Busy Day.* East Orange, NJ: Just Us Books, 1991. *(12)*

Hulme, Joy N. *Counting by Kangaroos: A Multiplication Concept Book.* New York: W. H. Freeman and Company, 1995. *(3)*

Hulme, Joy N. *Sea Squares.* New York: Hyperion Books, 1991. *(3, 11)*

Hutchins, Pat. *Changes, Changes.* New York: Aladdin Books, 1971. *(8, 13)*

Hutchins, Pat. *Clocks and More Clocks.* New York: Aladdin Books, 1970. *(12, 13)*

Hutchins, Pat. *The Doorbell Rang.* New York: Mulberry Books, 1986. *(3, 7)*

Hutchins, Pat. *1 Hunter.* New York: Mulberry Books, 1982. *(2)*

Jenkins, Steve. *Biggest, Strongest, Fastest.* New York: Ticknor & Fields Books, 1995. *(9, 15)*

Jonas, Ann. *Reflections.* New York: Greenwillow Books, 1987. *(8)*

Jonas, Ann. *Splash.* New York: Greenwillow Books, 1995. *(2)*

Kahn, Katherine Janus. *Alef Is One: A Hebrew Alphabet Counting Book.* Rockville, MD: Kar-Ben Copies, Inc., 1989. *(2, 14)*

Katz, Michael Jay. *Ten Potatoes in a Pot and Other Counting Rhymes.* New York: Harper & Row, Publishers, 1990. *(15)*

Kellogg, Steven. *Much Bigger than Martin.* New York: Dial Books, 1976. *(8, 9)*

Kitchen, Bert. *Somewhere Today.* Cambridge, MA: Candlewick Press, 1992. *(12)*

Kroll, Steven. *The Biggest Pumpkin Ever.* New York: Scholastic, 1984. *(9, 13, 15)*

Lasky, Kathryn. *The Librarian Who Measured the Earth.* Boston: Little, Brown and Company, 1994. *(9, 13, 14)*

Lewis, Paul Owen. *P. Bear's New Year's Party: A Counting Book.* Hillsboro, OR: Beyond Words Publishing, Inc., 1989. *(2, 12)*

Liebler, John. *Frog Counts to Ten.* Brookfield, CT: Millbrook Press, 1994. *(2)*

Lillegard, Dee. *Sitting in My Box.* New York: Puffin Books, 1989. *(9, 13)*

Linden, Ann Marie and Lynne Russell. *One Smiling Grandma: A Caribbean Counting Book.* New York: Dial Books, 1992. *(2, 14)*

Lionni, Leo. *The Biggest House in the World.* New York: Dragonfly Books, 1968. *(9)*

Lionni, Leo. *Inch by Inch.* New York: Mulberry Books, 1960. *(9)*

Llewellyn, Claire. *My First Book of Time.* New York: Dorling Kindersley, Inc., 1992. *(12)*

Lobel, Arnold. *Frog and Toad Together.* New York: HarperTrophy, 1971. *(13, 15)*

Mahy, Margaret. *The Seven Chinese Brothers.* New York: Scholastic, 1990. *(13, 14)*

Markle, Sandra. *Measuring Up: Experiments, Puzzles, and Games Exploring Measurement.* New York: Aladdin Books, 1995. *(9)*

(continued)

Marzollo, Jean. *Ten Cats Have Hats: A Counting Book.* New York: Scholastic, Inc., 1994. *(2)*

Mathews, Louise. *Bunches and Bunches of Bunnies.* New York: Scholastic, Inc., 1978. *(2, 3)*

McDermott, Gerald. *Anansi the Spider: A Tale from the Ashanti.* New York: Henry Holt and Company, 1972. *(13, 14)*

McGovern, Ann. *Stone Soup.* New York: Scholastic, Inc. 1968. *(13)*

McGrath, Barbara Barbieri. *The M&M's Counting Book.* Watertown, MA: Charlesbridge Publishing, 1994. *(2, 7, 8)*

McKissack, Patricia A. *A Million Fish . . . More or Less.* New York: Alfred A. Knopf, 1992. *(2, 14)*

McMillan, Brusce. *Counting Wildflowers.* New York: Mulberry Books, 1986. *(2)*

McMillan, Bruce. *Eating Fractions.* New York: Scholastic, Inc., 1991. *(4)*

Medearis, Angela Shelf. *The 100th Day of School.* New York: Scholastic, 1996. *(2, 12, 13)*

Medearis, Angela Shelf. *Picking Peas for a Penny.* New York: Scholastic, 1990. *(6, 14)*

Medearis, Angela Shelf. *Poppa's New Pants.* New York: Holiday House, 1995. *(9, 14)*

Merriam, Eve. *12 Ways to Get to 11.* New York: Simon & Schuster Books, 1993. *(3, 11)*

Min, Laura. *Mrs. Sato's Hens.* Glenview, IL: Goodyear Books, 1994. *(2)*

Moerbeek, Kees and Carla Dijs. *Six Brave Explorers.* Los Angeles: Intervisual Communications, Inc., 1988. *(2)*

Moncure, Jane Belk. *Apes Find Shapes.* Columbus, OH: American Education Publishing, 1993. *(8)*

Moncure, Jane Bell. *The Biggest Snowball of All.* Columbus, OH: American Education Publishing, 1993. *(8, 9)*

Morgan, Sally. *Squares and Cubes.* New York: Thomson Learning, 1994. *(8)*

Morozumi, Atsuko. *One Gorilla.* Hong Kong: Sunburst Book, 1990. *(2)*

Most, Bernard. *How Big Were the Dinosaurs?* San Diego: Voyager Books, 1994. *(9, 15)*

Murphy, Stuart J. *The Best Bug Parade.* New York: HarperCollins Publishers, 1996. *(8, 9)*

Murphy, Stuart J. *Give Me Half!* New York: HarperCollins Publishers, 1996. *(4)*

Murphy, Stuart J. *Ready, Set, Hop!* New York: HarperCollins Publishers, 1996. *(3, 11, 13)*

Myller, Rolf. *How Big Is a Foot?* New York: Dell Publishing, 1962. *(9)*

Nozaki, Akihiro and Mitsumasa Anno. *Anno's Hat Tricks.* New York: Philomel Books, 1985. *(13)*

O'Keefe, Susan Heyboer. *One Hungry Monster: A Counting Book in Rhyme.* Boston: Little, Brown and Company, 1989. *(2)*

Onyefulu, Ifeoma. *Emeka's Gift: An African Counting Story.* New York: Dutton/Cobblehill Books, 1995. *(2, 14)*

Onyefulu, Obi. *Chinye: A West African Folk Tale.* New York: Viking, 1994. *(13, 14)*

(continued)

Pallotta, Jerry. *The Icky Bug Counting Book.* Watertown, MA: Charlesbridge Publishing, 1992. *(2)*

Paul, Ann Whitford. *Eight Hands Round: A Patchwork Alphabet.* New York: HarperCollins Publishers, 1991. *(8, 14)*

Piers, Helen and Hannah Giffard. *Is There Room on the Bus? An Around-the-World Counting Story.* New York: Simon & Schuster Books, 1996. *(2, 14)*

Pinczes, Elinor J. *One Hundred Hungry Ants.* Boston: Houghton Mifflin, 1993. *(3, 7)*

Pinczes, Elinor J. *A Remainder of One.* Boston: Houghton Mifflin, 1995. *(3, 7)*

Pittman, Helena Clare. *A Grain of Rice.* New York: Bantam Skylark Book, 1986. *(3, 11, 14)*

Pluckrose, Henry. *Math Counts: Capacity.* Chicago: Children's Press, 1994. *(9)*

Pluckrose, Henry. *Math Counts: Counting.* Chicago, Children's Press, 1994. *(2)*

Pluckrose, Henry. *Math Counts: Length.* Chicago, Children's Press, 1994. *(9)*

Pluckrose, Henry. *Math Counts: Numbers.* Chicago, Children's Press, 1994. *(2, 15)*

Pluckrose, Henry. *Math Counts: Pattern.* Chicago, Children's Press, 1994. *(8)*

Pluckrose, Henry. *Math Counts: Shape.* Chicago, Children's Press, 1994. *(8)*

Pluckrose, Henry. *Math Counts: Size.* Chicago, Children's Press, 1994. *(8, 9)*

Pluckrose, Henry. *Math Counts: Sorting.* Chicago, Children's Press, 1994. *(1)*

Pluckrose, Henry. *Math Counts: Weight.* Chicago, Children's Press, 1994. *(9)*

Podwal, Mark. *The Book of Tens.* New York: Greenwillow Books, 1994. *(2, 7, 14)*

Reid, Barbara. *Two by Two.* New York: Scholastic, Inc., 1992. *(2, 7)*

Reid, Margarette S. *The Button Box.* New York: Puffin Unicorn, 1990. *(1)*

Rocklin, Joanne. *Musical Chairs and Dancing Bears.* New York: Henry Holt and Company, 1993. *(2, 3)*

Ryan, Pam Munoz. *One Hundred Is a Family.* New York: Hyperion Paperbacks for Children, 1994. *(2)*

San Souci, Robert D. *The Boy and the Ghost.* New York: Simon & Schuster Books, 1989. *(13, 14)*

Schwager, Istar. *Counting.* Lincolnwood, IL: Publications International, Ltd., 1993. *(2)*

Schwartz, David M. *How Much Is a Million?* New York: Mulberry Paperback Book, 1985. *(2, 3, 13)*

Schwartz, David M. *If You Made a Million.* New York: Lothrop, Lee & Shepard Books, 1989. *(2, 6, 13)*

Serfozo, Mary. *Who Wants One?* New York: Aladdin Books, 1989. *(2)*

Sharman, Lydia. *The Amazing Book of Shapes.* New York: Dorling Kindersley, 1994. *(8)*

Sharmat, Marjorie Weinman. *The 329th Friend.* New York: Four Winds Press, 1979. *(3, 13)*

Sheppard, Jerr. *The Right Number of Elephants.* New York: HarperCollins Publishers, 1990. *(2)*

(continued)

Shields, Carol Diggory. *Lunch Money and Other Poems About School.* New York: Dutton Children's Books, 1995. *(6, 15)*

Silverstein, Shel. *A Light in the Attic: Poems and Drawings by Shel Silverstein.* New York: HarperCollins Publishers, 1981. *(15)*

Silverstein, Shel. *Where the Sidewalk Ends: the Poems and Drawings of Shel Silverstein.* New York: HarperCollins Publishers, 1974. *(15)*

Slater, Teddy. *Stay in Line.* New York: Scholastic, Inc., 1996. *(8, 15)*

Time-Life for Children. *Alice in Numberland: Fantasy Math.* Alexandria, VA: Time-Life for Children, 1993. *(2, 4, 8, 9, 13, 15)*

Time-Life for Children. *The Case of the Missing Zebra Stripes: Zoo Math.* Alexandria, VA: Time-Life for Children, 1992. *(1, 3, 8, 12, 13, 15)*

Time-Life for Children. *From Head to Toe: Body Math.* Alexandria, VA: Time-Life for Children, 1993. *(3, 9, 12, 13, 15)*

Time-Life for Children. *The House That Math Built: House Math.* Alexandria, VA: Time-Life for Children, 1993. *(8, 9, 13, 15)*

Time-Life for Children. *How Do Octapi Eat Pizza Pie? Pizza Math.* Alexandria, VA: Time-Life for Children, 1992. *(3, 8, 9, 11, 13, 15)*

Time-Life Early Learning Program. *How Many Hippos? A Mix-and Match Counting Book.* Alexandria, VA: Time-Life for Children, 1990. *(2, 15)*

Time-Life for Children. *Look Both Ways: City Math.* Alexandria, VA: Time-Life for Children, 1992. *(3, 8, 13, 15)*

Time-Life for Children. *The Mystery of the Sunken Treasure: Sea Math.* Time-Life for Children, 1993. *(3, 4, 8, 9, 13, 15)*

Time-Life for Children. *Play Ball: Sports Math.* Alexandria, VA: Time-Life for Children, 1993. *(3, 8, 9, 10, 13, 15)*

Time-Life for Children. *Pterdactyl Tunnel: Amusement Park Math.* Alexandria, VA: Time-Life for Children, 1993. *(2, 3, 8, 10, 13, 15)*

Time-Life for Children. *Right in Your Own Backyard: Nature Math.* Alexandria, VA: Time-Life for Children, 1992. *(1, 3, 8, 12, 13, 15)*

Time-Life for Children. *The Search for the Mystery Planet: Space Math.* Alexandria, VA. Time-Life for Children, 1993. *(8, 9, 10, 11, 13, 15)*

Time-Life for Children. *See You Later, Escalator! Mall Math.* Alexandria, VA. Time-Life for Children, 1993. *(3, 6, 8, 9, 13, 15)*

Tompert, Ann. *Grandfather Tang's Story: A Tale Told with Tangrams.* New York: Crown Publishers, Inc., 1990. *(8, 14)*

Tompert, Ann. *Just a Little Bit.* Boston: Houghton Mifflin Company, 1993. *(9, 13)*

Viorst, Judith. *Alexander, Who Used to Be Rich Last Sunday.* New York: Aladdin Books, 1978. *(6)*

Walsh, Ellen Stoll. *Mouse Count.* San Diego: Harcourt Brace & Co., 1991. *(2)*

Weiss, Monica. *Mmmm . . . Cookies! Simple Subtraction.* Mahwah, NJ: Troll Associates, 1992. *(3)*

(continued)

Wells, Robert E. *Is a Blue Whale the Biggest Thing There Is?* Morton Grove, IL: Albert Whitman & Company, 1993. *(8, 9, 13, 15)*

Wells, Robert E. *What's Smaller Than a Pygmy Shrew?* Morton Grove, IL: Albert Whitman & Company, 1995. *(8, 9, 13, 15)*

West, Colin. *Ten Little Crocodiles.* Cambridge, MA: Candlewick Press, 1987. *(2)*

White, C.S. *The Monster's Counting Book.* New York: Platt & Munk, Publishers, 1978. *(2)*

Whittaker, Dora. *Will Gulliver's Suit Fit? Mathematical Problem-Solving with Children.* Cambridge, MA: Cambridge University Press. 1986. *(8, 9, 13)*

Williams, Rozanne Lanczak. *Who Took the Cookies from the Cookie Jar?* Cypress, CA: Creative Teaching Press, Inc., 1995. *(3)*

Wise, William. *Ten Sly Piranhas: A Counting Story in Reverse (A Tale of Wickedness—and Worse).* New York: Dial Books, 1993. *(2)*

Wood, Jakki. *One Tortoise, Ten Wallabies: A Wildlife Counting Book.* New York: Bradbury Press, 1994. *(2)*

Zimelman, Nathan. *How the Second Grade Got $8,205.50 to Visit the Statue of Liberty.* Morton Grove, IL: Albert Whitman & Company, 1992. *(6, 13)*

—. *Five Little Ducks.* New York: Crown Publishers, Inc., 1989. *(2)*

—. *I Can Add.* New York: Bantam Doubleday Dell, 1994. *(3)*

—. *I Can Subtract.* New York: Bantam Doubleday Dell, 1994. *(3)*

—. *Secret Shapes: A Changing Picture Book.* New York: Dorling Kindersley Publishing, Inc., 1995. *(8)*

10: Teacher Resource Books
Linking Mathematics to Literature and Writing

Atkinson, Sue. *Mathematics with Reason.* Portsmouth, NH: Heinemann, 1992.

Bartch, Marian R. *Math & Stories.* Glenview, IL: Goodyear Books, 1996.

Braddon, Kathryn L., Nancy J. Hall, and Dale Taylor. *Math Through Children's Literature: Making the NCTM Standards Come Alive.* Englewood, CO: Teacher Ideas Press, 1993.

Baker, Ann and Johnny. *Raps & Rhymes in Maths.* Portsmouth, NH: Heinemann, 1991.

Baker, Ann and Johnny. *Maths in the Mind.* Portsmouth, NH: Heinemann, 1991.

Baker, Dave, Cheryl Semples and Tony Stead. *How Big is the Moon?* Portsmouth, NH: Heinemann, 1990.

Baroody, Arthur J. *Children's Mathematical Thinking.* New York: Teachers College, Columbia University, 1987.

Bickmore-Brand, Jennie. *Language in Mathematics.* Portsmouth, NH: Heinemann, 1993.

Bresser, Rusty. *Math and Literature (Grades 4-6).* Sausalito, CA: Math Solutions Publications, 1995.

Burns, Marilyn. *Math and Literature (K-3): Book One.* Sausalito, CA: Math Solutions Publications, 1992.

Burns, Marilyn. *Writing in Math Class.* Sausalito, CA: Math Solutions Publications, 1995.

Corwin, Rebecca B. *Talking Mathematics.* Portsmouth, NH: Heinemann, 1996.

Countryman, Joan. *Writing to Learn Mathematics.* Portsmouth, NH: Heinemann, 1992.

Griffiths, Rachel and Margaret Clyne. *Books You Can Count On: Linking Mathematics and Literature.* Portsmouth, NH: Heinemann, 1988.

Lilburn, Pat and Pam Rawson. *Let's Talk Math.* Portsmouth, NH: Heinemann, 1993.

McKeown, Ross. *Learning Mathematics.* Portsmouth, NH: Heinemann, 1990.

Mathematical Association of the United Kingdom. *Math Talk.* Portsmouth, NH: Heinemann, 1987.

Parsons, Les. *Expanding Response Journals in All Subject Areas.* Portsmouth, NH: Heinemann, 1993.

Rommel, Carol A. *Integrating Beginning Math & Literature.* Nashville, TN: Incentive Publications, Inc., 1991.

Rowan, Thomas and Barbara Bourne. *Thinking Like Mathematicians.* Portsmouth, NH: Heinemann, 1994.

Satariano, Patricia. *Storytime Mathtime: Math Explorations in Children's Literature.* Palo Alto, CA: Dale Seymour Publications, 1994.

Schifter, Deborah. *What's Happening in Math Class? Volume One.* New York: Teachers College, Columbia University/International Reading Association, 1996.

(continued)

Schifter, Deborah. *What's Happening in Math Class? Volume Two.* New York: Teachers College, Columbia University/International Reading Association, 1996.

Sheffield, Stephanie. *Math and Literature (K-3): Book Two.* Sausalito, CA: Math Solutions Publications, 1995.

Thiessen, Diane and Margaret Mathias. *The Wonderful World of Mathematics: A Critically Annotated List of Children's Books in Mathematics.* Reston, VA: National Council of Teachers of Mathematics, 1992.

Welchman-Tischler, Rosamond. *How to Use Children's Literature to Teach Mathematics.* Reston, VA: National Council of Teachers of Mathematics. 1992.

Whitin, David J. and Sandra Wilde. *It's the Story That Counts: MORE Children's Books for Mathematical Learning, K-6.* Portsmouth, NH: Heinemann, 1995.

Whitin, David J. and Sandra Wilde. *Read Any Good Math Lately? Children's Books for Mathematical Learning, K-6.* Portsmouth, NH: Heinemann, 1992.

Zaslavasky, Claudia. *Multicultural Math: Hands-On Math Activities from Around the World.* New York: Scholastic Professional Books. 1994.

11: Occupations and Careers: People Who Use Mathematics in Their Jobs

Invite any one of these people into your classroom to explain how they use mathematics to perform their job and how mathematics is an important part of their job.

Accountant
Actuary
Administrator (hospital)
Advertising agent
Airline service person
Airline mechanics
Airline pilot
Airline attendant
Air traffic controller
Aide (teacher)
Appraiser
Architect
Artist
Attorney
Auditor
Auto mechanic
Bank Manager
Bank Teller
Bus driver
Building superintendent
Carpenter
Carpet cleaner
Cartographer
Chiropractor
Computer programmer
Computer salesperson
Computer technician
Contractor
Controller
County tax collector
Cook
Data processor
Dentist
Dental technician
Dietitian
Doctor (medical)

Draftsperson
Economist
Electrician
Engineer
Farmer
Firefighter
Forest ranger
Geologist
House painter
Income tax preparer
Insurance agent
Interior decorator
Investment broker
Landscaper
Librarian
Mail carrier
Manager (grocery)
Manager (department)
Manager (shopping mall)
Medical lab technician
Motor repair person
Navigator
Newspaper reporter
Nurse
Oceanographer
Optician
Office manager
Painting contractor
Personnel manager
Payroll bookkeeper
Pharmacist
Photographer
Physical therapist
Plumber
Police officer
Politician

I'm a nurse. I need to know math.

43

(continued)

Printer
Psychologist
Publisher
Purchasing agent
Roofer
School clerk
School teacher
School principal
Social worker
Stock broker

Surveyor
Surgeon
Taxi cab driver
Travel agent
Truck driver
TV repair person
Veterinarian
Waitress/Waiter
Zookeeper

12: Famous Mathematicians

Thales	*(c. 640–550 B.C.)*	Developed the logical system of a mathematical proof.
Pythagoras	*(c. 580–500 B.C.)*	Discovered the Pythagorean Theorem ($a^2 + b^2 = c^2$) used to find the length of a side of a right triangle when two other sides are known.
Plato	*(c. 427–347 B.C.)*	Philosopher who believed the secret of the universe lay in number and form.
Eratosthenes	*(c. 276–195 B.C.)*	Astronomer who discovered a system of identifying prime numbers.
Aristotle	*(c. 384–322 B.C.)*	Philosopher who developed the science of deductive logic.
Euclid	*(c. 300 B.C.)*	Wrote thirteen books on mathematics entitled *Elements*, a collection of all the known mathematics in his time. His book on geometry is the basis for textbooks on plane geometry.
Archimedes	*(c. 287–212 B.C.)*	Developed the principle of the lever.
Ptolemy	*(c. 100–170 A.D.)*	Wrote *System of Mathematics*, describing the systematic arrangement of the stars and planets.
Hypatia	*(c. 370–415 A.D.)*	First woman mathematician.
Leonardo Fibonacci	*(c. 1175–1250 A.D.)*	Identified the Fibonacci number sequence (1, 2, 3, 5, 8, 13, 21, 34, 55, 89, 144) in which each number is the sum of the preceding two numbers. This model is reflected in nature, art, and other sciences.
Niccolo Tartaglia	*(1500–1557)*	Developed the method for solving cubic equations and pioneered the application of mathematics to artillery.
Girolamo Cardano	*(1501–1576)*	Developed the idea of imaginary numbers and wrote the first study on the theory of probability.
Francois Viete	*(1540–1603)*	Developed symbolic algebra. He is sometimes referred to as the Father of Algebra.
Simon Stevin	*(1548–1617)*	Developed the first systematic definition of decimal fractions. His work became the basis for decimal coinage and decimal weights and measures.
John Napier	*(1550–1617)*	Inventor of logarithms; developed the first adding machine, by developing a system of number tables that make calculations easier and faster.

(continued)

Galileo Galilei	*(1564–1642)*	An astronomer who discovered the law of falling bodies.
Johannes Kepler	*(1571–1630)*	Astronomer whose mathematics laid the groundwork for calculus.
Rene Descartes	*(1596–1630)*	Philosopher and discoverer of analytical geometry.
Pierre de Fermat	*(1601–1665)*	Father of Modern Number Theory.
John Wallis	*(1616–1703)*	The first to use the symbol for infinity.
Blaise Pascal	*(1623–1662)*	Developed probability theory and devised a number system called Pascal's triangle.
Sir Isaac Newton	*(1642–1727)*	Discovered the laws of gravitation.
Gottfried Leibnix	*(1646–1716)*	Discovered the fundamental principles of infinitesimal calculus. Introduced the use of the decimal point, the equals symbol, and the single dot for multiplication.
Leonhard Euler	*(1707–1783)*	Prolific writer of mathematics, wrote the first book on analytic geometry, developed concepts in trigonometry, and made many discoveries in number theory.
Gaspard Monge	*(1746–1818)*	Studied descriptive geometry.
Jean Delambre	*(1749–1822)*	One of the leading astronomers of France. Established the basis for the metric system by measuring the arc of the meridian between Dunkirk and Barcelona.
Lorenzo Mascheroni	*(1750–1800)*	Studied the geometry of the compasses.
Joseph Jacquard	*(1752–1834)*	Developed the first successful loom, called the Jacquard weaving loom, which used the punchcard.
Lazare Carnot	*(1753–1823)*	Made contributions to modern geometry.
Sylvestre Lacroix	*(1765–1843)*	Wrote books on higher algebra, geometry, probability, and calculus.
Johann Pfaff	*(1765–1825)*	Wrote "Disquisitiones Analyticae" about integral calculus; also wrote on the subject of calculus or differential equations.
Joseph Fourier	*(1768–1830)*	Developed Fourier's series used in studying the flow of heat.
William Wallace	*(1768–1843)*	Wrote on logarithms, trigonometry, the pantograph, and geodesy. Also studied the quadrature of the hyperbola and hyperbolic functions.
Carl Gauss	*(1777–1855)*	His work is considered the beginning of modern number theory.

(continued)

Simeon Poisson	*(1781–1840)*	Contributed to the theory of probability, algebraic equations, differential equations, definite integrals, surfaces, and the calculus of variations.
Jean-Victor Poncelet	*(1788–1867)*	Contributed to the theory of projective geometry. One of the founders of modern geometry.
August Mobius	*(1790–1868)*	Contributed to the theory of modern geometry.
Charles Babbage	*(1792–1871)*	Worked on the calculating machine. Introduced the differential notation into British Mathematics.
N. I. Lobachevsky	*(1793–1856)*	Wrote about non-Euclidean geometry.
Theodore Olivier	*(1793–1853)*	Studied descriptive geometry.
Ernst August	*(1795–1870)*	Worked on mathematical physics.
Lambert Quetelet	*(1796–1874)*	A leader in the theory of probability. Wrote a history of mathematics.
Arthur Arneth	*(1802–1858)*	Wrote a history of mathematics and on geometry.
Niels Abel	*(1802–1829)*	Wrote memoirs on elliptic functions. Developed Abel's theorem which involves evaluating the sum of a number of integrals that have the same integrand, but different limits.
J. Bolyai	*(1802–1860)*	Wrote about non-Euclidean geometry.
Guglielmo Libri	*(1803–1869)*	Wrote a history of mathematics. Taught analysis.
Carl Jacobi	*(1804–1851)*	Studied elliptic functions, determinants, the theory of numbers, differential equations, the calculus of variations, and infinite series.
Peter Lejeune-Dirichlet	*(1805–1859)*	Studied algebra, number theory, and quadratic forms.
Augustus DeMorgan	*(1806–1871)*	Contributed to the theory of probability and to logic. Wrote a history of mathematics.
Ernst Kummer	*(1810–1893)*	Developed the theory of ideal prime factors of complex numbers and set forth the principles applicable to Kummer surfaces.
Evariste Galois	*(1811–1832)*	Contributed to modern advances in the theory of groups and modern theory of algebraic equations of higher degree.
Moritz Steinschneider	*(1813–1907)*	Wrote essays on Hebrew and Arabic mathematics.
George Boole	*(1815–1864)*	Made contributions to the theory of invariants and covariants and to the theory of logic.

(continued)

Karl Weierstrass	*(1815–1897)*	Father of Modern Analysis. One of the founders of the modern theory of functions.
Georg Cantor	*(1845–1918)*	Developed the theory of sets and the concept of transfinite numbers.
Henri Poincare	*(1854–1912)*	Wrote articles on electricity, optics, and theoretical mathematics in a style easy for readers to comprehend.
Alfred Whitehead	*(1861–1947)*	Studied pure mathematics. Co-authored "Principia Mathematica" with Bertrand Russell.
David Hilbert	*(1862–1943)*	Reduced Euclidean geometry to a series of axioms. Studied infinite-dimensional space, later called Hilbert space.
Bertrand Russell	*(1872–1970)*	Wrote "The Principles of Mathematics" to prove that mathematics could be derived from self-evident principles. Co-authored "Principia Mathematica" with Alfred Whitehead.
Herman Weyl	*(1885–1955)*	Made contribution to development of differential geometry, theory of continuous groups, and philosophy of mathematics. Added to Quantum and the theory of relativity.
John von Neumann	*(1903–1957)*	Pure mathematician. Developed and directed construction of a computer.
Kurt Godel	*(1906–1978)*	Developed Godel's proof in arithmetic. Also studied set theory.
Alan M. Turing	*(1912–1954)*	Made contributions to early computer theory. Wrote "On Computable Numbers" describing a universal computer called the Turing machine.
Grace Hopper	*(1906–)*	Coined the term "bug." Mother of COBOL.
Seymour Cray	*(1925–1996)*	Built speediest supercomputer.

SECTION 2

BEGINNING MATHEMATICS

Name _____

CUT OUT. ORDER THE FROGS FROM SHORTEST TO TALLEST.

13: Classification

Classification is sorting objects or ideas into sets or groups because they share a common attribute or characteristic, and separating those that do not. It is one of the most fundamental skills to be learned.

Progression of Skills

• *Graphic Collections.* Children carefully sort objects into groups and are able to describe the rational for the groupings. Unfortunately, others fail to follow the child's logic. The child may begin sorting by a certain characteristic (color, size, etc.), but then other objects with different characteristics are included for reasons that are clear only to the child.

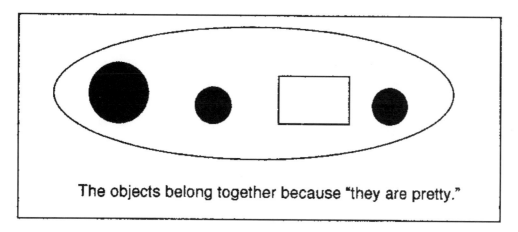

The objects belong together because "they are pretty."

• *Class Names.* Children begin to use class names before they understand the meaning of classes. The child may know peas by their name, but other foods are known by the class name of vegetables. When someone refers to peas as vegetables, confusion is created. This child does not comprehend that peas also belong to the class of vegetables.

• *Sorting by One Attribute.* The child is able to place all the red objects in one group and all the blue objects in another group, or all the squares in one group and all the circles in another.

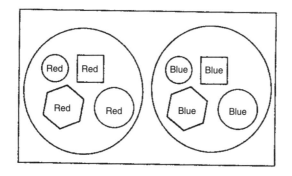

(continued)

• *Sorting by More Than One Attribute.* The child has built upon one attribute, sorting, and now is capable of sorting groups that contain multiple attributes. The red circles are placed in one group, the blue circles in another, the red squares in another, and the blue squares in still another.

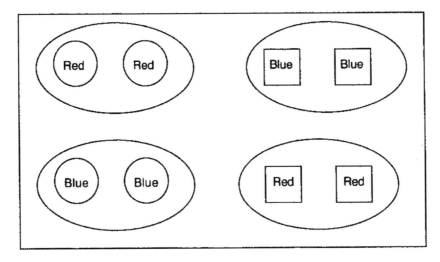

• *Class Inclusion.* The ability of the child to understand that the total number of the set is larger than any of its subsets. When looking at a family of gerbils (two adults and four offspring) in a cage, the child is asked, "Are there more gerbils (the set) or are there more babies (the subset)?" The child who has not attained a strong understanding of class inclusion will answer that there are more babies. The child who fully understands class inclusion realizes that the babies are a subset of the set of gerbils and answers accordingly. Children begin to attain class inclusion around the age of eight years.

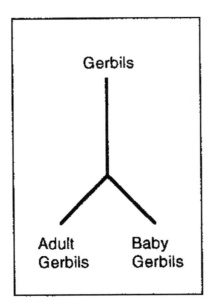

(continued)

Experiences for Developing Classification

- Describing the characteristics or attributes of objects.
- Describing how objects are the same or different.
- Describing the characteristics or attributes that objects do *not* have.
- Labeling the quantitative aspect of groups using some, all, or none.

14: Seriation

Seriation is ordering objects by their differences instead of just separating them. Seriation is *NOT* about sticks, or the objects being ordered. Seriation is about thought.

Progression of Skills

- *Unable to Seriate.* Children are unable to seriate or produce relationships between two objects at a time (larger–smaller; larger–smaller; etc.) instead of producing a series.

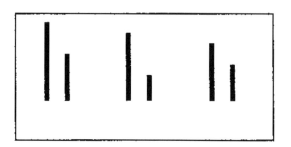

- *Trial and Error.* Children are able to produce a seriation but not by using systematic thought. Objects are added to the series, then removed when they do not fit and others tried. The child uses the shape of the seriation to help determine which objects are used next.

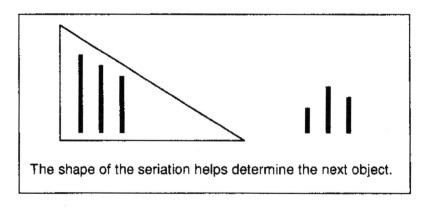

The shape of the seriation helps determine the next object.

- *Systematic Method.* At around the age of seven or eight children are capable of developing a logical system for seriating. The criterion lies in the process of *placing* the objects, not in the resulting arrangement. When ordering several sticks from largest to shortest, for example, the child takes all the sticks and chooses the longest one. Then the next longest one is chosen from the remaining group, which is also the next shortest object in the order. This process is repeated until the sticks are arranged in descending order. Again, it is the thought process that is considered seriation, not the final product.

(continued)

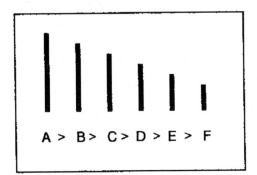

Several Seriation Relationships:

long to short   wide to narrow
high to low   deep to shallow
heavy to light   full to empty
dark to light   hot to cold

15: Number

Number is the combination of two relationships that children create among objects. The first is *counting order* and the second is *inclusion*.

When young children count objects, they tend to count some twice and skip others all together. As children become more conscious of accuracy, they begin to develop a process of putting the objects in a counting order. The order is not specific, any order will do, and it is usually done mentally.

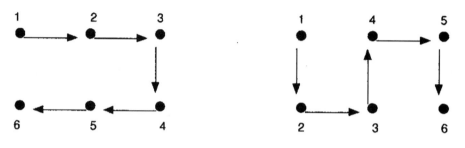

The counting order is not specific.

While the order is not specific, the process is. Once an object is counted, it is classified into the category "objects already counted." The remaining objects belong to the category "objects to be counted." As each object is counted, it is moved from the "to be counted" group to the "already counted" group. If children are able to maintain the accuracy of the two categories, the group of objects will be counted accurately.

The counting only reflects the children's considering one object at a time. The group of objects is not considered. When counting the group above, most children will arrive at the answer of six. If asked to show the six, they usually will point to the sixth object, not the entire group of six. What is necessary to determine the number of the group is combining the counting order with the idea of inclusion.

The relationship of inclusion means that children include "one" in "two," "two" in "three," and so on.

By combining counting order and inclusion into a single relationship, children develop the concept of number and quantify the entire set. They are able to correctly count the number of objects and show that the number is equal to the entire group.

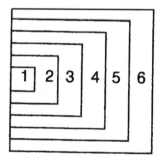

Inclusion

©1997 by The Center for Applied Research in Education

16: Spatial and Temporal Relationships

Spatial

• Topological Concepts

Before the age of four years, children begin to acquire topological concepts. These are such concepts as open/closed, separation/connection, inside/outside, and boundary. The children perceive their environment with themselves in the center and never consider other points of view. They draw themselves with a front view; eyes, nose and mouth inside a closed curve; the body connected to the head; and arms and legs connected to the body. Because the parts of the picture are in correct topological order, we perceive it as a picture of the child. Other items in the picture are randomly arranged with no thought of horizontal, vertical, or sizes in space.

• Euclidean Concepts

Between the ages of four and seven years, children begin to develop some Euclidean concepts such as shape, size, angle, and direction. They are able to distinguish circles from triangles and rectangles, and are able to draw rudimentary circles and rectangles. Drawing a triangle develops later. As their development progresses, they are able to discriminate further between circles and ellipses, and rectangles and squares.

They also begin to structure space, which is evidenced in their drawings. The sun is in the sky along with a bird, the child is next to the house which is also next to a tree. Additionally, a base line begins to develop in the drawing.

Space Relationships

• Positional

above	behind	below	between
bottom	in back of	in front of	inside
intersecting	into	off	on
on top of	outside	over	parallel
perpendicular	top	under	underneath

• Directional

across	around	away	away from
backward	diagonally	down	forward
from	left	right	up
through	to	toward	

• Distance

close	close to	far	far from
midway	near		

(continued)

Temporal Relationships

- Sunday, Monday, Tuesday, Wednesday, Thursday, Friday, Saturday
- January, February, March, April, May, June, July, August, September, October, November, December
- Second, Minute, Hour, Day, Month, Year
- Day Before Yesterday, Yesterday, Today, Tomorrow, Day After Tomorrow
- Morning, Noon, Afternoon, Evening, Night
- Summer, Fall, Winter, Spring

17: Estimation

The concept of estimation should be included in children's earliest mathematical experiences and should be utilized to assist children in their development of number sense and spatial relationships. Estimation gives children a different look at mathematics as they explore ideas such as "about," "close to," "near," and "a little less than."

As children become more familiar with estimation, they should also become more aware of when to estimate, relating information that is already known, and deciding how close an estimate is reasonable in different situations. As children are supported and encouraged to estimate, they will see that it is an important part of mathematics.

• *Estimation Activities*

1. *Estimate Quantities.* Use similar materials with varying sizes, and then varying containers. Estimate the number of 1-inch cubes in a 1-liter container, then the number of 1-centimeter cubes in the same container. Then the number of 1-inch cubes in a 2-liter container.

2. *Estimate Length.* Use nonstandard measures (paper clips, blocks, pencils) and standard measures (inch cubes, centimeter cubes, rulers). Ask, "About how many pencils long is the art table?"

3. *Estimate Volume.* Use various nonstandard containers and standard containers (liter bottle, quart cartons). Ask, "About how much water (rice, sand, etc.) would be needed to fill the vase?"

4. *Estimate Weight.* Use nonstandard measures (cubes, books, paper clips) and standard measures (grams, ounces, pounds). Ask, "About how many paper clips weigh the same as a pencil?"

• *Instructional Ideas*

1. *Estimating involves taking risks.* Make sure that there is a safe environment for estimating and investigating ideas.

2. *Ask students to justify whether or not their estimates appear to be reasonable.* The process of justifying an answer allows students to think through the estimation again and review their original conclusions.

3. *Use concrete materials that the students can manipulate and investigate.* Pictures or illustrations are not appropriate here.

4. *Vary the group size when estimating.* Estimate as individuals, in small groups, pairs, and as a whole class.

5. *Make sure all students get a chance to estimate.* Those who have already developed a sense of number should not dominate the activity at the expense of others.

18: Measurement

- *Measurement*

  1. *Standard.* Measurement involving a ruler, yard stick, meter stick, etc.

  2. *Non-standard Measurement.* Measurement involving pencils, paper clips, blocks, etc.

     According to Piagetian theory, measurement requires two operations, unit iteration and transitivity.

- *Unit Iteration.* This is placing a measuring unit (standard or non-standard) against what is being measured and transferring it as many times as the unit will go into the whole. Moving the measuring unit is called unit iteration. Laying out pencils or blocks and counting them is not unit iteration. For unit iteration one needs to:

  1. Place the unit at one end of what is being measured.

  2. Mark and move the unit and repeat as necessary.

  3. Keep track of the movements.

  4. Determine the last part.

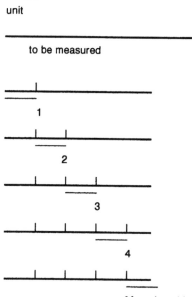

unit

to be measured

1

2

3

4

More than 4 but less than 5

(continued)

- *Transitivity.* This is the ability to infer a relationship from two or more other relationships. When asked to compare two lengths that cannot be placed side by side, young children use visual comparison ("That one is longer because I can see it!"). Later the children use a third item to make a comparison. When comparing length A to length B, the children compare both using length C.

  When comparing C to A and C to B, the results are that A > C and C > B. Therefore, it can be inferred that A > B.

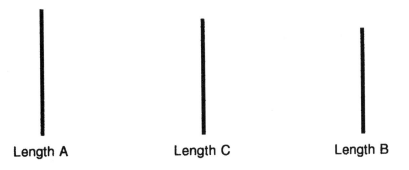

Length A	Length C	Length B

Unit iteration can be combined with transitivity. Length C is compared to Length A and Length B. Once again, it can be inferred that A > B.

Length A	Length C	Length B

19: Theories of Beginning Mathematics

Jean Piaget: Types of Knowledge

- *Physical Knowledge.* This is what we know about objects or what we can find out about objects by observing them or acting upon them. The source of physical knowledge is the object itself. *Examples:* The block is made of wood. The ball is red. The ball will roll down the ramp.

- *Social Knowledge.* This is agreed upon by society or social conventions. The source of social knowledge is oral or written communication through people. *Examples:* We do not run in school. The 4th of July is a holiday in the USA. Our written language.

- *Logico-mathematical Knowledge.* This is based on relationships that are created by the individual. The source of logico-mathematical knowledge is the individual in the way that he or she organizes the information. The relationships that the individual uses to organize information are:

  1. classification
  2. seriation
  3. number
  4. spatial relationships
  5. temporal (time) relationships

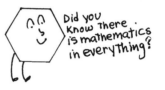

Examples: 1. The large red shapes go here. 2. This is the largest chair. 3. These groups have the same number since there are five in each group. 4. Place the books on top of the book shelf. 5. Tomorrow is Saturday.

For children to make sense of their world, physical, social and logico-mathematical knowledge must be going on all at the same time. They should not be addressed in isolation.

Jerome Bruner: Levels of Understanding

- *Enactive.* The child develops the ability to conceptualize by observing and manipulating objects. This level is also referred to as the concrete manipulative or hands-on level.

- *Iconic.* The child is able to think without manipulating objects and is able to replace the objects with pictures or diagrams that represent the objects. This is also referred to as the pictorial or representational level.

- *Symbolic.* The child is able to use symbols (4, ×, +, >, etc.) that represent numbers or ideas. This is also referred to as the abstract level.

The levels are presented as a suggested way for children to develop concepts. It is important for teachers to provide opportunities for children to work back and forth among all three levels as their abilities increase.

(continued)

Zoltan Dienes: Basic Principles for Working with Manipulative Materials

- *Dynamic Principle.* The true understanding of a math concept is a process that begins with time for undirected free play with materials, then structured activities, and finally application of the concept in real-world situations.

- *Constructive Principle.* Children should be allowed to develop concepts intuitively from their own experiences. Children should not be given concepts in analytical form until they have developed the concept in the concrete form. Children cannot analyze what they have not already constructed.

- *Mathematical Variability Principle.* Generalizing a concept is enhanced by providing many varying examples of the concept but keeping the relevant variables constant. For example, providing examples of triangles with varying angles, varying sides, and varying positions while keeping the relevant variable—a three-sided figure—constant.

- *Perceptual Variability Principle.* Provide multiple experiences using a variety of materials rather than the same experience many times. When children experience the same concept in different ways, they are more likely to generalize and understand the concept.

20: Resources for Beginning Mathematics

AIMS Educational Foundation. Fresno, CA.

Baratta-Lorton, M. *Workjobs: Activity-Centered Learning for Early Childhood.* Menlo Park, CA: Addison-Wesley, 1972.

Baratta-Lorton, M. *Workjobs II: Number Activities for Early Childhood.* Menlo Park, CA: Addison-Wesley, 1978.

Burk, D., Snider, A., and Symonds, P. *Math Excursions: Project-Based Mathematics for Kindergartners.* Portsmouth, NH: Heinemann, 1993.

Burns, M. *Mathematics and Literature. (K-3).* White Plains, NY: Cuisenaire Co., 1987.

Carson, P. and Dellosa, J. *All Aboard for Readiness Skills.* Greensboro, NC: Carson-Dellosa Publishing, 1995.

Griffiths, R. and Clyne, M. *Books You Can Count on: Linking Mathematics & Literature.* Portsmouth, NH: Heinemann, 1991.

Harcourt, L. *Explorations in Early Childhood.* Menlo Park, CA: Addison-Wesley, no date.

Kamil, C. and Jones-Livingston, S. *Young Children Reinvent Arithmetic, Third Grade: Implications of Piaget's Theory.* New York: Teachers College Press, 1994.

Kamil, C. and DeVries, R. *Group Games in Early Education: Implications of Piaget's Theory.* Washington, D.C.: NAEYC, 1980.

Ohanian, S. *Math as a Way of Knowing.* White Plains, NY: Cuisenaire Co., 1994.

Schultz, K., Colarusso, R., and Strawderman, V. *Mathematics for Every Young Child.* Columbus, OH: Merrill Education, 1990.

SECTION 3

GEOMETRY

Name _____

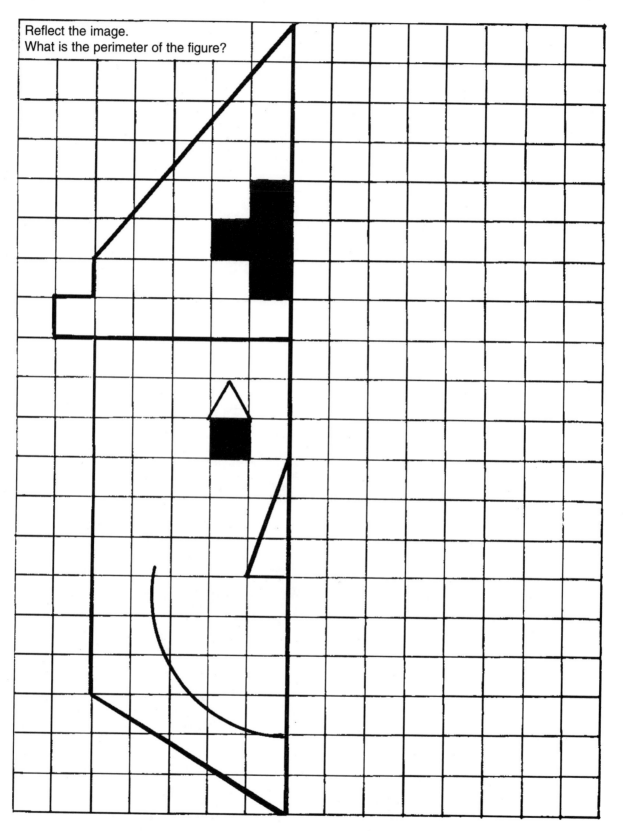

Reflect the image.
What is the perimeter of the figure?

Answer:_____

21: How Children Learn Geometric Concepts

A. Research of Pierre van Hiele and Dina van Hiele-Geldof (1959) suggests that children learn geometric ideas by proceeding through levels.

Level 0: Holistic Level
- Students perceive figures by their appearances as a whole entity.
- When students say "square," they react to the total figure, not to the specific properties of the square itself.
- They do not call Figure b shown below a square because it doesn't look like a square.

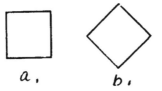

a,   b,

Level 1: Analysis of Figures
- Students are aware of various properties of figures: angles and size.
- They identify figures by knowing the figures' properties. For example: if each of the sides of a figure are parallel, then it must be a parallelogram; if the figure has three sides, then it must be a triangle.
- However, at this stage, students do not perceive any relationship between squares and rectangles. In other words, they are unable to see the relationship between figures with similar attributes as being a subset of the superset.

Level 2: Seeing the Relationships of Properties Among Figures
- Students understand that a square is also a rectangle and a special type of parallelogram.
- Students understand the relationships between figures, but have not developed the ability to prove theorems at this level.

Level 3: Deductive Reasoning
- Students begin to understand deductive reasoning and can follow the logic of an argument in proofs of statements presented to them.
- Students are able to develop sequences of statements to deduce one statement from another.
- Students are able to prove why a statement is true.

Level 4: Deep Understanding of Mathematical Structures
- Student is able to think like a mathematician.
- Student is able to justify to a very high degree statements made about mathematical structures.

(continued)

B. Research of Jean Piaget and Barbel Inhelder (1948) shows how children develop geometric ideas in developmental stages.

Stage 1: Before Age 4
- Children begin to acquire topological concepts.
- They understand closed/open, inside/outside, boundaries, separation, order, connectedness, and proximity.
- This understanding is used in the Goodenough-Harris Draw-a-Man test.

Stage 2: Ages 4 to 7
- Children begin to develop Euclidean concepts of shape, which include attributes such as size, shape, direction, angles, perpendicular, and parallel.
- In drawing they use a base line on which to place figures.

Stage 3: Ages 7 to 9
- Children relate to their physical environment.
- They are able to conserve length and area.
- They realize length and area do not change when figure is relocated in space.
- They become aware of horizontal and vertical points of references.
- They develop a sense of perspective.

State 4: Ages 9 to 11
- Children are concerned with filling space with details.
- They use perspective.

22: Vocabulary for Geometric Solid Shapes

1. *Geometric Shape:* A portion of 3-dimensional space that is occupied by a shape. Examples to use in classroom: any object.

2. *Polyhedron:* A geometric shape, especially one with more than six plane surfaces. A polygon is a closed plane figure, especially one with more than four sides and angles.

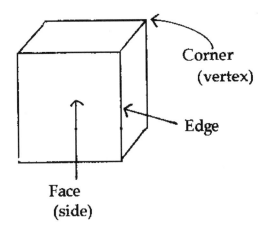

Corner (vertex)

Edge

Face (side)

a. *Face:* Any of the surfaces of a polyhedron.

b. *Base:* The face of the polyhedron to which the latitude is drawn.

c. *Edge:* The line formed when two faces of a geometric shape meet, as in an intersection.

d. *Vertex:* The point at which three or more faces of a geometric shape meet or intersect.

e. *Lateral face:* Any surface of a polyhedron that is not a base. Usually, a side is considered a lateral face.

f. *Height or altitude:* The perpendicular distance from the tallest point of the polyhedron to the base.

Shape	Faces	Corners	Edges
Pyramids			
Triangular based	4	4	6
Square based	5	5	8
Prisms			
Triangular	5	6	9
Square	6	8	12
Cube	6	8	12
Rectangular	6	8	12
Hexagonal	8	12	18
Curved			
Cone	2	1	1
Cylinder	3	0	2
Sphere	1	0	0

3. *Prism:* A polyhedron with two parallel and congruent faces. These faces are considered the bases of the prism.

69

(continued)

4. *Pyramid:* A geometric shape with one base (a polygon); the other faces are triangular. These faces come together at one point which is called the vertex or apex of the pyramid.

 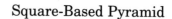

Triangular-Based Pyramid   Square-Based Pyramid

5. *Height or altitude (of a pyramid):* The perpendicular distance from the vertex to the base of the pyramid.

6. *Sphere:* A geometric shape consisting of all the points at the given (same) distance from a given point called the *center* of the sphere.

7. *Radius (of a sphere):* The distance from the center of the sphere to the sphere itself.

8. *Diameter (of a sphere):* The distance through the sphere from one surface point to another surface point, passing through the center of the sphere. The diameter of a sphere is twice the length of a radius.

9. *Cylinder:* A geometric shape with two congruent bases that are closed curves; a flat surface connects the bases.

(continued)

10. *Cone:* A geometric shape having a circle as a base figure and a point called the vertex that is not on the base.

11. *Volume:* The number of cubic units contained within the geometric shape.

23: Solid Shapes: Polyhedrons

Pyramids

Triangular-based pyramid

Square-based pyramid

Prisms

Triangular

Square

Cube

Rectangular

Hexagonal

Curved

Cylinder

Cone

Sphere

Read This. It has neat Parts.

©1997 by The Center for Applied Research in Education

24: Faces of Solid Shapes

Pyramids

Triangular-based pyramid

Square-based pyramid

Prisms

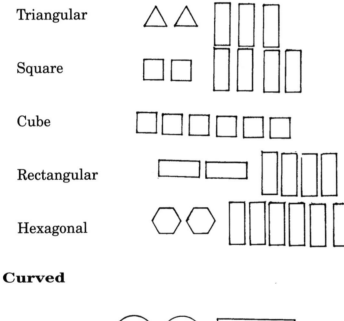

Triangular

Square

Cube

Rectangular

Hexagonal

Curved

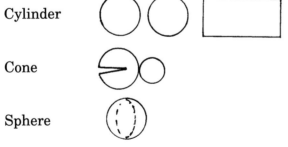

Cylinder

Cone

Sphere

25: Nets for Solid Shapes

Pyramids

Triangular-based phramid

Square-based pyramid

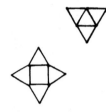

Prisms

Triangular

Square

Cube

Rectangular

Hexagonal

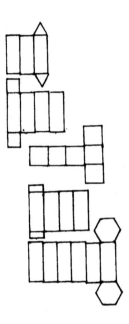

Curved

Cylinder

Cone

Sphere

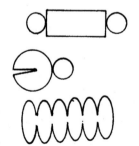

26: Vocabulary for Polygons

Basic Ideas in Geometry

1. Greeks received a physical concept of geometry from the Egyptians.
2. Greeks changed a physical concept into an abstract science peaking with Euclid.
3. Geometry is derived from Greek words that mean "earth measure."
4. The word geometry means the study of SPACE and shapes in space.
5. Elementary teachers need to develop the following concepts with children in grades 2-5:

> point
> space
> curve
> line
> line segment
> ray
> angle

Point:

1. A geometric point can be thought of as an immovable or fixed LOCATION in geometric space.
2. Similarly, geometric SPACE, which is undefined, can be thought of as the SET OF ALL POINTS.
3. A geometric point is a precise, fixed location in geometric space, but we cannot see a geometric point because it has no physical length, width, or thickness.
4. When we say space is the set of all points (location), we mean that we can think of the physical universe as being filled with these points.
5. Geometric points and geometric space are ideas with no physical existence. We represent geometric ideas by physical representations called symbols like dots, lines, etc.
6. Interestingly, no matter how small we make our dot, it still covers countless geometric points. However, a dot is the most satisfactory way of representing a geometric point. Points are labeled with a capital letter.

Symbol: • A

Line: A set of points and therefore a subset of space. A geometric line stretches endlessly.

Symbol: ←——————→

Intersection: The point at which two lines cross each other.

(continued)

Line Segment: A geometric line is a set of points (subset of geometric space) that represents the shortest distance between two given points.

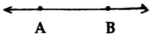

A   B

End Points: 1. A line segment has first and last points.
2. Every line segment is a subset of a line.
3. Segment means "part."

Symbol: ●—●
AB

Ray: 1. A ray is another kind of subset of a line. It consists of a point on the line and all points on the line extending in one direction from the point.

Symbol: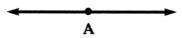

End Point
or
Initial Point

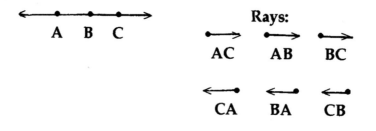

A

2. A ray begins at one point and continues endlessly in one direction.

A   B   C   **Rays:**
●→   ●→   ●→
AC   AB   BC

←●   ←●   ←●
CA   BA   CB

Angle: The union of two rays that have a common end point and do not lie on the same line.

(continued)

Vertex: The common end point of an angle.

Side: Names the two rays that form the angle.
                         Symbol: < BAC or < CAB

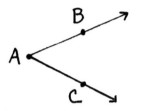

                         (The vertex is always the middle or second point indicated.)

Inside/Outside: All angles have an inside (interior) and an outside (exterior).

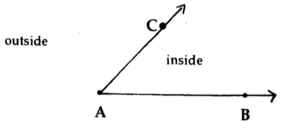

Degree: The standard unit of angle measure. The number of degrees measures the opening between the side of an angle.

Protractor: The instrument used to measure the degrees of an angle.

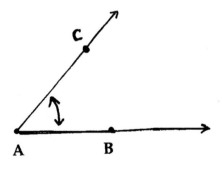

                         Symbol: °   < CAB = 50°

(continued)

Congruent: Two angles that have the same measure.

Symbols: ≅ means "is congruent to"
         ≇ means "is not congruent to"

Right Angle: An angle whose measure is 90°.

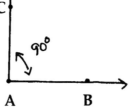

Perpendicular: Ray CD determines two angles: ACD and BCD. If they are congruent, they are right angles and said to be *perpendicular* to line AB.

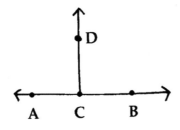

Symbol: CD ⊥ AB

Acute Angle: An angle that is less than a right angle or 90°.

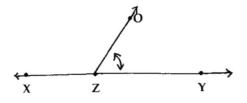

< YZO is an acute angle.

(continued)

Obtuse Angle: An angle that is greater than 90° but less than 180°.

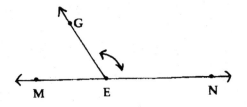

< NEG is an obtuse angle.

Adjacent Angles: Two angles with a common vertex, a common ray or side between them, and no common exterior points.

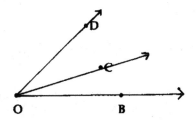

< DOC is *adjacent* to COB.
< DOC is *not adjacent* DOB.

Complementary Angles: If the sum of the measures of two angles is equal to the measure of a right angle (90°), the two angles are said to be complementary angles.

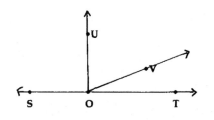

< UOV and < VOT are complementary angles.

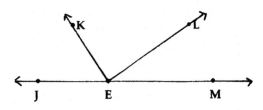

< JEK and < LEM are complementary angles.

(continued)

Supplementary Angles: If the sum of the two measures of angles is equal to 180°, the two angles are called supplementary angles.

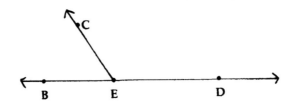

< BEC and < CED are supplementary angles.

Bisect: To divide an angle in half.

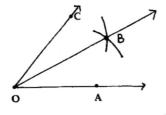

< OB bisects < AOC.

27: Polygons

Concept of a Geometric Plane: A plane is a subset of space. Any three points not in a straight line determine a plane.

Curves: 1. A line segment is a special kind of open curve.

Open Curve

2. A closed curve is a line or curve that returns to its beginning point. A closed curve has no end points.

Closed Curve

Polygons are *simple closed curves* composed of three or more line segments.

Number of sides	Prefix	Name
3	Tri	Triangle
4	Quad	Quadrilateral
5	Penta	Pentagon
6	Hexa	Hexagon
7	Hepta	Heptagon
8	Octa	Octagon
9	Nona	Nonagon
10	Deca	Decagon
11	Undeca	Undecagon
12	Dodeca	Dodecagon
Many	Poly	Polygon

28: Classification of Triangles

Triangles can be classified in two ways:

1. By the number of congruent sides:

   a. A *scalene* triangle has no congruent sides.

   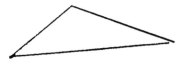

   b. An *isosceles* triangle has two congruent sides.

   c. An *equilateral* triangle has three congruent sides.

2. By the types of angles:

   a. An *acute* triangle has three acute angles.
      Acute angles are angles < 90°.

   b. A *right* triangle has a right angle.
      Right angles = 90°.

   c. An *obtuse* triangle has an obtuse angle.
      Obtuse angle is an angle > 90°.

29: Classification of Quadrilaterals: Definitions

Quadrilateral: Simple closed curves with a union of four sides, none of which lie on the same line.

Square: Four sides and angles are equal.

Rectangle: Opposite sides are congruent and parallel; angles are all 90°.

Parallelogram: Opposite sides are congruent and parallel; angles are not 90°.

Rhombus: All four sides are congruent and opposite sides are parallel; angles are less than 90°.

Trapezoid: Only one pair of sides is parallel.

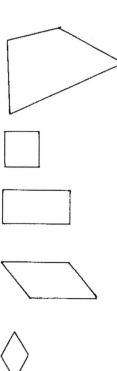

Venn Diagram of Quadrilaterals

Key: U = set of all quadrilaterals
    A = set of all parallelograms
    B = set of all rectangles
    C = set of all rhombuses
    D = set of all squares
    E = set of trapezoids
    F = all other quadrilaterals

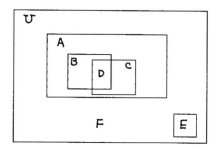

30: Nets for Pentomino Figures: Boxes

Pentomino nets that fold into a box.

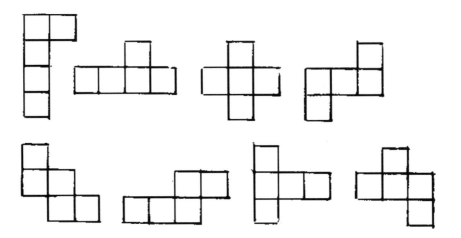

Pentomino nets that do not fold into a box.

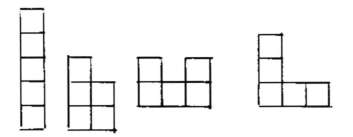

31: Nets for Hexonimo Figures: Cubes

The nets with black boxes will fold into cubes.

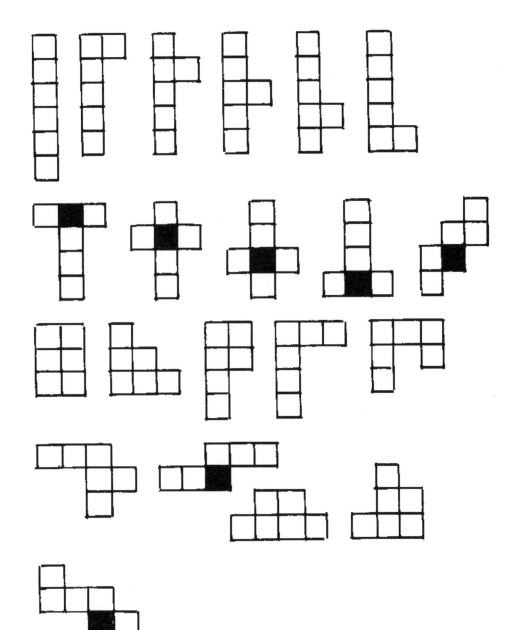

32: Circles:
Definitions

Circle: A set of all points in one plane that are an equal distance from a given point, called a center.

Radius: A line segment from the center to any point on the circle.

Diameter: The union of 2 radii lying on the same line.

Circumference: The distance around the circle.

Arc: Any two points that divide the circle into two parts.

Pi: An irrational number close to 3.14. It is the circumference of a circle divided by the diameter of that circle. The formula for establishing this ratio is $\pi = C/D$.

33: Formulas for Finding Perimeter and Area of Polygons

1. *Perimeter:* measuring the distance around a figure

   a. Square:

   P = s + s + s + s or 4(s)

   Example:

   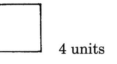

   4 units

   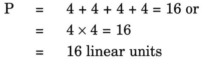

   P = 4 + 4 + 4 + 4 = 16 or

   = 4 × 4 = 16

   = 16 linear units

   b. Rectangle:

   P = 2 (l) + 2 (h)

   Example:

   5 units

   3 units

   P = (2 × 5) + (2 × 3)

   = 10 + 6

   = 16 linear units

2. *Area:* measuring the square units within the region of a figure

   a. Triangle:

   A = 1/2 (Base × Height)

   Example:

   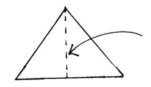

   5 units

   6 units

   A = 1/2 (6 × 5)

   = 1/2 of 30

   or 1/2 × 30

   1/2 × 30/1

   = 15 square units

(continued)

b. Square:

$$A = (\text{Length} \times \text{Width}) \text{ or } A = s^2$$

Example: A = (2×2) or 2^2

2 units   = 4 square units

2 units

c. Rectangle:

$$A = (\text{Length} \times \text{Width})$$

Example: A = (6×3)

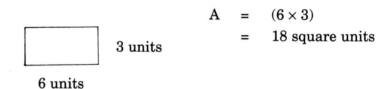

3 units   = 18 square units

6 units

d. Parallogram:

$$A = (\text{Base} \times \text{Height})$$

Example: A = (6×3)

3 units   = 18 square units

6 units

e. Trapezoid:

$$A = 1/2 \times \text{Height} \times (\text{Base 1} + \text{Base 2})$$

Example: A = $1/2 [3 \times (4 + 6)]$

4 units   = $1/2 (3 \times 10)$

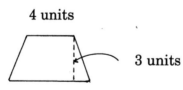   = $1/2$ of 30 or $1/2 \times 30/1$

3 units   = 15 square units

6 units

(continued)

f. Circle:

(Circumference)   C   = $\pi \times$ diameter

                                    or

                         C   = $\pi \times (2 \times \text{radius})$

Example: C   = $\pi \times d$
                              = 3.14×10
                              =   31.4 linear units

(Area)   A   = πr^2

Example: 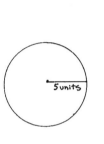   A   = πr^2
                              = 3.14×5^2
                              = $3.14 \times (5 \times 5)$
                              = 3.14×25
                              =   78.5 square units

34: Pick's Theorem:
Finding Area Using a Geoboard

A = the area of a polygon formed on a geoboard or on square grid paper.

N_p = the number of points on the perimeter of the polygon.

N_i = the number of points in the interior or inside the polygon.

With no pegs inside:

$A \quad = \quad 1/2 \, N_p - 1$

$A \quad = \quad 1/2 \text{ of } 5$

$\quad = \quad 2\,1/2 - 1$

$\quad = \quad 1\,1/2 \text{ square units}$

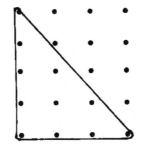

With pegs inside:

$A = 1/2 \, N_p - 1 + N_1$

$A \quad = \quad 1/2 \text{ of } 8 - 1 + N_i$

$\quad = \quad 4 - 1 + N_i$

$\quad = \quad 3 + 3$

$\quad = \quad 6 \text{ square units}$

35: Pythagorean Theorem

$a^2 + b^2 = c^2$

$4^2 + 3^2 = 5^2$

$16 + 9 = 25$

$25 = 25$

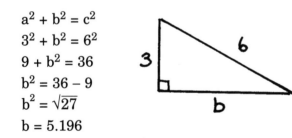

Find an unknown side of a right triangle using the Pythagorean theorem:

$a^2 + b^2 = c^2$

$3^2 + b^2 = 6^2$

$9 + b^2 = 36$

$b^2 = 36 - 9$

$b^2 = \sqrt{27}$

$b = 5.196$

36: Formulas for Finding
Volume of Polyhedras

Prism:

$$V = \text{Base} \times \text{Height}$$

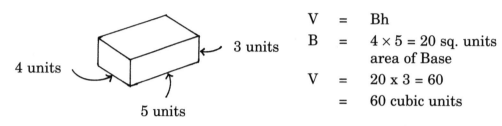

V	=	Bh
B	=	$4 \times 5 = 20$ sq. units area of Base
V	=	$20 \times 3 = 60$
	=	60 cubic units

1. Find the area of the Base figure.
2. Multiply it by the height.

Cube:

$$V = s^3$$

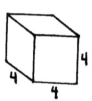

V	=	S^3
V	=	4^3
	=	$4 \times 4 \times 4 = 64$
	=	64 cubic units

Triangular Prism:

$$V = 1/2\ Bh$$

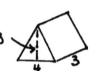

V	=	1/2 bh
	=	$[1/2 \times (4 \times 3) \times 3]$
	=	6×3
	=	18 cubic units

1. Find the area of the triangular face. A = 1/2 bh
2. Multiply by the height of the prism.

©1997 by The Center for Applied Research in Education

(continued)

Pyramid:

$$V = 1/3\ Bh$$

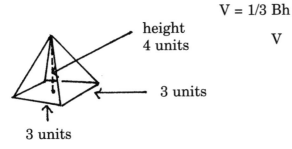

height
4 units

3 units

3 units

V	=	1/3 Bh
	=	1/3 (b × b) h
	=	1/3 × 9 × 4
	=	1/3 × 36 = 12
	=	12 cubic units

Cylinder:

$$V = Bh$$

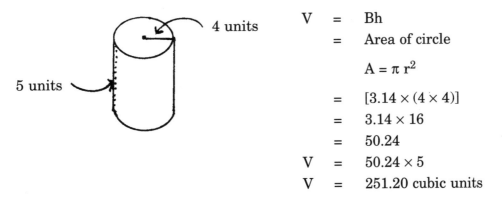

4 units

5 units

V	=	Bh
	=	Area of circle
		$A = \pi\ r^2$
	=	[3.14 × (4 × 4)]
	=	3.14 × 16
	=	50.24
V	=	50.24 × 5
V	=	251.20 cubic units

1. Find the area of the circle.
2. Multiply it by the height of the cylinder.

Cone:

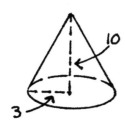

10

3

$$V = 1/3\ Bh$$

V	=	1/3 ($\pi\ r^2$) h
	=	1/3 (3.14 × 3^2) × 10
	=	1/3 × 28.26 × 10
	=	94.2 cubic units

1. Find the area of the circular figure.
2. Multiply the area times the height.
3. Divide the product by 1/3.

(continued)

Sphere:

$$V = 4/3\pi^3$$

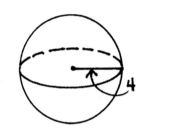

$$
\begin{aligned}
V \quad &= \quad 4/3 \ \pi \ r^3 \\
&= \quad 4/3 \times 3.14 \times 4^3 \\
&= \quad 4/3 \times 3.14 \times 64 \\
&= \quad 4/3 \times 3.14/1 \times 64/1 \\
&= \quad 267.95 \text{ cubic units}
\end{aligned}
$$

1. Cube the radius of the sphere.
2. Multiply by pi.
3. Multiply by 4/3.

37: 28 Symmetry Patterns

Any pattern, figure, or shape has *Symmetry* if there is harmony in the object. There are different kinds of symmetry patterns generated by basically two operations: rotations and reflections. These patterns can be translated by sliding them across a plane. Elementary students should become familiar with the two basic operations, along with figures that can be translated across a straight line in a plane. In the classroom these operations are called slides, flips, and turns.

There are exactly 28 known symmetry patterns.

Four Basic Patterns:

1. Ordinary motif or design. Motif is assymetrical.

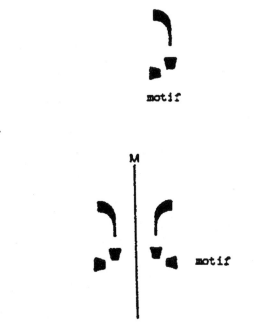

2. Simple reflection.

3. Rotation of a motif about a point. In this figure the motif is rotated 72° about the center point. This center point is called a rotocenter.

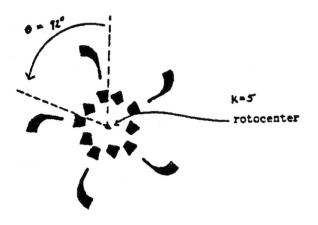

(continued)

4. Combining rotation with reflections.

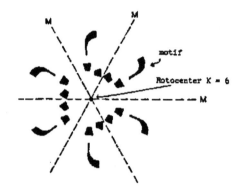

Seven Strip Patterns:

1. Motif is translated and repeated along a stright line.

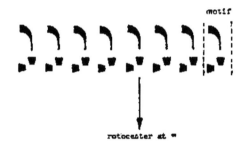

2. Motif is reflected about a mirror line.

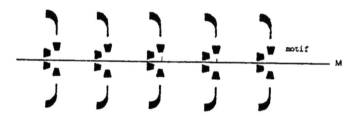

3. Motif is reflected through two parallel mirrors.

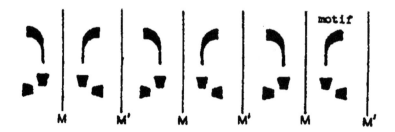

(continued)

4. Motif is reflected through three mirrors, two parallel to one another and the third mirror perpendicular to the two.

5. Motif is rotated through two distinct rotation points of order 2. (Rotations of 180°.)

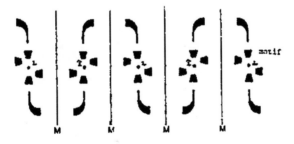

6. Motif uses a rotation point of order 2, is reflected followed by a translation.

7. Motif is translated followed by a reflection that has historically been called a glide reflection.

(continued)

Seventeen Plane Patterns:

There are exactly 17 different patterns that cover a plane. They become quite complicated to explain to elementary children. The 17 patterns are shown here. In order to simplify the pattern, rotoceters need to be understood.

A rotocenter is a rotation point of a certain order. The order is determined by the degree of the rotation itself. If a motif is rotated 180° about a point, then the rotation point or rotocenter is of order 2 because 180 divides 360 two times. The most important rotocenters to know are those of orders 2, 3, 4, and 6.

Order	Rotation
1	360°
2	180°
3	72°
4	90°
6	60°

By using a 2-3-6 rotation patttern, the right triangle motif will be rotated to cover the plane.

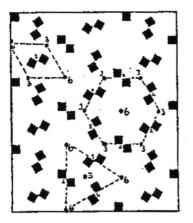 

2-3-6 Pattern.

(continued)

Patterns that cover the plane are defined by the rotation points through which the motif is rotated. The 17 plane patterns are names by these points. When a rotation point is at infinity, it generates a straight line. So the first pattern is explained as $1 \infty \infty$. For simplicity, the 17 different patterns are presented here without definition of the rotation points.

1.

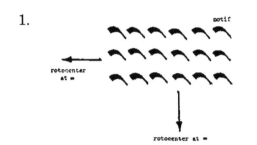

2.

3.

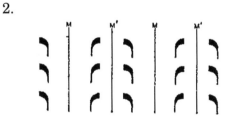

4.

5.

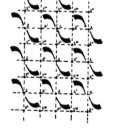

(continued)

6.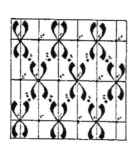

7.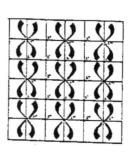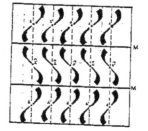

8.

9.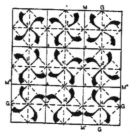

10.

11.

12.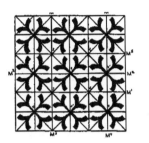

13.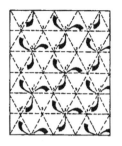

14.

15.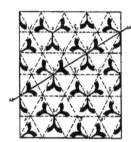

16.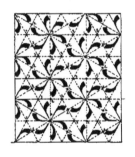

17.

38: Geometry Resources*

Angle Ruler	(ETA, Didax)
Brick by Brick	(ETA)
Circle Protractor	(ETA, Didax, Creative Publications)
Clear Plastic Geometric Volume Set	(ETA, Cuisenaire, Didax)
Foam Geometric Shapes	(ETA)
Geoblocks	(ETA, Didax)
Geoboards	(Cuisenaire, Didax, ETA, Dale Seymour)
Geo Board Stamps	(ETA, Didax)
Geo D-Stix	(Cuisenaire, Nasco, ETA)
Geometric Models	(Dale Seymour, Didax)
Geometry Dominoes	(Didax)
Geo-Rods	(Didax)
Geo Strips	(NASCO, Didax, ETA)
Large 3-D Geometric Shapes Stamps	(ETA, Didax)
Marvelous Mosaics ™	(ETA)
Mira Math	(NASCO, Didax, ETA, Creative Publications)
Notes on a Triangle	(Dale Seymour, Didax, Cuisenaire)
Pattern Block	(Cuisenaire)
Pattern Block Stamps	(Cuisenaire)
Pentablocks	(Cuisenaire)
Pentomino Puzzles Set	(ETA)
Plane Geometry Stamps	(ETA, Didax)
Polydron	(Dale Seymour, ETA, Cuisenaire)
Polydron Frameworks	(Dale Seymour, ETA, Cuisenaire)
Polygons + Power™ Pack	(ETA)
Polyhedra Blocks	(Dale Seymour, Cuisenaire)
Polyshapes	(ETA)
Power Blocks™	(ETA)
Power Polygons	(Cuisenaire, ETA)
Power Solids	(Dale Seymour, Cuisenaire)
Premier Pentominoes	(ETA)
Puzzle Cubes	(ETA)
Safe-T Compass®	(Didax, ETA, Creative Publications)
Shape Tracer Set	(ETA, Cuisenaire, Creative Publications)
Space Board	(Didax)
Tangoes	(ETA)
Tangrams	(ETA, Cuisenaire)
Template Set	(ETA)
Tessel-Grams™	(ETA)
Tessellation Shapes	(Didax, Dale Seymour, Cuisenaire, ETA, Creative Publications)
Tex Tiles	(Creative Publications)
Three-Dimensional Geometric Rubber Stamps	(Didax, NASCO)
3-D Geometric Shapes Stamps	(ETA, Didax, Cuisenaire)
Try It! Pentominoes	(Cuisenaire, ETA)
Wooden Geometric Solids	(ETA, Cuisenaire, Didax)

This might help you.

---

*See List 5 for addresses.

39: Geometry Activity Books*

Build it! Festival	(ETA, NASCO, Creative Publications)
Circles	(ETA, NASCO)
Circular Geoboard	(ETA, NASCO)
Cooperative Informal Geometry	(ETA, Cuisenaire, NASCO)
Elementary Geometry Lessons using the Polydron™ System	(Creative Publications, ETA)
Exploring Geoblocks	(ETA, Didax)
Exploring with Polydron™	(ETA, Dale Seymour, Cuisenaire)
Focus on Geometry	(NASCO)
Geoblocks and Geojackets	(ETA)
Geoblocks Jobcards®	(Creative Publications)
Geoboard Activity Books	(ETA, NASCO)
Geoboard Activity Cards	(ETA, NASCO)
Geoboard Collection Binders	(ETA)
Geometry Toolkit	(Dale Seymour)
Grandfather Tang's Story	(ETA, NASCO, Cuisenaire, Creative Publications)
Hands on Geoboards	(Creative Publications)
Hands-On Geometry	(ETA, NASCO)
Just for Geoboards	(Creative Publications)
K-5 Elementary Geometry Lessons Using the Polydron™ System	(Dale Seymour, Cuisenaire, Creative Publications)
'M' is for Mirror	(ETA)
Maneuvers with Circles	(ETA)
Math by All Means: Geometry	(NASCO, Creative Publications, ETA)
Mira Math Activities for Elementary School	(Didax)
Mirror Explorations	(ETA, NASCO)
Mirror Puzzle Book	(ETA)
Moving on with Geoboards	(Creative Publications)
Navigation	(ETA)
Patty Paper Geometry	(ETA)
Problem Solving with Pentominoes Book	(ETA, Cuisenaire, Didax)
Rainbow Geoboards in Action Activity Kits	(ETA)
Shapes Alive!	(ETA, NASCO)
Stretch it!	(ETA, NASCO)
Take Shape Geometry Binder	(ETA)
Tangramables™	(ETA, Didax)
Tangrams in Action Binder	(ETA, Didax)
Tessellation Jobcards®: Pattern Blocks	(Creative Publications)
Tessellation Teaching Masters	(ETA, Dale Seymour)
The Adventures of Terry Tangram™	(ETA)
The Circular Geoboard Book	(ETA)
20 Thinking Questions for Geoboards	(Creative Publications)
Windows to Tangrams	(ETA, NASCO)

---

*See List 5 for addresses.

NUMERATION AND COUNTING

Name _____

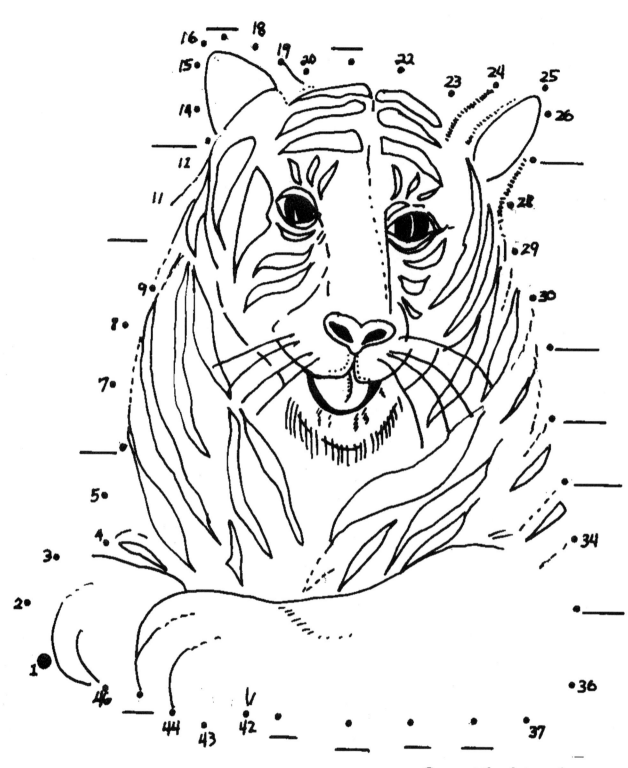

Connect the dots and
fill in the missing numbers.

40: The Egyptian Counting System

The Egyptian system of numeration was one of the earliest systems to be developed. It was a simple *additive* system in which the values of the symbols were *added* together. There was *no place value* and *no symbol for zero*.

Egyptian Symbol	Number Named	Meaning of Symbol
I	1	stroke
∩	10	oxen yoke
၅	100	coil of rope
⊥	1,000	lotus plant
∫	10,000	bent finger
	100,000	tadpole
	1,000,000	god supporting the sky

The symbols were written and then added, regardless of their order. For example, ∩ + I + I = 12. But I + ∩ + I also = 12, and I + I + ∩ again = 12.

1	I	21	∩∩I	3,000	⊥ ⊥
2	I I	22	∩∩II		
3	I I I	23	∩∩III	20,000	∫∫ ∫
4	I I I I			30,000	∫∫∫
		30	∩∩∩		
11	∩ I	40	∩∩∩∩	200,000	
12	∩ II			300,000	
13	∩ III	200	၅၅၅		
		300	၅၅၅	2,000,000	
20	∩∩	400	၅၅၅	3,000,000	

41: The Roman Counting System

The Roman system is an ancient numeration system that is still in use today. There is *no symbol for zero* and it is *not a place value system*. It does, however, utilize an order as the numerals of greater value were usually placed on the *left* of those of lesser value. The numerals were then *added* together.

Roman Numeral	Value of Numeral
I	1
V	5
X	10
L	50
C	100
D	500
M	1000

1	I	11	XI	30	XXX	400	CD
2	II	12	XII	40	XL	500	D
3	III	13	XIII	50	L	600	DC
4	IV	14	XIV	60	LX	700	DCC
5	V	15	XV	70	LXX	800	DCC
6	VI	16	XVI	80	LXXX	900	CM
7	VII	17	XVII	90	XC	1,000	M
8	VIII	18	XVIII	100	C	2,000	MM
9	IX	19	XIX	200	CC	3,000	*
10	X	20	XX	300	CCC	4,000	*

I can only be placed to the left of *V* or *X*.
X can only be placed to the left of *L* or *C*.
C can only be placed to the left of *D* or *M*.

*When representing large numbers the Romans sometimes used a bar over the numeral to increase its value by 1,000 times. Therefore, $\overline{\text{III}}$ = 3,000 and $\overline{\text{IV}}$ = 4,000.

©1997 by The Center for Applied Research in Education

42: The Chinese Counting System

The Chinese developed a system that used multiplication to indicate number value. There were symbols for the numbers 1 through 9 and different symbols for powers of ten. Symbols were multiplied by powers of tens to avoid repeating the symbols.

Chinese Symbol	Symbol Value
—	1
≡	2
≡	3
四	4
五	5
六	6
七	7
八	8
九	9
十	10
百	100

20	≡十	200	≡百
30	≡十	300	≡百
40	四十	400	四百
50	五十	500	五百
60	六十	600	六百
70	七十	700	七百
80	八十	800	八百
90	九十	900	九百

≡百 六十 五

$(3 \times 100) + (6 \times 10) + 5 = 365$

43: Ancient Number Systems

Ancient Greek

1	I
5	Γ
10	Δ
1,000	H
10,000	X
1,000,000	M

Ionic Greek

1	∝	10	L	100	ρ
2	β	20	κ	200	6
3	γ	30	λ	300	γ
4	ς	40	μ	400	υ
5	ε	50	ν	500	φ
6	ζ	60	⋿	600	χ
7	ς	70	ο	700	ψ
8	η	80	π	800	ω
9	θ	90	Q	900	π

Mayan

0	⊘	10	═
1	•	11	•̲
2	• •	12	••
3	• • •	13	•••
4	• • • •	14	••••
5	—	15	≡
6	•	16	•
7	••	17	••
8	•••	18	•••
9	••••	19	••••

44: The Hindu-Arabic Counting System

Decillions	hundreds	100,000,000,000,000,000,000,000,000,000,000,000
	tens	10,000,000,000,000,000,000,000,000,000,000,000
	ones	1,000,000,000,000,000,000,000,000,000,000,000
Nonillions	hundreds	100,000,000,000,000,000,000,000,000,000,000
	tens	10,000,000,000,000,000,000,000,000,000,000
	ones	1,000,000,000,000,000,000,000,000,000,000
Octillions	hundreds	100,000,000,000,000,000,000,000,000,000
	tens	10,000,000,000,000,000,000,000,000,000
	ones	1,000,000,000,000,000,000,000,000,000
Septillions	hundreds	100,000,000,000,000,000,000,000,000
	tens	10,000,000,000,000,000,000,000,000
	ones	1,000,000,000,000,000,000,000,000
Sextillions	hundreds	100,000,000,000,000,000,000,000
	tens	10,000,000,000,000,000,000,000
	ones	1,000,000,000,000,000,000,000
Quintillions	hundreds	100,000,000,000,000,000,000
	tens	10,000,000,000,000,000,000
	ones	1,000,000,000,000,000,000
Quadrillions	hundreds	100,000,000,000,000,000
	tens	10,000,000,000,000,000
	ones	1,000,000,000,000,000
Trillions	hundreds	100,000,000,000,000
	tens	10,000,000,000,000
	ones	1,000,000,000,000
Billions	hundreds	100,000,000,000
	tens	10,000,000,000
	ones	1,000,000,000
Millions	hundreds	100,000,000
	tens	10,000,000
	ones	1,000,000
Thousands	hundreds	100,000
	tens	10,000
	ones	1,000
Units	hundreds	100
	tens	10
	ones	1

45: Googol

What is a *googol*? A googol is the number 1 with one hundred zeros!

10,000,000,000,000, 000,000,000,000,000, 000,000,000,000,000, 000,000,000,000,000, 000,000,000,000,000, 000,000,000,000,000, 000,000,000,000.

Mathematicians write a googol like this, 10^{100}. It has been said that a googol is more than the number of grains of sand on earth.

46: Sets

- *Set.* A collection of objects or ideas (called elements) that are defined by a common attribute or characteristic. The collection can be described or the elements listed within set braces {___}.
- *Universal set.* A complete set of objects or ideas under consideration at that given time. It is usually symbolized by the letter U, as in U = {animals}.
- *Empty set (or null set).* A set that contains no elements. It can be shown by empty braces { }, or the Greek letter phi ø. The symbol {0} is not an empty set. It is a set of one zero.
- *Cardinal number.* The number of elements in the set. For example, the set of alphabet letters {a, b, c, d, e, f} contains six elements. Cardinality is symbolized as n: n{a, b, c, d, e, f} = 6. Sets are usually named by capital letters. Designating the set of letters as set A produces n(A) = 6.
- *Equal sets.* Two sets are equal if they contain the exact same elements, including the same cardinal number.
- *Equivalent sets.* Two sets are equivalent if they have the same cardinal number, but not the same elements.

$$J = \{? \; ? \; \# \; ?\} \quad K = \{? \; ? \; ? \; \#\} \quad L = \{! \; ? \; ! \; ?\}$$

Set J and set K are equal sets since they contain the exact same elements; their order does not matter. Set L is equivalent but not equal to set J and set K since we could match the elements in one-to-one correspondence and they all contain four elements.

The following examples illustrate these ideas:

U = { ○ □ △ ▭ ● ■ ▲ ▬ }

C is the set of circles, so C = { ○ ● }

D is the set of dark shapes, so D = { ● ■ ▲ ▬ }

H is the set of hexagons, so H = { }, or H = { ø }, the empty set.

The cardinality of the sets are:

$$n(C) = 2 \quad n(D) = 4 \quad n(H) = 0 \quad n(U) = 8$$

T is the set of triangles, so T = { △ ▲ } . Set T and set C are equivalent, but they are not equal.

(continued)

- *Union, or joining, of two sets.* This yields a set of all the elements that are in one set, the other set, or both sets. The symbol for union (∪) is written between two set names to designate the appropriate sets; D ∪ C, the union of the set of dark and the set of circles. D ∪ C = {○ ● ■ ▲ ▬} . Each element is a member of set C *or* D, *or* both sets.

- *Intersection of two sets.* This yields a set of all the elements that are in both sets. The symbol for intersection (∩) is also written to designate the appropriate sets; the intersection of the dark set and the set of circles has one common element, a dark circle. D ∩ C = { ● }. Each element of the intersection is a member of set C *and* set D.

The following is an example of the intersection of two sets. One hoop contains the set of large shapes with no large shapes outside the hoop. The other hoop contains the set of circles, with no circles outside the hoop. Large circles belong in both sets but may not be outside either hoop. We indicate that by placing them in the intersection of the two hoops, which shows that the large circles are members of both sets.

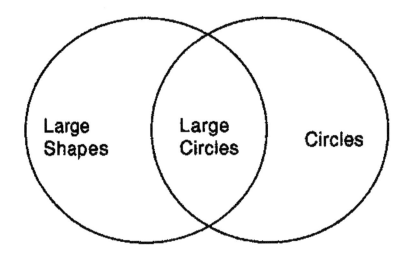

47: Ordering Sets

When comparing two sets, the only relationships that exist are:

- *Equal* (=). The elements in the two sets match in one-to-one correspondence, or each has as many as the other.
- *Greater than* (>). The elements cannot be matched one-to-one. One set has more than the other set.
- *Less than* (<). The elements cannot be matched one-to-one. One set has less than the other set.

Children an be introduced to the hungry alligator who loves to eat big numbers. The alligator's mouth always opens toward the big number and then the sentence is read.

Three is less than five.   Four is greater than two.

48: Cardinal and Ordinal Numbers

Cardinal numbers answer the question *"How many?"* and are usually determined by counting. *Ordinal numbers* show order.

Cardinal Number	Symbol	Ordinal Number	Abbreviated Form
One	1	First	1st
Two	2	Second	2nd
Three	3	Third	3rd
Four	4	Fourth	4th
Five	5	Fifth	5th
Six	6	Sixth	6th
Seven	7	Seventh	7th
Eight	8	Eighth	8th
Nine	9	Ninth	9th
Ten	10	Tenth	10th
Eleven	11	Eleventh	11th
Twelve	12	Twelfth	12th
Thirteen	13	Thirteenth	13th
Fourteen	14	Fourteenth	14th
Fifteen	15	Fifteenth	15th
Sixteen	16	Sixteenth	16th
Seventeen	17	Seventeenth	17th
Eighteen	18	Eighteenth	18th
Nineteen	19	Nineteenth	19th
Twenty	20	Twentieth	20th
Twenty-one	21	Twenty-first	21st
Twenty-two	22	Twenty-second	22nd
Twenty-three	23	Twenty-third	23rd
Twenty-four	24	Twenty-fourth	24th
Twenty-five	25	Twenty-fifth	25th
Twenty-six	26	Twenty-sixth	26th
Twenty-seven	27	Twenty-seventh	27th
Twenty-eight	28	Twenty-eighth	28th
Twenty-nine	29	Twenty-ninth	29th
Thirty	30	Thirtieth	30th

The same pattern is repeated for subsequent numbers.

Cardinal Number	Symbol	Ordinal Number	Abbreviated Form
Forty	40	Fortieth	40th
Fifty	50	Fiftieth	50th
Sixty	60	Sixtieth	60th
Seventy	70	Seventieth	70th
Eighty	80	Eightieth	80th
Ninety	90	Ninetieth	90th
One hundred	100	One hundredth	100th
One hundred one	101	One hundred first	101st
One hundred two	102	One hundred second	102nd
One hundred three	103	One hundred third	103rd
Two hundred	200	Two hundredth	200th
Three hundred	300	Three hundredth	300th
One thousand	1,000	One thousandth	1000th
One thousand one	1,001	One thousand first	1001st

49: Prime Numbers

Prime numbers are integers other than 1 whose factors are one and themselves. The factors for 2 are 2×1 or 1×2—only one and itself—making it a prime number. The factors for 7 are 7×1 or 1×7; therefore it is also a prime number.

Prime numbers can be illustrated using an array.

```
                2                          7
1 × 2    * *             1 × 7    * * * * * *
                                  *
2 × 1    *                        *
         *                        *
                        7 × 1     *
                                  *
                                  *
                                  *
```

The first 50 prime numbers.

2	31	73	127	179
3	37	79	131	181
5	41	83	137	191
7	43	89	139	193
11	47	97	149	197
13	53	101	151	199
17	59	103	157	211
19	61	107	163	223
23	67	109	167	227
29	71	113	173	229

50: Composite Numbers

Composite numbers are integers not including 1 that have factors other than one and themselves. The factors for 4 are 4 × 1 and 2 × 2 (1, 2, 4). The factors for 12 are 12 × 1, 6 × 2, and 4 × 3 (1, 2, 3, 4, 6, 12). Therefore, both are composite numbers. By definition, 1 is neither prime nor composite.

Composite numbers can be illustrated using an array.

```
1 × 4    * * * *        4 × 1    *           2 × 2    * *
                                 *                    * *
                                 *
                                 *
```

The first 50 composite numbers.

4	20	33	46	58
6	21	34	48	60
8	22	35	49	62
9	24	36	50	63
10	25	38	51	64
12	26	39	52	65
14	27	40	54	66
15	28	42	55	68
16	30	44	56	69
18	32	45	57	70

©1997 by The Center for Applied Research in Education

51: Expanded and Exponential Notations

Expanded Notation

Expanded notation displays numbers in specific component parts. The component parts show the place value of the digits.

2,435 written in expanded notation is 2,000 + 400 + 30 + 5. The expanded number can also be written as:

$$(2 \times 1{,}000) + (4 \times 100) + (3 \times 10) + (5 \times 1)$$

Exponential Notation

Exponential notation is the process of writing a numeral called an *exponent* to the right and above a 10 to indicate how many times 10 is used as a factor. The 10 is then raised to the power of the exponent.

10^1 means 10×1 or 10, and is read "ten to the first power."

10^2 means 10×10 or 100, and is read "ten to the second power."

10^3 means $10 \times 10 \cdot 10$ or 1,000, and is read "ten to the third power."

In a special case, ten to the zero power (10^0) is considered to be equal to one.

Thousands	Hundreds	Tens	Ones
10^3	10^2	10^1	10^0

Using Exponential Notation

10^3	10^2	10^1	10^0
2	4	3	5

$$(2 \times 10^3) + (4 \times 10^2) + (3 \times 10^1) + (5 \times 10^0) =$$
$$(2 \times 10 \times 10 \times 10) + (4 \times 10 \times 10) + (3 \times 10) + (5 \times 1) =$$
$$(2 \times 1000) + (4 \times 1000) + (3 \times 10) + (5 \times 1) = 2{,}435$$

Exponential notation can also be used to express numbers less than 1. A negative exponent is written to the right and above a 10 to indicate powers of ten on the right side of the decimal point.

10^3	10^2	10^1	10^0		10^{-1}	10^{-2}	10^{-3}
1000	100	10	1	.	.1	.01	.001

$$(6 \times 10^2) + (8 \times 10^1) + (1 \times 10^0) + (7 \times 10^{-1}) + (9 \times 10^{-2}) + (4 \times 10^{-3}) =$$
$$(6 \times 100) + (8 \times 10) + (1 \times 1) + (7 \times .1) + (9 \times .01) + (4 \times .001) =$$
$$600 + 80 + 1 + .7 + .09 + .004 = 681.794$$

52: Scientific Notation

The principles of exponential notation are used in scientific notation. Here a number is expressed as being greater than 1 and less than 10, multiplied by a certain power of ten. For example, 3.6 (> 1 and < 10) is multiplied by 10^2, or $3.6 \times 10^2 = 360$. Similarly, 2.5 multiplied by 10^5 is $2.5 \times 10^5 = 250,000$.

Scientific notation is an efficient way to express and work with large numbers.

Planet	Distance (miles) from the Sun
Mercury	3.6×10^7
Venus	6.71×10^7
Earth	9.29×10^7
Mars	1.42×10^8
Jupiter	4.83×10^8
Saturn	8.86×10^8
Uranus	1.78×10^9
Neptune	2.79×10^9
Pluto	3.67×10^9

Scientific notation can express very small numbers just as easily as large numbers. The principles of exponential notation are still used.

$$1 \text{ centimeter} = 6.214 \times 10^{-6} \text{ miles}$$
$$1 \text{ centimeter} = 3.281 \times 10^{-2} \text{ feet}$$
$$1 \text{ inch} = 1.578 \times 10^{-5} \text{ miles}$$
$$1 \text{ inch} = 8.333 \times 10^{-2} \text{ feet}$$

©1997 by The Center for Applied Research in Education

53: 100 Number Array

1	2	3	4	5	6	7	8	9	10
11	12	13	14	15	16	17	18	19	20
21	22	23	24	25	26	27	28	29	30
31	32	33	34	35	36	37	38	39	40
41	42	43	44	45	46	47	48	49	50
51	52	53	54	55	56	57	58	59	60
61	62	63	64	65	66	67	68	69	70
71	72	73	74	75	76	77	78	79	80
81	82	83	84	85	86	87	88	89	90
91	92	93	94	95	96	97	98	99	100

54: Counting by 1's, 2's, 5's, and 10's

Instruct the children to record their counting exercise in journals or have them create a recordkeeping counting book. After collecting data, have them make a graph of the objects.

Things to Count and Record by 1's

Classroom

- stuff inside the desk
- books on shelves
- wastepaper baskets
- flags
- animals in classroom
- plants
- bugs
- stuff in wastebasket
- crayons
- artists' materials
- computers
- math manipulatives
- storybooks
- textbooks
- pencils
- stickers

People wearing

- blue, red, green, etc.
- checks
- sneakers
- glasses
- watches
- earrings
- ribbons
- T-shirts
- dresses
- shorts
- long pants
- short
- tall
- hair: black, red, yellow, etc.

School

- boys, girls, teachers
- women, men
- office clerks
- visitors, police officers, prinicpal

Things to Count and Record by 2's

Classroom

- eyes in classroom, school, playground, animals
- two fingers held up by children standing in line

Things to Count and Record by 5's

- Line children up, raise hands one child at a time, record by 5's
- Number of feet in classroom to find out number of toes
- Number of cars that pass by classroom window, tally in sets of 5
- Tally in sets of 5 number of:
  —children going into lunchroom
  —people going into store
  —ants going into mound
  —candy in a big bag
  —coins in a piggy bank
  —cans in a pantry
  —eating utensils in cabinets
  —bowls in kitchen cabinets
  —pots and pans
  —socks in a dresser
  —clothes in a closet

Things to Count and Record by 10's

- Tally in sets of 10 number of:
  —flakes in a cereal box
  —raisins in a cereal box
  —leaves on a branch
  —pebbles in three-hand scoops
  —flock of birds
  —herd of cows
  —candy in a large bag
  —apples in a grocery store
  —shoes in a store window

Try This.

©1997 by The Center for Applied Research in Education

55: Counting Up to 10 in Other Languages

Japanese

1	一	ee-CHEE
2	二	NEE
3	三	SAHN
4	四	SHEE
5	五	GO
6	六	ro-KOO
7	七	shee-CHEE
8	八	ha-CHEE
9	九	KOO
10	十	JCOO

Russian

1	один	oh-DEEN
2	два	DVA
3	три	TREE
4	четыре	chye-tir'ye
5	пять	pyat
6	шесть	shyest'
7	семь	syem'
8	восемь	vo syem'
9	девять	dye'vyat'
10	десять	dye'syat'

Spanish

1	uno	OO-no
2	dos	DOHSS
3	tres	TRAYSS
4	quatro	KWAH-troh
5	cinco	SEEN-koh
6	seis	SAYS
7	siete	SYAY-tay
8	ocho	O-cho
9	nueve	NWEV-ay
10	diez	DYESS

French

1	un	UNG
2	deux	DUH
3	trois	TRWAH
4	quatre	KAHTR
5	cinq	SANK
6	six	SEESS
7	sept	SET
8	huit	WEET
9	neuf	NUF
10	dix	DEES

Norwegian

1	en	AYN
2	to	TIH
3	tre	TRAY
4	fire	FEE-reh
5	fem	FEM
6	seks	SEKS
7	sju	SHOO
8	atte	AWT-TEH
9	ni	NEE
10	ti	TEE

German

1	eins	INS
2	zwei	TSVI
3	drei	DRI
4	vier	FEER
5	funf	FEWNF
6	sechs	ZEKS
7	sieven	ZEE-ben
8	acht	AHKT
9	neun	NOYN
10	zehn	TSANE

(continued)

Hebrew

1	אַחַת	a-CHAT
2	שְׁתַּיִם	sh-TA-yim
3	שָׁלֹשׁ	sh-LOSH
4	אַרְבַּע	ar-BAH
5	חָמֵשׁ	cha-MAISH
6	שֵׁשׁ	shaish
7	שֶׁבַע	SHE-vah
8	שְׁמוֹנֶה	shmoe-NEH
9	תֵּשַׁע	TAI-shah
10	עֶשֶׂר	EH-ser

Italian

1	uno	OO-no
2	due	DOO-ay
3	tre	TRAY
4	quattro	KWAHT-tro
5	cinque	CHEEN-kway
6	sei	SAY
7	sette	SET-tay
8	otto	OHT-to
9	nove	NO-vay
10	dieci	DYAY-chee

Oglala Lakota (Sioux)

1	Wanji	wan-JEE
2	Numpa	noo-pah
3	Yamni	ya-MNEE
4	Topa	toh-pah
5	Zaptan	zahp-than
6	Sakpe	sha-kpay
7	Sakowin	sha-koh-ween
8	Saglogan (gutteral g's)	sha-glo-ghan
9	Napeinyunka	nahp-chee-yoon-kah
10	Wikcemma	week-cheeh-mnah

Dineh (Navajo)

1	t'áá lá"	*Ɬáá'ii Ɬa'i
2	naaki	nakə
3	táá'	ta
4	díí'	dng
5	'ashdla'	ashglə
6	hastáá	hasta
7	tsosts'id	tsostsid
8	tseebíí	tsebe
9	náhást'éí	nahaste
10	neeznáá	nezna

Special thanks to:

Robert Two Crow
Oglala Lakota
Batesland, SD

Lula M. Begay
Navajo/Bilingual Instructor
Shiprock, NM

---

*This sound is not used in the English language. To make it, place your tongue in position behind your teeth to make a soft "L" sound, but say the "CH" in cheese, allowing the air to flow freely through the sides of your tongue.

(continued)

Arabic

1	١	Wahed
2	٢	Ethnain
3	٣	Thalatha
4	٤	Arbah
5	٥	Kamsa
6	٦	Sitah
7	٧	Sabah
8	٨	Thamania
9	٩	Tisah
10	١٠	Asharah

Swahili

1	mojo	MOH-jah
2	mbili	MBEE-lee
3	tatu	TAH-tu
4	nne	EN-nay
5	tano	Tah-noh
6	sita	SEE-tah
7	saba	SAH-bah
8	nane	NAH-nay
9	tisa	TEE-sah
10	kumi	KOO-mee

SECTION 5

BASIC
OPERATIONS

Name _____

How Many Feet?

1. Count the number of pairs of feet in your class. _____

2. Multiply the pairs by 2 to tell how many feet there are in all.

   _____ × 2 = _____ feet

3. Multiply the product you just found by 8.

   _____ × 8 = _____

4. Add 45 to the product.

   _____ + 45 = _____

5. How many sets of 5 are in your new sum? *Hint:* 5 √

   _____

6. If you have a remainder, can you explain why? _____

   _____

   _____

   _____

56: Properties of Addition and Subtraction of Whole Numbers

Property	Addition	Subtraction
Identity	Zero is the identity element. Any number plus zero gives the identity: $2 + 0 = 2$, $0 + 5 = 5$.	Subtraction does not have an identity element: $2 - 0 = 2$ but $0 - 2 \neq 2$.
Commutative	The order of the two addends does not affect the sum: $3 + 2 = 5$ and $2 + 3 = 5$.	Subtraction is not commutative: $3 - 2 = 1$ but $2 - 3 \neq 1$.
Associative	When three or more numbers are to be added, the way the addends are grouped does not affect the sum: $(3 + 2) + 1 = 3 + (2 + 1)$.	Subtraction is not associative: $(3 - 2) - 1 \neq 3 - (2 - 1)$.

Identity Property: $a + 0 = a$ or $0 + a = a$.   ($2 + 0 = 2$ or $0 + 5 = 5$)

• *Cuisenaire Rods®*

$$\boxed{\text{r}} + 0 = \boxed{\text{r}} \quad \text{or} \quad 0 + \boxed{\text{y}} = \boxed{\text{y}}$$

• *Manipulative Materials*

$$\square\,\square + 0 = \square\,\square \quad \text{or} \quad 0 + \square\square\square\square\square = \square\square\square\square\square$$

Commutative Property: $a + b = b + a$.   ($3 + 2 = 5$ and $2 + 3 = 5$)

• *Cuisenaire Rods®*

green + red
yellow
red + green

• *Manipulative Materials*

$$\square\square\square + \square\square = \square\square + \square\square\square$$

Associative Property: $(a + b) + c = a + (b + c)$. $[(3 + 2) + 1 = 3 + (2 + 1)]$

• *Cuisenaire Rods®*

(green + red) + white   green + (red + white)
yellow + white   green + green
dark green   dark green

For whole numbers, subtraction is neither commutative, associative, nor does it have an identity property. These properties do not apply to the operation of subtraction.

57: Properties of Multiplication and Division of Whole Numbers

Property	Multiplication	Division
Identity	One is the identity element for multiplication Any number times one gives the identity: $2 \times 1 = 2, 1 \times 5 = 5$.	Division does not have an identity element.
Commutative	The order of the two factors does not affect the product: $3 \times 2 = 6$ and $2 \times 3 = 6$.	Division is not commutative: $6 \div 3 = 2$ but $3 \div 6 \neq 2$.
Associative	When three or more numbers are to be multiplied, the way the factors are grouped does not affect the product: $(3 \times 2) \times 1 = 3 \times (2 \times 1)$.	Division is not associative: $(3 \div 2) \div 1 \neq 3 \div (2 \div 1)$.
Distributive	The product of a number and a sum may be expressed as a sum of two products: $3 (4 + 5) = (3 \times 4) + (3 \times 5)$.	Division is not distributive.

Identity Property: $ax1 = a$ or $1xa = a$. $(2 \times 1 = 2$ or $1 \times 7 = 7)$

Cuisenaire Rods®

w		w

2 white rods
2×1 or 2 groups of 1= 2

k

1 black rod
1×7 or 1 group of 7= 7

Commutative Property: $a \times b = b \times a$. $(3 \times 5 = 5 \times 3)$

• *Cuisenaire Rods®*

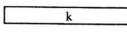

y	y	y

3 yellow rods

$3 \times 5 = 15$

g	g	g	g	g

5 green rods

$5 \times 3 = 15$

Associative Property: $(a \times b) \times c = a \times (b \times c)$. $(3 \times 4) \times 5 = 3 \times (4 \times 5)$

$$
\begin{aligned}
(3 \times 4) \times 5 &= 3 \times (4 \times 5) \\
(12) \times 5 &= 3 \times (20) \\
60 &= 60
\end{aligned}
$$

Distributive Property of Multiplication Over Addition: $a (b + c) = (a \times b) + (a \times c)$.

$$
\begin{aligned}
3 (4 + 5) &= (3 \times 4) + (3 \times 5) \\
3 (9) &= (12) + (15) \\
27 &= 27
\end{aligned}
$$

For whole numbers, division is neither commutative, associative, nor does it have an identity property. These properties do not apply to the operation of division.

©1997 by The Center for Applied Research in Education

58: 100 Basic Addition Facts

0	1	2	3	4	5	6	7	8	9
+0	+0	+0	+0	+0	+0	+0	+0	+0	+0
0	1	2	3	4	5	6	7	8	9

0	1	2	3	4	5	6	7	8	9
+1	+1	+1	+1	+1	+1	+1	+1	+1	+1
1	2	3	4	5	6	7	8	9	10

0	1	2	3	4	5	6	7	8	9
+2	+2	+2	+2	+2	+2	+2	+2	+2	+2
2	3	4	5	6	7	8	9	10	11

0	1	2	3	4	5	6	7	8	9
+3	+3	+3	+3	+3	+3	+3	+3	+3	+3
3	4	5	6	7	8	9	10	11	12

0	1	2	3	4	5	6	7	8	9
+4	+4	+4	+4	+4	+4	+4	+4	+4	+4
4	5	6	7	8	9	10	11	12	13

0	1	2	3	4	5	6	7	8	9
+5	+5	+5	+5	+5	+5	+5	+5	+5	+5
5	6	7	8	9	10	11	12	13	14

0	1	2	3	4	5	6	7	8	9
+6	+6	+6	+6	+6	+6	+6	+6	+6	+6
6	7	8	9	10	11	12	13	14	15

0	1	2	3	4	5	6	7	8	9
+7	+7	+7	+7	+7	+7	+7	+7	+7	+7
7	8	9	10	11	12	13	14	15	16

0	1	2	3	4	5	6	7	8	9
+8	+8	+8	+8	+8	+8	+8	+8	+8	+8
8	9	10	11	12	13	14	15	16	17

0	1	2	3	4	5	6	7	8	9
+9	+9	+9	+9	+9	+9	+9	+9	+9	+9
9	10	11	12	13	14	15	16	17	18

59: 100 Basic Subtraction Facts

0	1	2	3	4	5	6	7	8	9
-0	-0	-0	-0	-0	-0	-0	-0	-0	-0
0	1	2	3	4	5	6	7	8	9

1	2	3	4	5	6	7	8	9	10
-1	-1	-1	-1	-1	-1	-1	-1	-1	-1
0	1	2	3	4	5	6	7	8	9

2	3	4	5	6	7	8	9	10	11
-2	-2	-2	-2	-2	-2	-2	-2	-2	-2
0	1	2	3	4	5	6	7	8	9

3	4	5	6	7	8	9	10	11	12
-3	-3	-3	-3	-3	-3	-3	-3	-3	-3
0	1	2	3	4	5	6	7	8	9

4	5	6	7	8	9	10	11	12	13
-4	-4	-4	-4	-4	-4	-4	-4	-4	-4
0	1	2	3	4	5	6	7	8	9

5	6	7	8	9	10	11	12	13	14
-5	-5	-5	-5	-5	-5	-5	-5	-5	-5
0	1	2	3	4	5	6	7	8	9

6	7	8	9	10	11	12	13	14	15
-6	-6	-6	-6	-6	-6	-6	-6	-6	-6
0	1	2	3	4	5	6	7	8	9

7	8	9	10	11	12	13	14	15	16
-7	-7	-7	-7	-7	-7	-7	-7	-7	-7
0	1	2	3	4	5	6	7	8	9

8	9	10	11	12	13	14	15	16	17
-8	-8	-8	-8	-8	-8	-8	-8	-8	-8
0	1	2	3	4	5	6	7	8	9

9	10	11	12	13	14	15	16	17	18
-9	-9	-9	-9	-9	-9	-9	-9	-9	-9
0	1	2	3	4	5	6	7	8	9

60: 100 Basic Multiplication Facts

0	1	2	3	4	5	6	7	8	9
×0	×0	×0	×0	×0	×0	×0	×0	×0	×0
0	0	0	0	0	0	0	0	0	0

0	1	2	3	4	5	6	7	8	9
×1	×1	×1	×1	×1	×1	×1	×1	×1	×1
0	1	2	3	4	5	6	7	8	9

0	1	2	3	4	5	6	7	8	9
×2	×2	×2	×2	×2	×2	×2	×2	×2	×2
0	2	4	6	8	10	12	14	16	18

0	1	2	3	4	5	6	7	8	9
×3	×3	×3	×3	×3	×3	×3	×3	×3	×3
0	3	6	9	12	15	18	21	24	27

0	1	2	3	4	5	6	7	8	9
×4	×4	×4	×4	×4	×4	×4	×4	×4	×4
0	4	8	12	16	20	24	28	32	36

0	1	2	3	4	5	6	7	8	9
×5	×5	×5	×5	×5	×5	×5	×5	×5	×5
0	5	10	15	20	25	30	35	40	45

0	1	2	3	4	5	6	7	8	9
×6	×6	×6	×6	×6	×6	×6	×6	×6	×6
0	6	12	18	24	30	36	42	48	54

0	1	2	3	4	5	6	7	8	9
×7	×7	×7	×7	×7	×7	×7	×7	×7	×7
0	7	14	21	28	35	42	49	56	63

0	1	2	3	4	5	6	7	8	9
×8	×8	×8	×8	×8	×8	×8	×8	×8	×8
0	8	16	24	32	40	48	56	64	72

0	1	2	3	4	5	6	7	8	9
×9	×9	×9	×9	×9	×9	×9	×9	×9	×9
0	9	18	27	36	45	54	63	72	81

61: 100 Basic Division Facts

$0\overline{)0}$	$0\overline{)1}$	$0\overline{)2}$	$0\overline{)3}$	$0\overline{)4}$	$0\overline{)5}$	$0\overline{)6}$	$0\overline{)7}$	$0\overline{)8}$	$0\overline{)9}$
$1\overline{)0}$	$1\overline{)1}$	$1\overline{)2}$	$1\overline{)3}$	$1\overline{)4}$	$1\overline{)5}$	$1\overline{)6}$	$1\overline{)7}$	$1\overline{)8}$	$1\overline{)9}$
$2\overline{)0}$	$2\overline{)2}$	$2\overline{)4}$	$2\overline{)6}$	$2\overline{)8}$	$2\overline{)10}$	$2\overline{)12}$	$2\overline{)14}$	$2\overline{)16}$	$2\overline{)18}$
$3\overline{)0}$	$3\overline{)3}$	$3\overline{)6}$	$3\overline{)9}$	$3\overline{)12}$	$3\overline{)15}$	$3\overline{)18}$	$3\overline{)21}$	$3\overline{)24}$	$3\overline{)27}$
$4\overline{)0}$	$4\overline{)4}$	$4\overline{)8}$	$4\overline{)12}$	$4\overline{)16}$	$4\overline{)20}$	$4\overline{)24}$	$4\overline{)28}$	$4\overline{)32}$	$4\overline{)36}$
$5\overline{)0}$	$5\overline{)5}$	$5\overline{)10}$	$5\overline{)15}$	$5\overline{)20}$	$5\overline{)25}$	$5\overline{)30}$	$5\overline{)35}$	$5\overline{)40}$	$5\overline{)45}$
$6\overline{)0}$	$6\overline{)6}$	$6\overline{)12}$	$6\overline{)18}$	$6\overline{)24}$	$6\overline{)30}$	$6\overline{)36}$	$6\overline{)42}$	$6\overline{)48}$	$6\overline{)54}$
$7\overline{)0}$	$7\overline{)7}$	$7\overline{)14}$	$7\overline{)21}$	$7\overline{)28}$	$7\overline{)35}$	$7\overline{)42}$	$7\overline{)49}$	$7\overline{)56}$	$7\overline{)63}$
$8\overline{)0}$	$8\overline{)8}$	$8\overline{)16}$	$8\overline{)24}$	$8\overline{)32}$	$8\overline{)40}$	$8\overline{)48}$	$8\overline{)56}$	$8\overline{)64}$	$8\overline{)72}$
$9\overline{)0}$	$9\overline{)9}$	$9\overline{)18}$	$9\overline{)27}$	$9\overline{)36}$	$9\overline{)45}$	$9\overline{)54}$	$9\overline{)63}$	$9\overline{)72}$	$9\overline{)81}$

62: Algorithms for Addition

Operation	Definition	Symbolic	Representation
Addition	**Addend plus addend equals sum**	**a + b = c**	**3 + 5 = 8**
Subtraction	Sum minus addend equals addend	c − a = b c − b = a	8 − 3 = 5 8 − 5 = 3
Multiplication	Factor times factor equals product	a × b = c	3 × 4 = 12
Division	Product divided by factor equals factor	c ÷ a = b c ÷ b = a	12 ÷ 3 = 4 12 ÷ 4 = 3

Addition: Addend plus addend equals sum

Without Regrouping

- *Manipulative Materials*

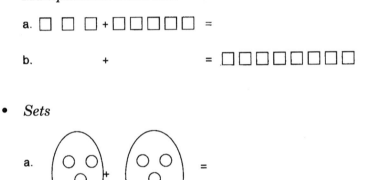

- *Sets*

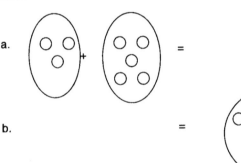

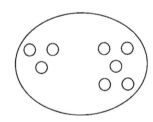

- *Cuisenaire Rods®*

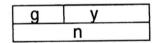   green + yellow = brown

- *Number Line*

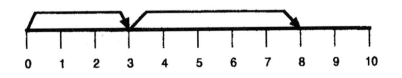

135

(continued)

• *Place Value Blocks*

No symbolic representation: thirty five plus twenty three.

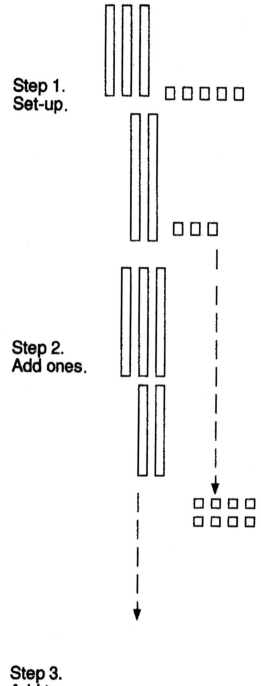

Step 1.
Set-up.

Step 2.
Add ones.

Step 3.
Add tens,
solution.

(continued)

Combining symbolic representation and blocks.

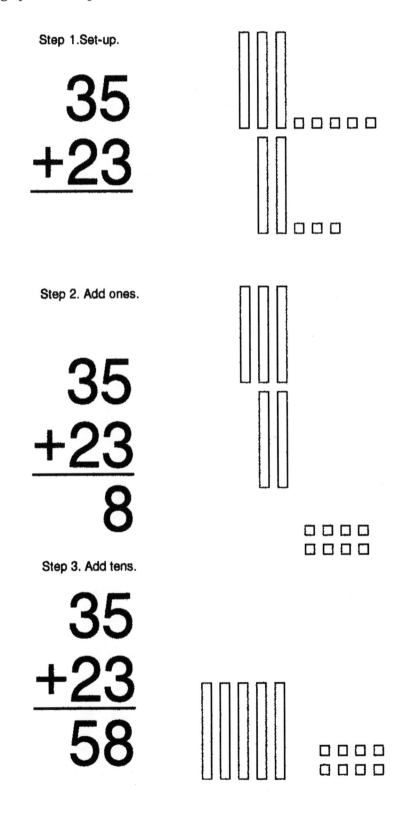

Step 1. Set-up.

35
+23

Step 2. Add ones.

35
+23
———
8

Step 3. Add tens.

35
+23
———
58

(continued)

With Regrouping

• *Place Value Blocks*

Step 1.Set-up.

37
+46

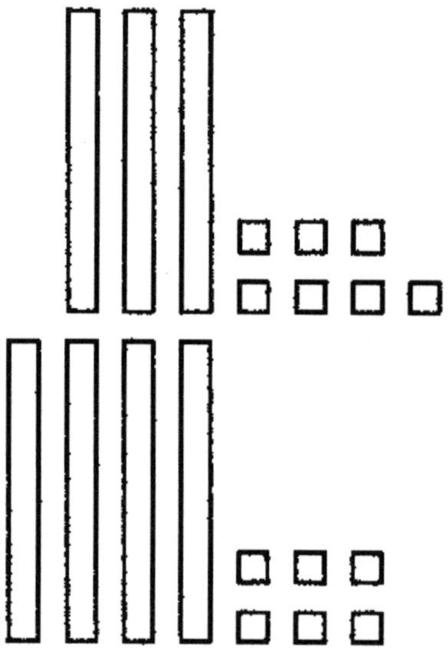

Step 2. Add ones.

37
+46

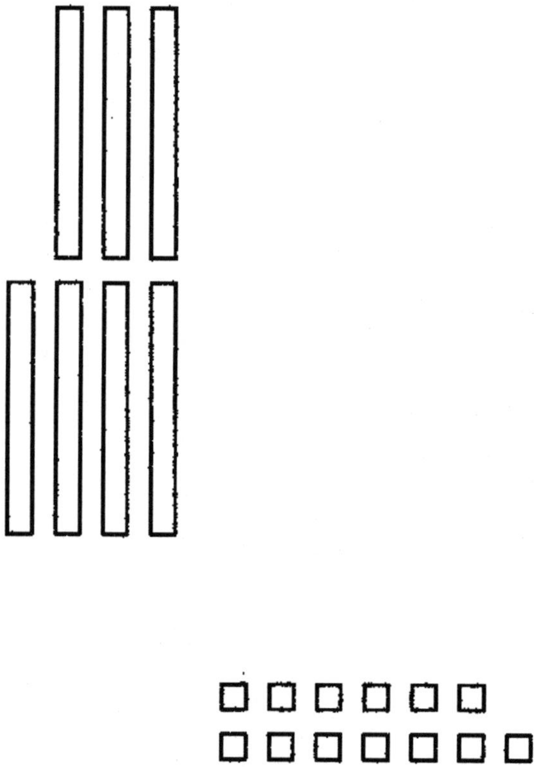

(continued)

**Step 3. Trade 10
ones for 1 ten.**

$$\begin{array}{r} 1 \\ 37 \\ +46 \\ \hline 3 \end{array}$$

Step 4. Add tens.

$$\begin{array}{r} 1 \\ 37 \\ +46 \\ \hline 83 \end{array}$$

63: Algorithms for Subtraction

Operation	Definition	Symbolic	Representation
Addition	Addend plus addend equals sum	$a + b = c$	$3 + 5 = 8$
Subtraction	**Sum minus addend equals addend**	$c - a = b$	$8 - 3 = 5$
		$c - b = a$	$8 - 5 = 3$
Multiplication	Factor times factor equals product	$a \times b = c$	$3 \times 4 = 12$
Division	Product divided by factor equals factor	$c \div a = b$	$12 \div 3 = 4$
		$c \div b = a$	$12 \div 4 = 3$

Subtraction: Sum minus addend equals addend

Without Regrouping

- *Manipulative Materials*

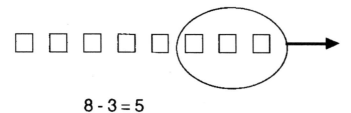

$$8 - 3 = 5$$

- *Sets*

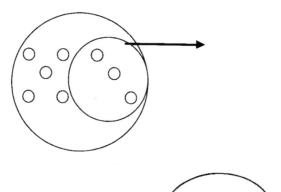

- *Cuisenaire Rods*®

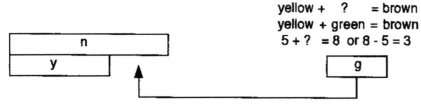

What rod is needed to make the two rods the same length as the single rod?

yellow +   ?   = brown
yellow + green = brown
5 + ? = 8 or 8 - 5 = 3

(continued)

- *Number Line*

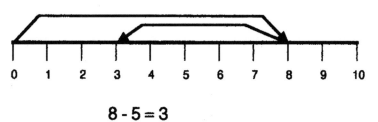

$$8 - 5 = 3$$

- *Place Value Blocks*

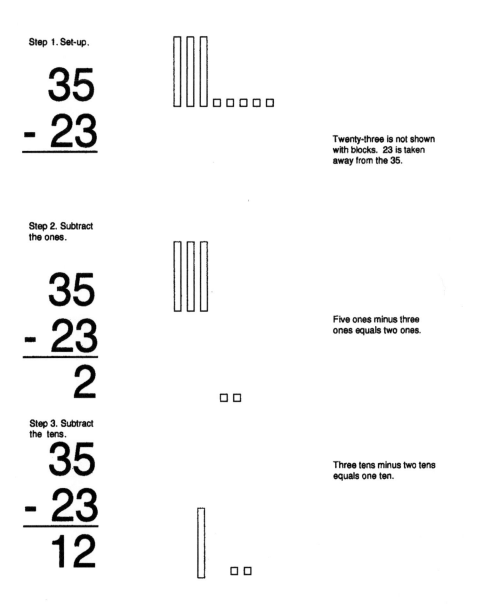

Step 1. Set-up.

35
- 23

Twenty-three is not shown with blocks. 23 is taken away from the 35.

Step 2. Subtract the ones.

35
- 23
2

Five ones minus three ones equals two ones.

Step 3. Subtract the tens.

35
- 23
12

Three tens minus two tens equals one ten.

(continued)

With Regrouping

Step 1. Set-up.

42
- 27

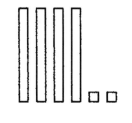

Twenty-seven is not
shown with blocks. 27 is
taken away from the 42.

Step 2. Cannot subtract the
ones. Trade 1 ten for 10 ones.

312
4̶2̶
- 27

(continued)

Step 3. Subtract the ones.

$$
\begin{array}{r}
3\;\!1\!2 \\
\cancel{4}\cancel{2} \\
-\;2\;7 \\
\hline
5
\end{array}
$$

minus 7 ones

Step 3. Subtract the tens.

$$
\begin{array}{r}
3\;\!1\!2 \\
\cancel{4}\cancel{2} \\
-\;2\;7 \\
\hline
1\;5
\end{array}
$$

minus 2 tens

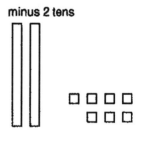

64: Algorithms for Multiplication

Operation	Definition	Symbolic Representation	
Addition	Addend plus addend equals sum	a + b = c	3 + 5 = 8
Subtraction	Sum minus addend equals addend	c − a = b	8 − 3 = 5
		c − b = a	8 − 5 = 3
Multiplication	**Factor times factor equals product**	**a × b = c**	**3 × 4 = 12**
Division	Product divided by factor equals factor	c ÷ a = b	12 ÷ 3 = 4
		c ÷ b = a	12 ÷ 4 = 3

Multiplication: Factor times factor equals product

> $3 \times 4 = 3$ groups of 4 or 3(4) = 12

> $4 \times 23 = 4$ groups of 23 or 4(23) = 92

> 23
> ×4 = 4 × 23 = 4 groups of 23 or 4(23)
> 92

- *Manipulative Materials*

3 groups of 4; 3 x 4; 3(4)

- *Sets*

3 groups of 4; 3 x 4; 3(4)

- *CuisenaireRods*®

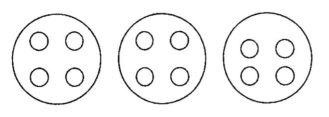

3 groups of 4; 3 x 4; 3(4)

(continued)

144

- *Array*

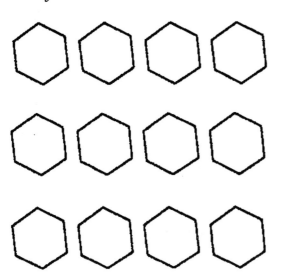

3 groups of 4; 3 x 4; 3(4)

- *Number Line*

3 x 4 ; 3(4)

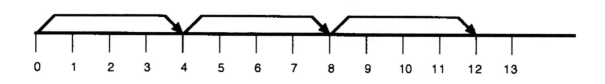

(continued)

• *Place Value Blocks*

Step 1. Set-up.

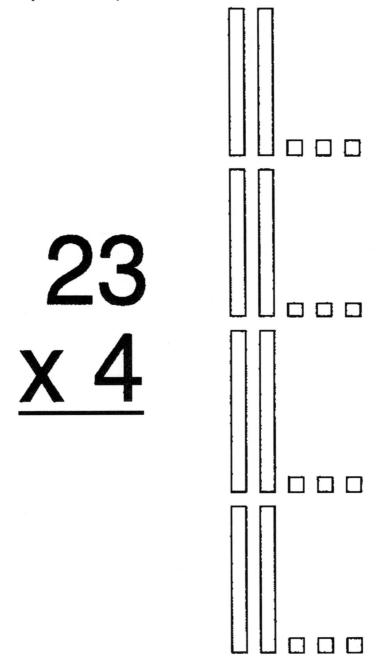

$$23$$
$$\underline{\times 4}$$

(continued)

Step 2. Group ones,
4x3=12. Trade 10
ones for 1 ten, keep 2
ones.

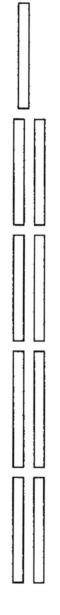

(continued)

Step 3. Group tens,
4x2=8 plus 1 more
makes 9.

$$\begin{array}{r} 1 \\ 23 \\ \times\,4 \\ \hline 92 \end{array}$$

(continued)

Expanded Algorithm

$$
\begin{array}{r}
24 \\
\times 16 \\
\hline
24 \\
120 \\
40 \\
+200 \\
\hline
384
\end{array}
$$

16 groups of 24 or 16×24
6 groups of 4 or 6×4
6 groups of 20 or 6×20
10 groups of 4 or 10×4
10 groups of 20 or 10×20

Step 1.

16 x 24 or 16 groups of 24.

Step 2.

20   4

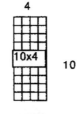

Step 3.

20   4

10x20   10x4   10

6x20   6x4   6

(continued)

Grid Multiplication

```
 24                    20        4
×16          10   |  200   |   40   |  240
384               |        |        |
              6   |  120   |   24   |  144
                  |  320   |   64   |  384
```

```
245                  200       40        5
×37          30  | 6000  |  1200  |  150  |  7350
9065             |       |        |       |
              7  | 1400  |   280  |   35  |  1715
                 | 7400  |  1480  |  185  |  9065
```

65: Algorithms for Division

Operation	Definition	Symbolic	Representation
Addition	Addend plus addend equals sum	$a + b = c$	$3 + 5 = 8$
Subtraction	Sum minus addend equals addend	$c - a = b$ $c - b = a$	$8 - 3 = 5$ $8 - 5 = 3$
Multiplication	Factor times factor equals product	$a \times b = c$	$3 \times 4 = 12$
Division	**Product divided by factor equals factor**	$c \div a = b$ $c \div b = a$	$12 \div 3 = 4$ $12 \div 4 = 3$

Division

- *Sharing*

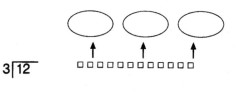

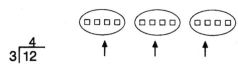

- *Repeated Subtraction*

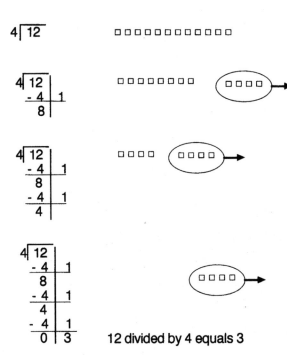

12 divided by 4 equals 3

(continued)

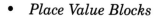

- *Place Value Blocks*

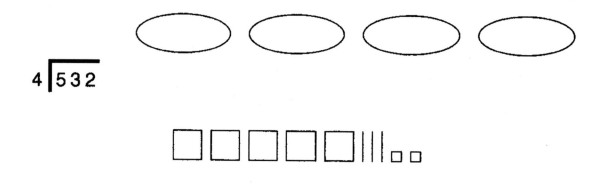

$$4\overline{)532}$$

Share hundred blocks—had 5 hundreds, shared 4, 1 remaining.

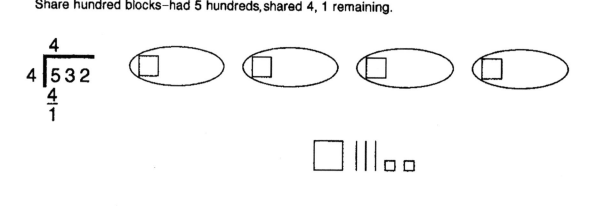

Trade the 1 hundred for 10 tens.

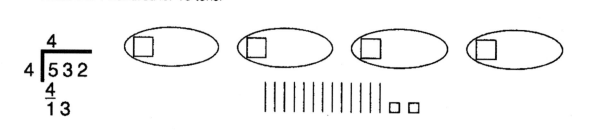

(continued)

Share tens blocks—had 13 tens, shared 12, 1 remaining.

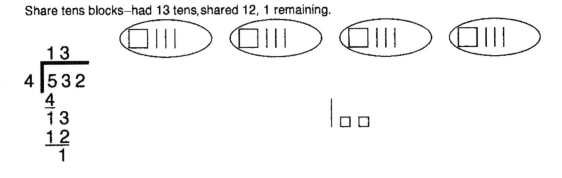

```
      13
   ┌──────
 4 │ 5 3 2
     4
     ──
     1 3
     1 2
     ───
       1
```

Trade the 1 ten for 10 ones.

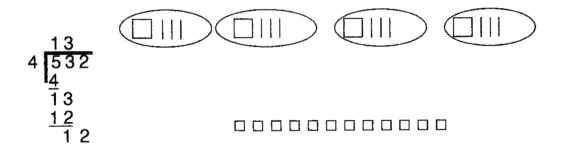

```
      13
   ┌──────
 4 │ 5 3 2
     4
     ──
     1 3
     1 2
     ───
       1 2
```

Share ones blocks—had 12 ones, shared 12.

```
      1 3 3
   ┌──────
 4 │ 5 3 2
     4
     ──
     1 3
     1 2
     ───
       1 2
       1 2
       ───
         0
```

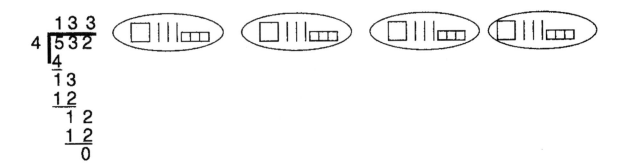

(continued)

• *Place Value Distribution*

$$4\overline{)532}$$

Step 1.
Show 532.

100	10 10 10 10 10 10 10 10 10	1 1 1 1 1 1 1 1
100	10 10 10 10 10 10 10 10 10	1 1 1 1 1 1 1 1
100	10 10 10 10 10 10 10 10 10	1 1 1 1 1 1 1 1
100	10 10 10 10 10 10 10 10 10	1 1 1 1 1 1 1 1
100	10 10 10 10 10 10 10 10 10	1 1 1 1 1 1 1 1
100	10 10 10 10 10 10 10 10 10	1 1 1 1 1 1 1 1
100	10 10 10 10 10 10 10 10 10	1 1 1 1 1 1 1 1
100	10 10 10 10 10 10 10 10 10	1 1 1 1 1 1 1 1
100	10 10 10 10 10 10 10 10 10	1 1 1 1 1 1 1 1

1 group of 4

Step 2.
How many
groups of
4 Hundreds?

100	10 10 10 10 10 10 10 10 10	1 1 1 1 1 1 1 1
100	10 10 10 10 10 10 10 10 10	1 1 1 1 1 1 1 1
100	10 10 10 10 10 10 10 10 10	1 1 1 1 1 1 1 1
100	10 10 10 10 10 10 10 10 10	1 1 1 1 1 1 1 1
100	10 10 10 10 10 10 10 10 10	1 1 1 1 1 1 1 1
100	10 10 10 10 10 10 10 10 10	1 1 1 1 1 1 1 1
100	10 10 10 10 10 10 10 10 10	1 1 1 1 1 1 1 1
100	10 10 10 10 10 10 10 10 10	1 1 1 1 1 1 1 1
100	10 10 10 10 10 10 10 10 10	1 1 1 1 1 1 1 1

1 group of 4

Step 3.
Regroup
the
remaining
100 to 10
tens.

100	10 10 10 10 10 10 10 10 10	1 1 1 1 1 1 1 1
100	10 10 10 10 10 10 10 10 10	1 1 1 1 1 1 1 1
100	10 10 10 10 10 10 10 10 10	1 1 1 1 1 1 1 1
100	10 10 10 10 10 10 10 10 10	1 1 1 1 1 1 1 1
100	10 10 10 10 10 10 10 10 10	1 1 1 1 1 1 1 1
100	10 10 10 10 10 10 10 10 10	1 1 1 1 1 1 1 1
100	10 10 10 10 10 10 10 10 10	1 1 1 1 1 1 1 1
100	10 10 10 10 10 10 10 10 10	1 1 1 1 1 1 1 1
100	10 10 10 10 10 10 10 10 10	1 1 1 1 1 1 1 1

(continued)

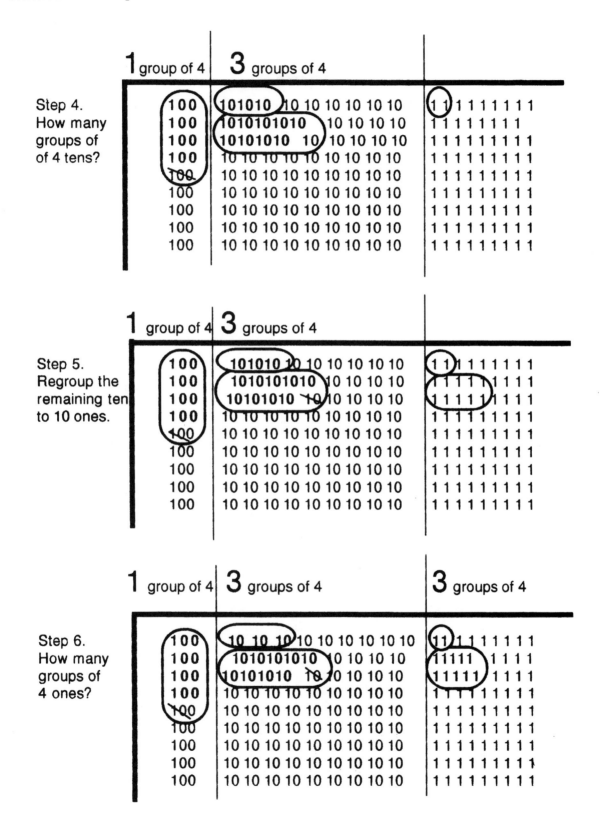

Step 4.
How many
groups of
of 4 tens?

Step 5.
Regroup the
remaining ten
to 10 ones.

Step 6.
How many
groups of
4 ones?

(continued)

- *Estimation Algorithm*

Step 1.

```
  ┌─────────
4 │ 5 3 2
```

Step 2.

```
      1 0 0
  ┌─────────
4 │ 5 3 2
    4 0 0  │ 4 × 100
  ─────────
    1 3 2
```

Step 3.

```
        3 0
      1 0 0
  ┌─────────
4 │ 5 3 2
    4 0 0  │ 4 × 100
  ─────────
    1 3 2
    1 2 0  │ 4 × 30
  ─────────
      1 2
```

Step 4.

```
    1 3 3
        3
      3 0
    1 0 0
  ┌─────────
4 │ 5 3 2
    4 0 0  │ 4 × 100
  ─────────
    1 3 2
    1 2 0  │ 4 × 30
  ─────────
      1 2
      1 2  │ 4 × 3
  ─────────
        0
```

66: The Basic Facts Families for Addition

- *Zero Facts:* Any number plus zero equals the original number.

  > 0+0, 1+0, 2+0, 3+0, 4+0, 5+0, 6+0, 7+0, 8+0, and 9+0.

- *Plus One Facts:* Any number plus one equals the next number in order.

  > 0+1, 1+1, 2+1, 3+1, 4+1, 5+1, 6+1, 7+1, 8+1, and 9+1.

- *Double Facts:* Numbers added to themselves equal a unique sum.

  > 0+0 , 1+1, 2+2, 3+3, 4+4, 5+5, 6+6, 7+7, 8+8, and 9+9.

- *Double Facts Plus One:* 8 is one more than 7, so 7+8 is 7+7=14 + 1=15.

  > 0+1, 1+2, 2+3, 3+4, 4+5, 5+6, 6+7, 7+8, and 8+9.

Some facts, such as 0+0 and 1+1, reside within more than one family,

Using the Basic Facts Families

There are 100 basic addition facts that students should learn. The traditional method of learning these has been memorization. However, by using the facts families and properties of addition, the student's task becomes easier. Each time a property of family fact is understood and utilized by the student, the amount of facts to be memorized is reduced. Instead of having to memorize 100 basic facts, the number of facts is reduced to 21.

Property or Family	Number of Non-duplicated Facts	Addition Basic Facts to Be Learned
		100
Zero Facts	10	90
Plus 1	9	81
Double	8	73
Double Plus 1	7	66
Commutative Property	45	21

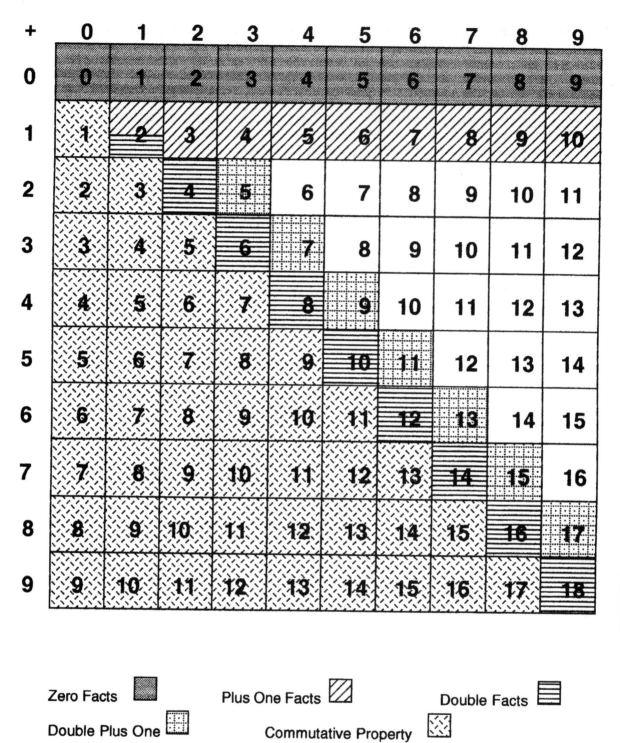

+	0	1	2	3	4	5	6	7	8	9
0	0	1	2	3	4	5	6	7	8	9
1	1	2	3	4	5	6	7	8	9	10
2	2	3	4	5	6	7	8	9	10	11
3	3	4	5	6	7	8	9	10	11	12
4	4	5	6	7	8	9	10	11	12	13
5	5	6	7	8	9	10	11	12	13	14
6	6	7	8	9	10	11	12	13	14	15
7	7	8	9	10	11	12	13	14	15	16
8	8	9	10	11	12	13	14	15	16	17
9	9	10	11	12	13	14	15	16	17	18

Zero Facts   Plus One Facts   Double Facts

Double Plus One   Commutative Property

67: The Basic Facts Families for Multiplication

- *Zero Facts:* Any number times zero equals the zero.

  $0 \times 0, 1 \times 0, 2 \times 0, 3 \times 0, 4 \times 0, 5 \times 0, 6 \times 0, 7 \times 0, 8 \times 0,$ and $9 \times 0.$

- *Times One Facts:* Any number times one equals the original number.

  $0 \times 1, 1 \times 1, 2 \times 1, 3 \times 1, 4 \times 1, 5 \times 1, 6 \times 1, 7 \times 1, 8 \times 1, 9 \times 1.$

- *Double Facts:* Numbers multiplied by themselves equal a unique sum.

  $0 \times 0, 1 \times 1, 2 \times 2, 3 \times 3, 4 \times 4, 5 \times 5, 6 \times 6, 7 \times 7, 8 \times 8, 9 \times 9.$

Property or Family	Number of Non-duplicated Facts	Multiplication Basic Facts to Be Learned
		100
Zero Facts	10	90
Times One	9	81
Double Facts	8	72
Commutative Property	45	27

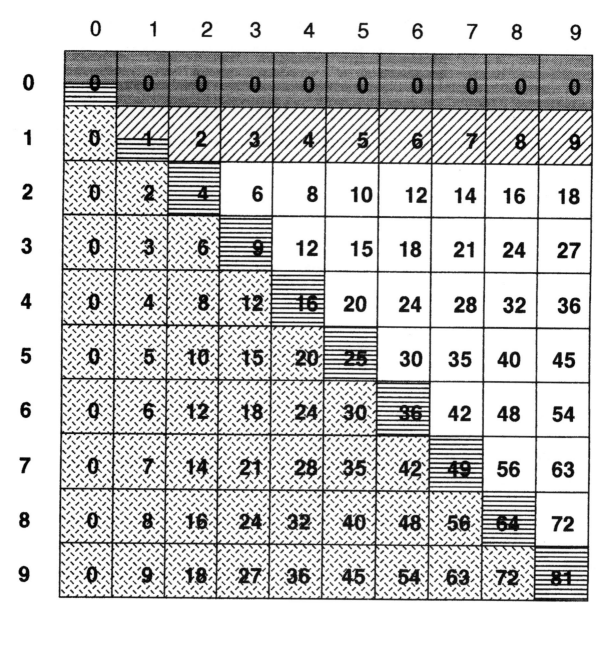

	0	1	2	3	4	5	6	7	8	9
0	0	0	0	0	0	0	0	0	0	0
1	0	1	2	3	4	5	6	7	8	9
2	0	2	4	6	8	10	12	14	16	18
3	0	3	6	9	12	15	18	21	24	27
4	0	4	8	12	16	20	24	28	32	36
5	0	5	10	15	20	25	30	35	40	45
6	0	6	12	18	24	30	36	42	48	54
7	0	7	14	21	28	35	42	49	56	63
8	0	8	16	24	32	40	48	56	64	72
9	0	9	18	27	36	45	54	63	72	81

Zero Facts ▨   Times One Facts ▧

Double Facts ▤   Commutative Property ▨

68: Story Problems

Addition

• *Active:* Demonstrates or implies the action of combining two sets.

Maria had 3 cats and she bought 2 more. How many cats does she have now? (3 + 2 = 5)

• *Static:* More of a classification than an active combination of two sets. Both subsets are there already and no action is implied.

Shanika has 4 goldfish and 2 dogs. How many pets does Shanika have? (4 + 2 = 6)

Subtraction

• *Take away:* An active removal of part of a set.

Lu had 12 ounces of cola and gave 6 ounces to a friend. How many ounces of cola does Lu have left?

(12 − 6 = 6)

• *Comparison:* Comparing two sets to determine how many more in one than the other. Usually answers the question "How much (many) more . . . than . . . ?"

Teri has 9 pencils and Shante' has 6 pencils. How many more pencils does Teri have than Shanté?

(9 − 6 = 3)

• *Missing Addend:* Represented as an addition problem but solved by using subtraction. The problem is shown as 5 + □ = 9 but is solved by 9 − 5 = 4. The answer determines the amount needed to complete a set.

Muhammad has 9 rabbits and 5 cages. He wants to have a cage for each rabbit. How many more cages does Muhammad need? (5 + □ = 9)

Multiplication

• *Grouping:* Designates the number of groups and the number in each group.

Juanita had 4 packs of juice with 6 cans of juice in each pack. How many cans of juice did Juanita have? (4 groups of 6 or 4 × 6 = 24)

• *Array:* Deals with rows and columns in a rectangular arrangement. Rows are horizontal and columns are vertical. The problem states the number of rows and how many in each row.

Ruth made a garden with 5 rows. She planted 6 flowers in each row. How many flowers did Ruth plant? (5 rows of 6 or 5 × 6 = 30)

• *Combination:* Determines the number of different combinations that can be made from two or more variables. The combinations are usually best illustrated with a grid or a tree.

Margaret had 4 shirts, red, blue, yellow, and white. She had 2 pair of slacks of black and brown. How many different outfits could Margaret make? (4 × 2 = 8)

The ice cream store served 2 kinds of cones (sugar and plain), 4 flavors of ice cream (vanilla, chocolate, mint, and cherry), and 3 kinds of toppings (nuts, whipped cream, and fudge). How many different combinations of cone, 1 flavor of ice cream and 1 topping can be made? (2 × 4 × 3 = 24)

161

(continued)

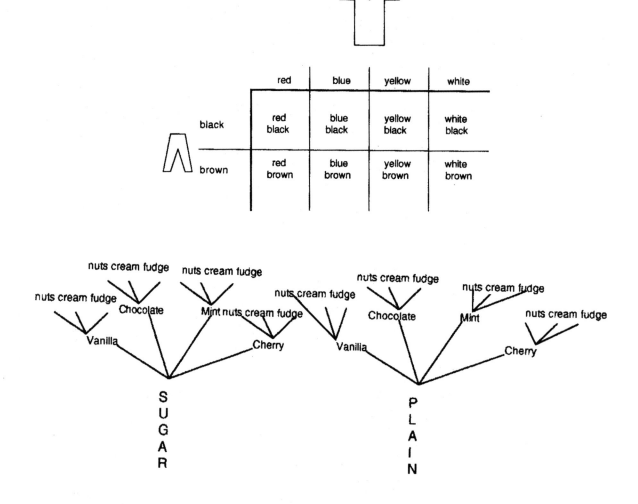

Division

• *Partitive or Sharing:* Determines the amount that each would get if a total is equally shared. The number of shares is known and each individual share is determined.

Sonia had a 24-inch piece of candy that she wanted to share equally with each of her six friends. How much candy should Sonia give to each friend? (24 ÷ 6 = 4)

• *Measurement or Repeated Subtraction:* Determines the number of shares if a total is divided into equal portions. The amount of each share is known and the number of shares is determined.

Carlina had 18 beads. She uses 3 beads when making a bracelet. How many bracelets can Carlina make from the 18 beads? (18 ÷ 3 = 6)

69: Grid Addition

36 + 27

1. Find 36 on the chart.
2. Count 7 ones to the right. If you reach the end of the row, move to the row below and continue counting from the left.
3. Move straight down 2 rows to represent the 2 tens.
4. 36 + 27 = 63.

```
 1   2   3   4   5   6   7   8   9   10
11  12  13  14  15  16  17  18  19   20
21  22  23  24  25  26  27  28  29   30
31  32  33  34  35  36  37  38  39   40
41  42  43  44  45  46  47  48  49   50
51  52  53  54  55  56  57  58  59   60
61  62  63  64  65  66  67  68  69   70
71  72  73  74  75  76  77  78  79   80
81  82  83  84  85  86  87  88  89   90
91  92  93  94  95  96  97  98  99  100
```

45 + 47

```
 1   2   3   4   5   6   7   8   9   10
11  12  13  14  15  16  17  18  19   20
21  22  23  24  25  26  27  28  29   30
31  32  33  34  35  36  37  38  39   40
41  42  43  44  45  46  47  48  49   50
51  52  53  54  55  56  57  58  59   60
61  62  63  64  65  66  67  68  69   70
71  72  73  74  75  76  77  78  79   80
81  82  83  84  85  86  87  88  89   90
91  92  93  94  95  96  97  98  99  100
```

70: Finger Multiplication

This method of multiplying on your fingers works for those children who have trouble remembering the multiplication facts for 6's, 7's, 8's, 9's. It works for multiplication sentences with these factors only. If the factors are 1, 2, 3, 4, or 5, it will not work.

How to multiply on your fingers

1. Note the value of each finger before starting. Values are the same for both hands.

   1 finger up represents 6
   2 fingers up represents 7
   3 fingers up represents 8
   4 fingers up represents 9

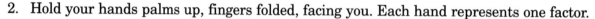

2. Hold your hands palms up, fingers folded, facing you. Each hand represents one factor.

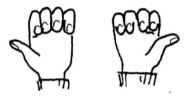

3. To multiply 6 × 7 = ? Hold up 1 finger to represent 6 and touch the remaining fingers with your thumb on your left hand. Hold up 2 fingers to represent 7 and touch the remaining fingers with your thumb on your right hand.

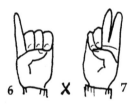

4. Multiply the fingers pointing up by 10. (3 × 10 = 30). Then count the thumb and fingers held down on the left hand (3) and on the right hand (4). (3 × 4 = 12). Finally add 30 + 12 = 42!

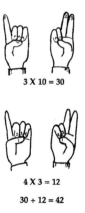

3 X 10 = 30

4 X 3 = 12

30 + 12 = 42

71: Products of Nines

The products of the factors involving nine can be demonstrated using the fingers on both hands. Begin with the fingers outstretched, palms down. For 9×1 the left small finger is folded down. The remaining fingers represent the product 9. For 9×2 the second finger from the left, the left ring finger, is folded. The product is represented by the tens place to the left of the folded finger and the ones place to the right. One finger on the left equals 10 and eight more on the right equals the product of 18.

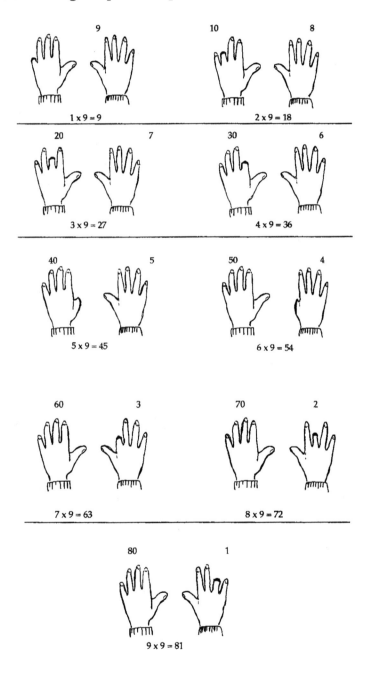

72: Chisanbop

Chisanbop is a method of solving basic calulations using your fingers which was invented by a Korean mathemetician named Sung Jin Pai. It has since been adapted so it can be used by elementary school children. In the Chisanbop method, numerical values are assigned to the fingers and thumbs of each hand. By pressing down combinations of fingers and thumbs, you can represent numbers from 1 to 99 and perform calculations.

How Chisanbop Works

Each of the four left fingers is worth ten. The left thumb is worth fifty.

Each of the four right fingers is worth one. The right thumb is worth five.

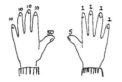

Hands are held over a surface, fingers suspended above the surface. Numbers are indicated by pressing a finger, or combinations of fingers, to the surface.

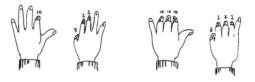

For 17, press the *left* index finger and the *right* thumb, index, and middle fingers (10 + 5 + 1 + 1).

For 38 press the *left* index, middle, and ring fingers, and the *right* thumb, index, and middle fingers (10 + 10 + 10 + 5 + 1 + 1 + 1).

To Add 17 + 24

Begin by pressing down the fingers to show 17.

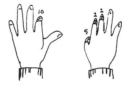

Add 24 by pressing the middle and ring fingers of the left hand (10, 20).

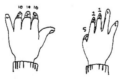

Press the right ring and small fingers (21, 22), raise the right hand (23) which now has a value of ten, and transfer that ten by pressing the small finger on the left hand. Press the right index finger (24). The pressed fingers reveal the result of 41.

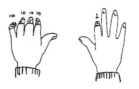

SECTION 6

NUMBER THEORY

Name _____

73: Complex Number System

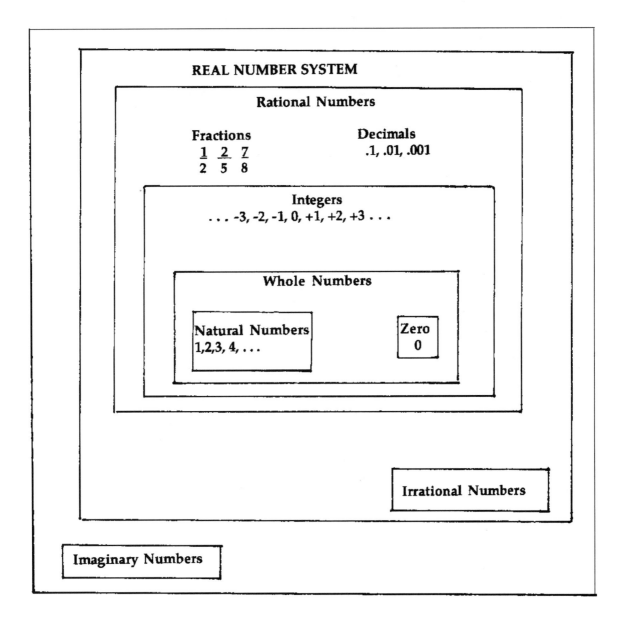

74: Rules of Divisibility

A number can be divided by another number if that number can be divided into it evenly, without leaving any remainder.

Example: $35 \div 5 = 7$

There are various symbols that indicate the operation of division:

$$\div \quad / \quad \sqrt{\quad}$$

Divisibility Rules:

A number is divisible by:	If:	Example:
2	the last digit is divisible by 2.	14,576
3	the sum of its digits is divisible by 3. $1 + 4 + 5 + 2 + 3 = 15$	14,523
4	if the last two digits are divisible by 4 24 is divisible by 4	23,724
5	if the last digit is a 5 or 0	35,595 35,950
6	if the number is divisible by 2 or 3. 2 and 3 are factors of 6. Apply rules for 2 and 3.	12, 912
8	if the last three digits are divisible by 8.	14,104
9	if the sum of its digits is divisible by 9. $3 + 9 + 8 + 3 + 3 + 1 = 27$ 27 is divisible by 9	398,331
10	if the number ends in 0.	675,940

This is interesting.

75: Product Expressions: Finding Prime Numbers

Factors

When two numbers are multiplied together, they produce a product. The two numbers are called *factors*. The number they produce is called a *product*.

$$\underset{\text{Factor}}{\underset{\downarrow}{2}} \quad \times \quad \underset{\text{Factor}}{\underset{\downarrow}{3}} \quad = \quad \underset{\text{Product}}{\underset{\downarrow}{6}}$$

2 is a *factor* of *6*
3 is a *factor* of *6*
6 is the *product* of *2 and 3*
6 is a *multiple* of *2*
6 is a *multiple* of *3*

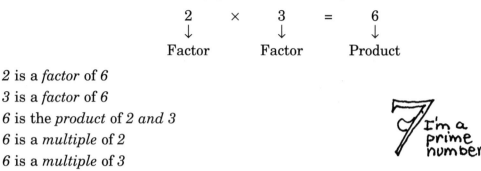

The multiples of 2 are 0, 2, 4, 6, 8, 10, 12 . . .
The multiples of 3 are 0, 3, 6, 9, 12, 15, 18 . . .

Product Expressions are multiplication sentences that name a product.

Example: 3 × 4 or 2 × 6 or 1 × 12

The product expressions for 12 are: *1 × 12*
                                          2 × 6
                                          3 × 4

Because of the commutative property, we need to name only three product expressions.

Activity: Have students list the product expressions and show the array for the numbers 1 through 20.

Number	Product Expression	Array
1	1 × 1	•
2	1 × 2	• •
3	1 × 3	• • •
4	1 × 4	• • • •
	2 × 2	• •
		• •
5	1 × 5	• • • • •
6	1 × 6	• • • • • •
	2 × 3	• • •
		• • •
7	1 × 7	• • • • • • •

(continued)

8	1×8	• • • • • • • •
	2×4	• • • •
		• • • •
9	1×9	• • • • • • • • •
	3×3	• • •
		• • •
		• • •
10	1×10	• • • • • • • • • •
	2×5	• • • • •
		• • • • •
11	1×11	• • • • • • • • • • •
12	1×12	• • • • • • • • • • • •
	2×6	• • • • • •
		• • • • • •
	3×4	• • • •
		• • • •
		• • • •
13	1×13	• • • • • • • • • • • • •
14	1×14	• • • • • • • • • • • • • •
	2×7	• • • • • • •
		• • • • • • •
15	1×15	• • • • • • • • • • • • • • •
	3×5	• • • • •
		• • • • •
		• • • • •
16	1×16	• • • • • • • • • • • • • • • •
	4×4	• • • •
		• • • •
		• • • •
		• • • •
17	1×17	• • • • • • • • • • • • • • • • •
18	1×18	• • • • • • • • • • • • • • • • • •
	2×9	• • • • • • • • •
		• • • • • • • • •
	3×6	• • • • • •
		• • • • • •
		• • • • • •

(continued)

19   1×19 • • • • • • • • • • • • • • • • • • •

20   1×20 •

            2×10 • • • • • • • • • •
                                   • • • • • • • • • •

            4×5 • • • • •
                                   • • • • •
                                   • • • • •
                                   • • • • •

Summary:

1. A product expression for a number is another name for the number itself.

2. Every whole number greater than 1 can be named by at least 2 product expressions:

   1 × itself and the *number × 1*

   1 × 12   12 × 1

   However, because of the commutative attribute, one can conclude that every whole number greater than 1 can be named by at least 1 product expression.

3. Many numbers can be expressed by 2 or more product expressions:

   4, 6, 8, 9, 10, 14, 20

4. Whole numbers greater than *1* that have only *1* and themselves as factors and are called *Prime Numbers*.

5. Whole numbers greater than *1* that have whole number factors other than *1* and themselves are called *Composite Numbers*.

6. The number *1* is neither prime nor composite; it is unique.

   • It is a factor of every number.

   • It is the identity for multiplication.

7. All of the prime numbers, other than the number 2, are all odd numbers.

76: Sieve of Eratosthenes

1. Draw a circle around 2.
2. Cross out all the multiples of 2.
3. Draw a circle around 3.
4. Cross out all the multiples of 3.
5. Draw a circle around 5.
6. Cross out all the multiples of 5.
7. Draw a circle around 7.
8. Cross out all the multiples of 7.
9. What is the next number that is not crossed out? 11
10. Circle all the numbers that are not crossed out. They are prime numbers.

(2, 3, 5, 7, 11, 13, 17, 19, 23, 29, 31, 37, 41, 43, 47, 53, 59, 59, 61, 67, 71, 73, 79, 83, 89, 97)

2	3	4	5	6	7	8	9	10
11	12	13	14	15	16	17	18	19	20
21	22	23	24	25	26	27	28	29	30
31	32	33	34	35	36	37	38	39	40
41	42	43	44	45	46	47	48	49	50
51	52	53	54	55	56	57	58	59	60
61	62	63	64	65	66	67	68	69	70
71	72	73	74	75	76	77	78	79	80
81	82	83	84	85	86	87	88	89	90
91	92	93	94	95	96	97	98	99	100

	2	3	4	5	6	7	8	9	10
11	12	13	14	15	16	17	18	19	20
21	22	23	24	25	26	27	28	29	30
31	32	33	34	35	36	37	38	39	40
41	42	43	44	45	46	47	48	49	50
51	52	53	54	55	56	57	58	59	60
61	62	63	64	65	66	67	68	69	70
71	72	73	74	75	76	77	78	79	80
81	82	83	84	85	86	87	88	89	90
91	92	93	94	95	96	97	98	99	100

77: Prime Factorization: Making Factor Trees

When a composite number is expressed as a product of prime numbers, it is called *prime factorization*. A fundamental theorem of arithmetic states that except for the order of the factors, a composite number can be expressed as a product of prime numbers in only one way.

24 can be renamed as 4×6 or 3×8 or 2×12

To find the prime factors for 24, any multiplication sentence that produces the product can be selected. Rename each number with another multiplication sentence until you no longer can rename the number.

    Students should be able to recognize prime numbers up to 50.

Example A:

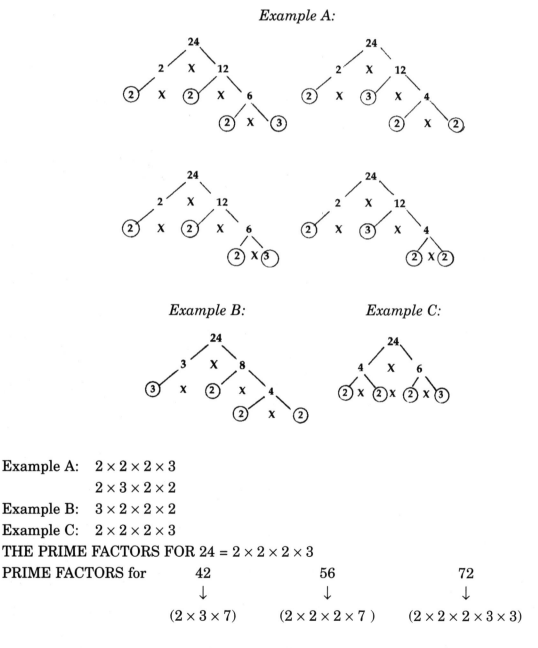

Example B: *Example C:*

Example A: $2 \times 2 \times 2 \times 3$
               $2 \times 3 \times 2 \times 2$
Example B: $3 \times 2 \times 2 \times 2$
Example C: $2 \times 2 \times 2 \times 3$
THE PRIME FACTORS FOR 24 = $2 \times 2 \times 2 \times 3$
PRIME FACTORS for   42   56   72
                   ↓   ↓   ↓
           ($2 \times 3 \times 7$)   ($2 \times 2 \times 2 \times 7$)   ($2 \times 2 \times 2 \times 3 \times 3$)

78: Prime Factoring Large Numbers

92

2)$\underline{92}$
2)$\underline{46}$
  23

92 = 2 × 2 × 23

468

2)$\underline{468}$
2)$\underline{234}$
3)$\underline{117}$
3)$\underline{\ 39}$
  13

100

2)$\underline{100}$
2)$\underline{\ 50}$
5)$\underline{\ 25}$
   5

100 = 2 × 2 × 5 × 5

945

5)$\underline{955}$
3)$\underline{189}$
7)$\underline{\ 63}$
3)$\underline{\ \ 9}$
   3

468 = 2 × 2 × 3 × 3 × 13   **945 = 3 × 3 × 3 × 5 × 7[*]**

*Order the factors from smallest to largest.

When a number such as 144 is prime factored, some of the factors repeat themselves. A student can use exponential notation to shorten the expression. The prime factorization of 144 = 2 × 2 × 2 × 2 × 3 × 3.

To write the prime factors that name 144 using exponential notation, count the number of times a factor is repeated and write the factor using a superscript.

$$144 = 2^4 \times 3^2$$

79: Finding the LCM
(Least Common Multiple)

Finding the LCM:

1. The LCM must be a multiple of the two numbers.
2. It must be the least of all such common multiples.
3. The LCM is a number greater than or equal to the larger of the two numbers.

There are two ways to find the LCM.

Find the LCM of (24, 36).

Method #1:   1. List multiples of each number.
   2. Identify least common multiple.
      Multiples of 24 = {24, 48, 72, 96, *144* . . .}
      Multiples of 36 = {36, *72*, 108, *144* . . .}
      (Italic indicates common multiples.)
      LCM = 72

Method #2:   1. Prime factor each number.
      $24 = 2 \times 2 \times 2 \times 3$ $36 = 2 \times 2 \times 3 \times 3$
   2. Match prime factors that are the same.

      $24 = \boxed{2 \times 2} \times 2 \times \boxed{3}$
      $36 = \boxed{2 \times 2} \times 3 \times \boxed{3}$

   3. Multiply to find the GCF (Greatest Common Factor). (See List 80.)
      $GCF = 2 \times 2 \times 3 = 12$
   4. Multiply the GCF by the remaining factors 2 and 3.
      $LCM = 12 \times 2 \times 3 = 72$

80: Finding the GCF
(Greatest Common Factor)

Finding the GCF:

1. The GCF must be a factor of the two numbers.
2. It must be the greatest of all such common factors.
3. The GCF is a number less than or equal to the lower of the two numbers.

There are three ways to find the GCF.

Find the GCF of (24, 36).

Method #1:
1. List factors of each number.
2. Identify greatest common factor.
   Factors of 24 = {*1, 2, 3, 4, 6, 8,* (12) 24}
   Factors of 36 = {*1, 2, 3, 4, 6, 9,* (12) 18, 36}
   (Italic indicates common factors.)
   GCF = 12

Method #2:
1. Prime factor each number.
2. Match prime factors that are the same.
3. Multiply.

$$24 = 2 \times 2 \times 2 \times 3$$
$$36 = 2 \times 2 \times 3 \times 3$$

GCF = $2 \times 2 \times 3 = 12$

Method #3:
1. Divide.
2. Keep dividing the remainder into the divisor until the remainder is zero.

(24, 36)   (42,100)

$$
\begin{array}{cc}
1 & 2 \\
24\overline{)36} & 12\overline{)24} \\
\underline{-24} & \underline{-24} \\
 & 0
\end{array}
$$

or

$$
\begin{array}{ccc}
2 & 2 & 1 \\
42\overline{)100} & 16\overline{)42} & 10\overline{)16} \\
\underline{-\,84} & \underline{-32} & \underline{-10} \\
16 & 10 & 6
\end{array}
$$

$$
\begin{array}{ccc}
1 & 1 & 2 \\
6\overline{)10} & 4\overline{)6} & 2\overline{)4} \\
\underline{-\,6} & \underline{-4} & \underline{-4} \\
4 & 2 & 0
\end{array}
$$

GCF = 12 for (24, 36)   GCF = 2 for (42, 100)

81: Finding Square Roots

When a number is raised to a second power, we say that the number is squared.

Example: 5^2 $5 \times 5 = 25$

So, 5 *squared* is 25 or 5×5.

A perfect square is when you multiply a number by itself. The product is a *perfect square*.

Example: *81* is *perfect square* because $9 \times 9 = 81$.

The symbol for a square root is $\sqrt{}$.

The *square root* of a number is a number that when multiplied by itself produces the given number.

Example: $\sqrt{49} = 7$

How to Calculate Square Root

1. Finding the square root of a number that is *not* a perfect square requires you to estimate.

   For example, what is the square root of *40*?

2. Since the perfect squares of 36 = 6 and 49 = 7, than you can conclude that the square root of 40 is closer to 36 than it is to 49. You could reason that the square root is approximately 6.4.

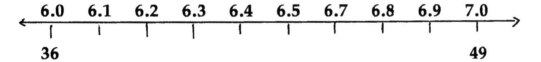

3. Estimate approximations by simple mental calculations:
   a. Difference between the two numbers: $49 - 36 = 13$.
   b. Midpoint between the two numbers would be
      1/2 of 13 = 6.5
      36 + 6.5 = 42.5

   c. Is 40 closer to 36 or 49? It is closer to 36.
   d. You could reason that the square root of 40 is approximately 6.4 or 6.3 since 40 is less than 42.5, the mid point, and closer to 42.5 than 36.

4. Calculating:

$$
\begin{array}{r}
6.4 \\
\times 6.4 \\
\hline
256 \\
+3840 \\
\hline
40.96
\end{array}
\qquad
\begin{array}{r}
6.3 \\
\times 6.3 \\
\hline
189 \\
+3780 \\
\hline
39.69
\end{array}
$$

179

(continued)

39.69 is closer to 40.

You can conclude that *6.3* is the approximate square root of 40.

5. Check by using the calculator. The square root of *40 = 6.3245553*.

Most math books will have a square root table. Since the square root of most numbers are irrational, they are all approximations.

82: Digital Roots

The process of adding the digits of whole numbers and repeating the process for each sum, which eventually produces a single digit, is called the digital root.

(1) Add to find the sum of the digits in 237.

$$237 \rightarrow 2 + 3 + 7 = 12$$

(2) If the sum is not a single digit, continue the process until it produces the digital root.

$$1 + 2 = 3$$

The digits of the whole number may be added in any fashion, always leading to the same digital root.

$$371 \rightarrow 3 + 7 + 1 = 11 \rightarrow 1 + 1 = 2$$
$$371 \rightarrow 37 + 1 = 38 \rightarrow 3 + 8 = 11 \rightarrow 1 + 1 = 2$$
$$371 \rightarrow 3 + 71 = 74 \rightarrow 7 + 4 = 11 \rightarrow 1 + 1 = 2$$

$$35{,}482 \rightarrow 35 + 48 + 2 = 85 \rightarrow 8 + 5 = 13 \rightarrow 1 + 3 = 4$$
$$35{,}482 \rightarrow 3 + 5 + 4 + 8 + 2 = 22 \rightarrow 2 + 2 = 4$$

Using Digital Roots as an Alternative Method for Checking Computation

- *Addition*

  The digital root of each addend, when added, equal the digital root of the sum.

254	$2 + 5 + 4 =$	2	576	$5 + 7 + 6 = 18 \rightarrow 1 + 8 = 9$	
+187	$1 + 8 + 7 =$	+7	+247	$2 + 4 + 7 = 13 \rightarrow 1 + 3 = \underline{4}$	
441	$4 + 4 + 1 =$	9		$13 \rightarrow 1 + 3 = 4$	
			823	$8 + 2 + 3 = 13 \longrightarrow 1 + 3 = 4$	

  However, if the sum is of exactly a multiple of 9, the digital root will incorrectly validate the sum.

254	$2 + 5 + 4 =$	2
+187	$1 + 8 + 7 =$	+7
432	$4 + 3 + 2 =$	9

- *Multiplication*

  The digital root of each factor, when multiplied, equal the digital root of the product.

46	$4 + 6 = 10 \rightarrow 1 + 0 =$	1
×23	$2 + 3 =$	×5
1058	$1 + 0 + 5 + 8 = 14 \rightarrow 1 + 4 =$	5

17	$1 + 7 =$	8
×14	$1 + 4 =$	×5
	$40 \rightarrow 4 + 0 = 4$	
238	$2 + 3 + 8 = 13 \rightarrow 1 + 3 = 4$	

(continued)

- *Subtraction*

  For subtraction, it is more convenient to check the problem using the inverse operation, addition.

If	251	*then*	184	$1 + 8 + 4 = 13 \rightarrow 1 + 3 = 4$
	$- \ 67$		$\underline{+67}$	$6 + 7 = 13 \rightarrow 1 + 3 = \underline{+4}$
	184		251	$2 + 5 + 1 = 8$

If	213	*then*	124	$1 + 2 + 4 = 7$
	$- \ 89$		$\underline{+89}$	$8 + 9 = \underline{+8}$
	124			$15 \rightarrow 1 + 5 = 6$
			213	$2 + 1 + 3 = 6$

- Division

  For division, it is more convenient to check the problem using the inverse operation, multiplication.

If	14	*then*	26	$2 + 6 = 8$
	$26)\overline{364}$		$\underline{\times 14}$	$1 + 4 = \underline{\times 5}$
				$40 \rightarrow 4 + 0 = 4$
			364	$3 + 6 + 4 = 13 \rightarrow 1 + 3 = 4$

  The digital root process also works for division with a remainder.

If	20	*then*	$(27 \times 20) + 23 = 563$	
	$27)\overline{563}$			
	$\underline{54}$		The digital root of 27	9
	23		Times the digital root of 20	$\underline{\times 2}$
				18
			Plus the digital root of 23	$\underline{+ \ 5}$
				$23 \rightarrow 2 + 3 = 5$
			Equals the digital root of 563	$14 \rightarrow 1 + 4 = 5$

SECTION 7

FRACTIONS

Name _____

Color 1/2 of my sections yellow.

Draw green spots on 1/3 of my sections.

Draw black stripes on 3/4 of my sections.

Color 6/12 of my sections red.

83: Teaching the Concept of Fractions

In the elementary classroom, there are three models used to teach fractions:

Part of a Whole (geometric figures)

Parts of Sets (arrays)

Measurement

1. Part of a Whole (geometric figures): Whole part divided into pieces. This popular method uses figures divided into *regions* or *sectors* in circles, rectangular regions, and square regions.

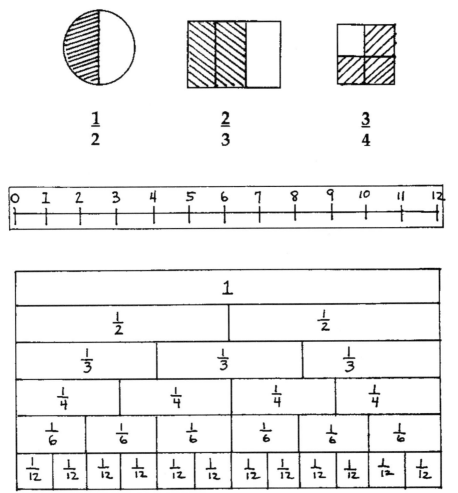

2. Parts of Sets (arrays): The difference between the *region* fraction concept and the Parts of Sets fraction concept is that the parts are distinct entities in their own right and they do not have to be physically connected. They may not be the same size or shape.

For example: Flowers in a bouquet, members in a family, students in a class, members of a baseball team, gems in a bracelet. Excellent models that can be used with elementary children are colored chips arranged in an array and colored eggs in an egg carton.

185

(continued)

3. Measurement: Reading parts of a number line.

In elementary school seven measurement concepts are taught: length, area, volume, weight, temperature, time, and angles. Any of these measurement concepts can be selected as a model for representing fractions. The most popular is the number line (length). Other models include the use of Cuisenaire Rods® and Unifix™ cubes.

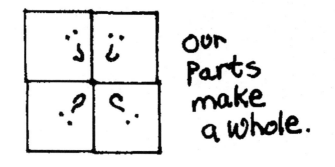

84: Fraction Vocabulary

Rational numbers are not whole numbers. They are numbers less than 1. A rational number is written either expressed in fraction form or decimal form.

Fraction: A fraction is a number of the form $\dfrac{a}{b}$ where $b \neq 0$.

Numerator: The number named above the fraction bar.

$$\dfrac{5}{9} \qquad \leftarrow \qquad Numerator$$

Denominator: The number named below the fraction bar. The denominator must not be 0.

$$\dfrac{5}{9} \qquad \leftarrow \qquad Denominator$$

Equivalent fractions: Fractions that name the same number.

$$\dfrac{2}{3} \quad = \quad \dfrac{4}{6} \quad = \quad \dfrac{8}{12}$$

Mixed numeral: A number that contains a whole number and a fraction.

$$2\tfrac{3}{4} \quad \text{is an abbreviated form of} \quad 2 + \tfrac{3}{4}$$

Improper fraction: A fraction in which the numerator is greater than or equal to the denominator.

$$1\tfrac{4}{5} = \dfrac{9}{5} \qquad \dfrac{4}{4} = 1 \qquad \dfrac{6}{2} = 3$$

Proper fraction: A fraction in which the numerator is less than the denominator.

$$\dfrac{1}{5} \qquad\qquad \dfrac{2}{3} \qquad\qquad \dfrac{13}{15}$$

Simplest form: The form in which a fraction is written if the numerator and the denominator have no common factors other than *1*.

$$\dfrac{7}{8} \qquad\qquad \dfrac{2}{5} \qquad\qquad \dfrac{7}{25}$$

Reciprocal or multiplicative inverse: When dividing fractions the reciprocal must be used. The reciprocal or multiplicative inverse of any nonzero number is the number whose product with the given number is *1*.

(continued)

$$\frac{3}{4} = \frac{4}{3} \times \frac{3}{4} = \frac{12}{12} = 1$$

Use the reciprocal of the divisor and change the operation symbol from division to multiplication.

$$\frac{a}{b} \div \frac{c}{d} = \qquad\qquad \frac{3}{4} \div \frac{2}{5} =$$

$$\downarrow \ \downarrow \qquad\qquad\qquad \downarrow \ \downarrow$$

$$\frac{a}{b} \times \frac{d}{c} = \frac{e}{f} \qquad\qquad \frac{3}{4} \times \frac{5}{2} = \frac{15}{8} = 1\frac{7}{8}$$

85: Adding Fractions

Adding Proper Fractions

Like Denominators

$$\frac{1}{3} + \frac{2}{3} = \frac{3}{3}$$

$$\begin{array}{r} \frac{5}{6} \\ \frac{2}{6} \\ + \\ \hline \frac{7}{6} = 1\frac{1}{6} \end{array}$$

Unlike Denominators

$$\begin{array}{r} \frac{2}{6} \\ \frac{4}{9} \\ + \\ \hline \end{array}$$

1. Find the LCM (lowest common multiple).
2. A quick way to determine the LCM is to Prime Factor each denominator:

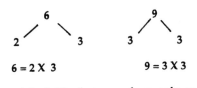

$$6 = 2 \times 3 \qquad 9 = 3 \times 3$$

Match like factors and use only once.

$$6 = 2 \times \boxed{3}$$
$$9 = 3 \times \boxed{3}$$

LCM = 2 X 3 X 3   LCM = 18

3.   Change fractions into equivalent fractions by dividing the denominator into the LCM (18) and multiplying the numerator and denominator of the original fraction by the quotient written in fraction form. *Or think like this:* What number times 6 will give me 18 as a product? (3) and what number times 9 will give me 18? (2)

$$\begin{array}{r} \left(\frac{2 \times 3}{6 \times 3}\right) = \frac{6}{18} \\ \left(\frac{4 \times 2}{9 \times 2}\right) = \frac{8}{18} \\ \hline \frac{14}{18} = \frac{7}{9} \\ \uparrow \\ \text{Simplest form} \end{array}$$

Mixed Numerals with Unlike Denominators

$$3\frac{3}{5} = 3\left(\frac{3 \times 2}{5 \times 2}\right) = 3\frac{6}{10}$$
$$+8\frac{9}{10} \qquad\qquad +8\frac{9}{10}$$
$$11\frac{15}{10} = 12\frac{5}{10} = 12\frac{1}{2}$$

Simplest form ↗

189

86: Subtracting Fractions

Proper Fractions

$$\frac{5}{6}$$
$$-\frac{3}{6}$$
$$\frac{2}{6} = \frac{1}{3}$$

$$\frac{5}{6} = \left(\frac{4 \times 5}{4 \times 6}\right) = \frac{20}{24}$$

$$-\frac{3}{8} = \left(\frac{3 \times 3}{3 \times 8}\right) = -\frac{9}{24}$$

$$\frac{11}{24}$$

1. Find the LCM when denominators are not alike.
2. Find equivalent fraction.
3. Subtract.

Mixed Fractions

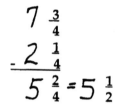

$$5\frac{3}{8} = 4 + \left(\frac{8}{8} + \frac{3}{8}\right) = 4\frac{11}{8}$$
$$-4\frac{5}{8}$$
$$-4\frac{5}{8}$$
$$0\frac{6}{8} = \frac{3}{4}$$

1. Regroup a whole number and write it in fraction form.
2. Add the numerators together to write the renamed fraction.
3. Subtract.

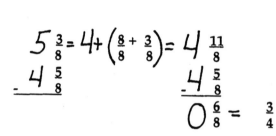

$$9\frac{1}{3} = 9 + \left(\frac{2 \times 1}{2 \times 3}\right) = 9\frac{2}{6} = 8 + \left(\frac{6}{6} + \frac{2}{6}\right) = 8\frac{8}{6}$$
$$-4\frac{5}{6}$$
$$\frac{5}{6}$$
$$-4\frac{5}{6}$$
$$4\frac{3}{6} = 4\frac{1}{2}$$

1. Find the LCM.
2. Regroup a whole number and write it in fraction form and add the numerators together to write the renamed fraction.
3. Subtract.

©1997 by The Center for Applied Research in Education

(continued)

$$11\tfrac{1}{5} = 11\left(\tfrac{4\times1}{4\times5}\right) = 11\tfrac{4}{20} = 10+\left(\tfrac{20+4}{20\quad20}\right) = 10\tfrac{24}{20}$$
$$-2\tfrac{3}{4} \qquad 2\left(\tfrac{5\times3}{5\times5}\right) \qquad -2\tfrac{15}{20} \qquad\qquad\qquad -2\tfrac{15}{20}$$
$$\overline{\qquad\qquad\qquad\qquad\qquad\qquad\qquad\qquad\qquad\qquad 8\tfrac{9}{20}}$$

1. Find the LCM.
2. Divide the denominator into the LCM and multiply the first fraction's numerator and denominator by the quotient, which is written in fraction form.
3. Regroup a whole number and write it in fraction form.
4. Add the numerators together to write the renamed fraction.
5. Subtract.

87: Multiplying Fractions

Proper Fractions

1. Multiply the numerator by the numerator.
2. Multiply the denominator by the denominator.

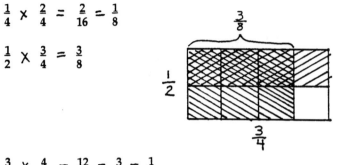

$$\frac{1}{4} \times \frac{2}{4} = \frac{2}{16} = \frac{1}{8}$$

$$\frac{1}{2} \times \frac{3}{4} = \frac{3}{8}$$

$$\frac{3}{8} \times \frac{4}{5} = \frac{12}{40} = \frac{3}{12} = \frac{1}{4}$$

Mixed Fractions

1. Change the whole number into a fraction.

$$3 \times \frac{1}{4} = \left(\frac{3}{1} \times \frac{1}{4}\right) = \frac{3}{4}$$

2. To change a mixed fraction into an improper fraction,

multiply the whole number by the denominator
($6 \times 2 = 12$),

then add the numerator to the product
($12 + 5 = 17$).

$$\frac{5}{6} = \frac{17}{6}$$

3. To simplify multiplication problems, check to see if cross products can be divided by the same number. In this example, 8 and 14 are cross products because both can be divided by 2.

$$1\tfrac{3}{8} \times 4\tfrac{2}{3} = \quad \frac{11}{\cancel{8}_4} \times \frac{\cancel{14}^{7}}{3} = \frac{77}{12} = 6\tfrac{5}{12}$$

$$2\tfrac{4}{5} \times 1\tfrac{3}{7} = \quad \frac{\cancel{14}^{2}}{\cancel{5}_{1}} \times \frac{\cancel{10}^{2}}{\cancel{7}_{1}} = \frac{4}{1} = 4$$

88: Dividing Fractions

To divide fractions, multiply by the reciprocal of the divisor. Reciprocal or multiplicative inverse of any nonzero number is the number whose product with the given number is 1.

$$\frac{3}{4} = \left(\frac{4}{3} \times \frac{3}{4}\right) = \frac{12}{12} = 1$$

Invert the denominator with the numerator.

A rule to remember: To divide one number expression in fraction form by another number expressed in fraction form, multiply the first number by the reciprocal of the second number.

$$\frac{1}{7} \div \frac{1}{3} = \left(\frac{1}{7} \times \frac{3}{1}\right) = \frac{3}{7}$$

Proper Fractions

$$\frac{2}{8} \div \frac{1}{8} = \left(\frac{2}{8} \times \frac{8}{1}\right) = \frac{16}{8} = 2$$

$$\frac{6}{7} \div \frac{4}{5} = \left(\frac{\overset{3}{\cancel{6}}}{7} \times \frac{5}{\underset{2}{\cancel{4}}}\right) = \frac{15}{14} = 1\frac{1}{14}$$

$$\frac{8}{9} \div \frac{4}{18} = \left(\frac{\overset{2}{\cancel{8}}}{\underset{1}{\cancel{9}}} \times \frac{\overset{2}{\cancel{18}}}{\underset{1}{\cancel{4}}}\right) = \frac{4}{1} = 4$$

Mixed Fractions

$$2\frac{5}{6} \div 3\frac{1}{4} = \left(\frac{17}{6} \div \frac{13}{4}\right) = \left(\frac{17}{\underset{3}{\cancel{6}}} \times \frac{\overset{2}{\cancel{4}}}{13}\right) = \frac{34}{39}$$

$$1\frac{3}{10} \div 2\frac{1}{2} = \left(\frac{13}{10} \div \frac{5}{2}\right) = \left(\frac{13}{\underset{5}{\cancel{10}}} \times \frac{\overset{1}{\cancel{2}}}{5}\right) = \frac{13}{25}$$

89: Ratios

A ratio is a set of numbers that is given in a certain order to describe the relationship that exists between two or more groups. A ratio is *not* a fraction.

Example 1:   5 toes for every foot.   Ratio is 5 toes to 1 foot

or

1 foot to 5 toes.

$$\frac{1}{5}$$

- When a ratio is only 2 numbers, you can write it as a fraction.

Example 2:

You have a bag with ten pieces of candy in it. Four of the pieces are gumdrops, three are lemon drops, two are chocolate-covered cherries, and one is a malted milk ball.

- When a ratio has 3 or more numbers in it, it is written like this:
  1 : 2 : 3 : 4 : 10
- Order the numbers from least to most in value.
- Make sure all the numbers, except the last, will add up to the total number in the set.

Example 3:

When a ratio is written 5 : 7 : 8, you know the first two numbers do not add up to 8. The ratio defining the complete set of the relationship of the parts to its whole will be 20 because 5 + 7 + 8 = 20. The correct way to write this is 5 : 7 : 8 : 20.

Proportion: A statement of equality between two ratios. If 2 pieces of gum cost 15¢, then 4 pieces cost 30¢. The equality can be shown as 2 : 15 = 4:30, or 2/15 = 4/30.

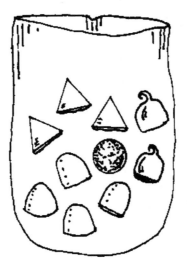

195

(continued)

Solving a Proportion

Example 1: A missing number of a proportion can be found if the other three numbers are given. If the equivalent ratios are written in fractional form, the products formed by multiplying the numerator of one fraction by the denominator of the other are equal.

2/4 = 4/8 $2 \times 8 = 4 \times 4$

3/5 = 9/15 $3 \times 15 = 5 \times 9$

Example 2:

If 2 pieces of gum sell for 15¢, how much would 8 pieces cost?

2/15 = 8/n

- Multiply the numerator of one fraction by the denominator of the other.

  $2 \times n = 15 \times 8$, or $2n = 120$

- Then solve for the unknown.

  n = 120/2

  n = 60

  8 pieces of gum would cost 60¢

90: Fraction Resources*

Birthday Party Fractions	(NASCO)
Connecting Fraction Circles	(ETA, Cuisenaire)
Exploring Fractions and Decimals Kit	(Didax)
Frac Jack	(ETA, NASCO)
Fractions Are Easy as Pie	(NASCO)
Fraction Arrows	(Didax)
Fraction Bars®	(NASCO, Dale Seymour, ETA, Didax)
Fraction Bar Games	(NASCO, Didax)
Fraction Bars® Transparencies	(NASCO)
Fraction Cakes Game	(NASCO)
Fraction Chart	(NASCO)
Fraction Circle Rings	(NASCO, Dale Seymour, Cuisenaire, ETA)
Fraction Circles	(NASCO, Dale Seymour, Didax, Cuisenaire)
Fraction Circles PLUS™	(Creative Publications)
Fraction Dice	(Cuisenaire, ETA, Didax, Creative Publications)
Fraction Dominoes	(NASCO, Cuisenaire, Didax)
Fraction Finder	(Cuisenaire)
Fraction Flashcards	(NASCO, Didax)
Fraction Flip Books and Activity Cards	(NASCO, Didax)
Fractions Kit	(NASCO, Didax)
Fraction Pattern Blocks	(NASCO)
Fractions Pie Game	(Dale Seymour, ETA)
Fraction Rubber Stamps	(Cuisenaire, Didax)
Fraction Squares	(NASCO, Cuisenaire, Didax)
Fraction Squares PLUS™	(Creative Publications)
Fraction Stax®	(NASCO, ETA, Didax)
Fraction Strips	(Dale Seymour, Cuisenaire)
Fraction Tiles	(Dale Seymour, Cuisenaire)
Fraction Tower™ Activity Set	(NASCO, ETA)
Fraction Tower™ Cubes	(NASCO, ETA)
Fractions Tray	(ETA)
Fractions with Tangrams	(ETA)
Fraction 500	(NASCO)
Fruit Salad: An introduction to fractions	(NASCO)

*See List 5 for addresses.

©1997 by The Center for Applied Research in Education

(continued)

Geometric Fraction Shapes	(Dale Seymour, ETA)
Geometry and Fractions with Pattern Blocks Kit	(ETA)
Learning Wrap-Ups® Fractions	(NASCO)
Magnetic Fraction Circles and Squares	(NASCO, ETA)
Making Sense of Fractions Set	(ETA)
NASCO Fraction Circles & Squares Set	(NASCO)
Overhead Fraction Circles	(Cuisenaire, NASCO, ETA, Didax)
Overhead Fraction Squares	(Cuisenaire, NASCO, ETA, Didax)
Overhead Fraction Strips	(Cuisenaire)
Overhead Fractions Circles PLUS™	(Creative Publications)
Overhead Fractions Squares PLUS™	(Creative Publications)
Percentage Fraction Shapes	(Didax)
PieCulator™	(Cuisenaire)
Pizza Party™	(NASCO, ETA, Didax, Creative Publications)
Rainbow Fraction™ Flashcards	(NASCO, ETA)
Rainbow Fraction™ Tiles Set	(ETA, Didax)
Rectangle Fraction Sets	(NASCO)
Square Parts	(Didax)
Vegetable Soup: More fun with fractions!	(NASCO)
Versa-Tiles® Fractions and Decimal Set	(ETA)

91: Fraction Activity Books*

Activities for Fraction Circles PLUS™	(Creative Publications)
Connections	(Creative Publications)
Constructing Ideas about Fractions™	(Creative Publications)
Developing Mathematical Thinking: Fractions	(Dale Seymour)
Eating Fractions	(ETA)
Exploring Fractions and Decimals with Manipulatives	(Didax)
Focus on Fractions	(ETA)
Fraction Action	(ETA)
Fraction Circle Activities	(NASCO, Didax, ETA, Dale Seymour)
Fraction Concepts: Using Fraction Circles and The Math Explorer™ Calculator	(NASCO)
Fraction Factory® Activity Binder	(Creative Publications)
Fraction Factory® Games & Puzzles	(Creative Publications)
Fraction Factory® Jobcards®	(Creative Publications)
Fraction Flip Books and Activity Cards	(NASCO)
Fractions in Action	(ETA, NASCO)
Fraction Tower™ Activity Cards	(ETA)
Fractions with Relational Attributes Activity Cards	(ETA)
Geometry & Fractions Book	(ETA)
Just for Fraction Circles	(Creative Publications)
Key to Fractions	(ETA)
Learning with Fraction Circles	(Cuisenaire)
Learning with Fraction Squares	(Cuisenaire)
Learning with Geometric Fraction Shapes	(Cuisenaire)
Making Sense of Fractions	(ETA)
Word Problems with Fractions	(ETA)
20 Thinking Questions™ for Fractions Circles	(Creative Publications)

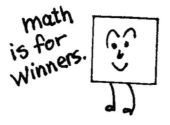

---

*See List 5 for addresses.

SECTION 8

DECIMALS

Name _____

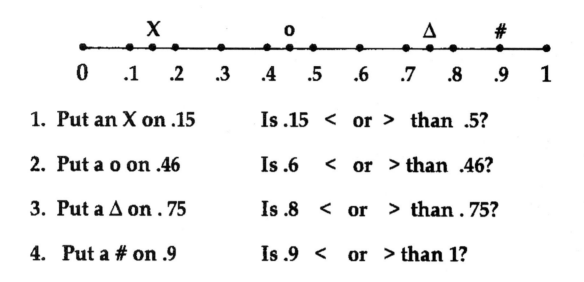

0   .1   .2   .3   .4   .5   .6   .7   .8   .9   1

1. Put an X on .15   Is .15 < or > than .5?

2. Put a o on .46   Is .6   < or > than .46?

3. Put a △ on .75   Is .8   < or > than .75?

4. Put a # on .9   Is .9   < or > than 1?

Color the grid the decimal portion indicated.

.6   .37

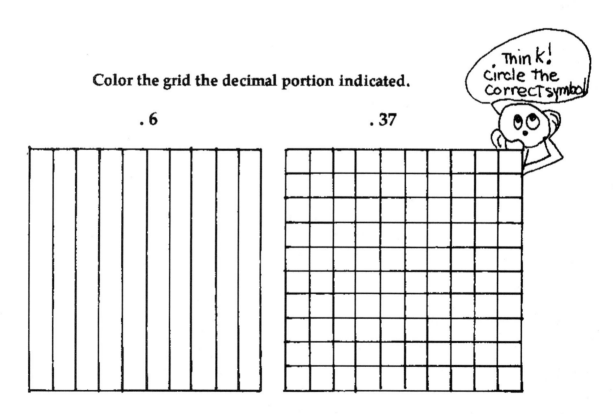

92: The Decimal System: Exponential and Expanded Notation

The Decimal System

thousands	hundreds	tens	ones	.	tenths	hundredths	thousandths
1	2	3	4	.	1	2	3

- The value of a digit is its place or position in a number.
- Each position has a name as shown in the number listed.
- A decimal point is placed to sort whole numbers from those numbers less than 1.
- The number word for 1234.123 is

> *One thousand, two hundred, thirty-four and one hundred*
> *twenty-three thousandths.*

- The first place to the right of the decimal point is 1/10 or the *tenths* place.
- The second place to the right of the decimal point is 1/100 or the *hundredths* place.
- The third place to the right of the decimal point is 1/1000 or the *thousandths* place.

Exponential Notation

- Exponential Notation is a short way of writing a number naming its position in the place value system to its tens power.

  500 is $5 \times (10 \times 10)$ or 5×10^2

  80 is $8 \times (10)$ or 8×10^1

  3 is 3×1 or 3×10^0

- *583,* a whole number, is written as $(5 \times 10^2) + (8 \times 10^1) + (3 \times 10^0)$
- *14.123,* a whole number, plus a decimal, is written as

$$(1 \times 10^1) + (4 \times 10^0) + (1 \times 10^{-1}) + (2 \times 10^{-2}) + (3 \times 10^{-3})$$

Number	Notation	Number Word
1 0 0 0	10^3	One thousand
1 0 0	10^2	One hundred
1 0	10^1	Ten
1	10^0	One
.1	10^{-1}	One-tenth
.0 1	10^{-2}	One-hundredth
.0 0 1	10^{-3}	One-thousandth

5674.123 written in:

©1997 by The Center for Applied Research in Education

203

(continued)

Expanded Notation

$(5 \times 1000) + (6 \times 100) + (7 \times 10) + (4 \times 1) + (1 \times 1/10) + (2 \times 1/100) + (3 \times 1/1000)$

Exponential Notation

$(5 \times 10^3) + (6 \times 10^2) + (7 \times 10^1) + (4 \times 10^0) + (1 \times 10^{-1}) + (2 \times 10^{-2}) + (3 \times 10^{-3})$

93: Teaching the Concept of Decimals

In the elementary classroom, there are three models used to teach decimals:

Place Value (manipulative: Place Value Blocks)
Geometric (grids and figures)
Measurement (fractions changed to decimals on number line)

Place Value (Manipulatives: Place Value Blocks)

1. Place value is fundamental to understanding decimals.
2. Review place value concepts before teaching decimals.

Thousands	Hundreds	Tens	Ones
$10 \times 10 \times 10$	10×10	10×1	1
10^3	10^2	10^1	10^0

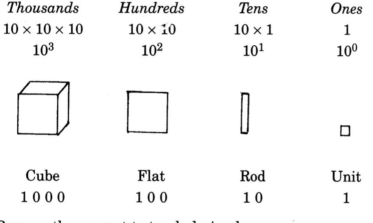

Cube	Flat	Rod	Unit
1 0 0 0	1 0 0	1 0	1

3. Reverse the concept to teach decimals.

Ones	Tenths	Hundredths	Thousandths
$\dfrac{1}{1}$	$\dfrac{1}{10}$	$\dfrac{1}{100}$	$\dfrac{1}{1000}$
10^0	10^{-1}	10^{-2}	10^{-3}

1	.1	.01	.001

It takes 1000 units to make the cube.

1000 units = 1

100 rods = 1

10 flats = 1

4. 1 in the hundredths place is $\dfrac{1}{10}$ the value of the 1 in the tenths place. We can write this using a number that is not a fraction. A decimal point is used to designate the number. The decimal point is the reference point indicting the separation of the whole number from the fractions number.

205

(continued)

$$\frac{11}{10} \quad = \quad 1\frac{1}{10} \quad = \quad 1.1$$

Geometric (grids and figures)

1 unit	1 out of 10	1 out of 100	1 out of 1000
1	$\frac{1}{10}$	$\frac{1}{100}$	$\frac{1}{1000}$
1.	.1	.01	.001
one	tenths	hundredths	thousandths

Circles can be used to show these relationships.

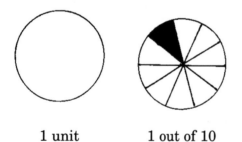

1 unit   1 out of 10

Measurement (fractions changed to decimals on number line)

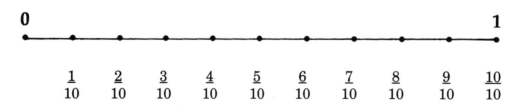

$$0 \qquad\qquad\qquad\qquad\qquad\qquad\qquad\qquad\qquad\qquad\qquad 1$$

$$\frac{1}{10} \quad \frac{2}{10} \quad \frac{3}{10} \quad \frac{4}{10} \quad \frac{5}{10} \quad \frac{6}{10} \quad \frac{7}{10} \quad \frac{8}{10} \quad \frac{9}{10} \quad \frac{10}{10}$$

(continued)

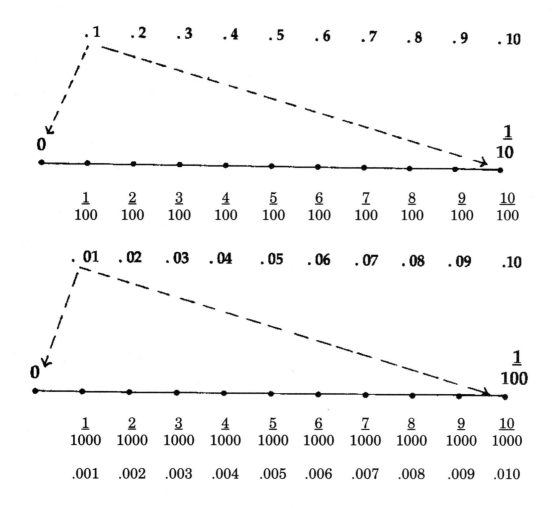

94: Addition and Subtraction of Decimals

Adding and subtracting decimals is fairly easy for elementary students. The rule students need to practice is:

Line up the decimal points.

Examples: $29.076 + 567.39 =$ $30.0005 - 2.1 =$

$$\begin{array}{r} 29.076 \\ + 567.39 \\ \hline \end{array}$$ $$\begin{array}{r} 29.076 \\ + 567.39 \\ \hline \end{array}$$ $$\begin{array}{r} 30.0005 \\ - 2.1 \\ \hline \end{array}$$ $$\begin{array}{r} 30.0005 \\ - 2.1 \\ \hline \end{array}$$

Correct   *Incorrect*   *Correct*   *Incorrect*

1. Remember to line up the decimal points before adding or subtracting.
2. Place the tenths in the tenths column, the hundredths in the hundredths column, and the thousandths in the thousandths column.
3. Remember, the decimal point (•) separates the whole number from the decimal number. It indicates that the numbers to the right of the decimal point are less than 1.
4. When adding or subtracting decimals and regrouping is required, regroup as normally exercised when adding or subtracting whole numbers.

Problem   **Rewrite**

                              add zeros for each place value

$$\begin{array}{r} 30.5 \\ - 2.0009 \\ \hline \end{array}$$ $$\begin{array}{r} 30.5000 \\ - 2.0009 \\ \hline \end{array}$$

Solve

$$\begin{array}{r} \overset{2}{\cancel{3}}0.\overset{4}{\cancel{5}}\overset{9}{\cancel{0}}\overset{9}{\cancel{0}}0 \\ - 2.0009 \\ \hline 28.4991 \end{array}$$

©1997 by The Center for Applied Research in Education

95: Multiplication and Division of Decimals

Multiplying Decimals

When multiplying decimals you do *not* line up the decimal points. Your answer will be determined by the number of decimal places in the two factors used to find the product.

```
   32.59          32.59             32.59
X      4       X    1.4          X    1.45
 130.36          13036             16295
                 32590           1 30360
                 45.626          3 25900
                                 47.2555
```

```
         32.59
X      .00045
         16295
       130360
 0.0146655
```

When dividing decimals the divisor must be changed into a whole number. This is easily done by multiplying the divisor and the dividend by the decimal value of the divisor. Students can easily do this by counting the place value positions to the right of the decimal and moving the decimal in the dividend the same number of positions to the right.

Example:

```
         3339.                    18.                20.
.002)6.678.                4.56)82.08.         .15)3.
    -6                        -456                -30
     6                        3648                 00
    -6                       -3648
     7                        0000
    -6
    18
   -18
    00
```

(continued)

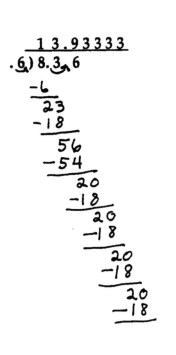

The answer is 13.93

96: Changing a Fraction to a Decimal

Decimals, like fractions, represent a part of a whole. It is sometimes necessary to change a fraction into a decimal. Division is used to change a fraction into a decimal.

1. To change a fraction into a decimal, divide the denominator into the numerator.

$$\frac{3}{4}$$

$$
\begin{array}{r}
.75 \\
4\overline{)3.00} \\
-28 \\
\hline
20 \\
-20 \\
\hline
00
\end{array}
$$

2. Some fractions, when changed into decimals, will be nonterminating. You will see a pattern in which the digits begin to repeat themselves. An example of this kind of fraction is:

$$\frac{1}{6}$$

$$
\begin{array}{r}
.166 \\
6\overline{)1.00} \\
-6 \\
\hline
40 \\
-36 \\
\hline
40 \\
-36
\end{array}
$$

3. The bar over the digits indicates that the digit or digits are repeating .

$.\overline{16} = .16666666 \ldots$

$.\overline{16} = .16161616 \ldots$

97: Terminating and Nonterminating Fractions/Decimals

1. There are two kinds of decimals when fractions are changed into a decimal. A fraction can be a terminating decimal or a nonterminating decimal.

   Example: $\frac{1}{4}$ $\frac{1}{6}$

```
        .25                        .166
    4)1.00                     6)1.000
      - 8                        - 6
       20                         40
                                - 36
                                  40
                                 -36
```

   (Terminating)   *(Nonterminating)*

2. Terminating and nonterminating decimals are easily determined:

   Fractions whose *denominators* when factored into primes containing 2's and 5's form *Terminating Decimals*.

Fraction	Prime Factors	Decimal
$\frac{1}{4}$	2×2	.250 or .25
$\frac{1}{10}$	2×5	.50 or .5

   Fractions whose *denominators* are other than 2 or 5 when prime factored form *Nonterminating or Repeating Decimals*.

Fraction	Prime Factors	Decimal
$\frac{1}{3}$	3	.333 . . .
$\frac{1}{6}$	2×3	.166 . . .
$\frac{1}{12}$	$2 \times 2 \times 3$	.08333 . . .

©1997 by The Center for Applied Research in Education

98: Changing a Percent into a Fraction and Changing a Decimal into a Percent

The term *percent* means parts per hundred.

The symbol for PERCENT is %.

In simple form, percent is used when comparing a number to 100.

1. Change a Percent into Its Fraction Equivalent

$$58\% \quad = \quad \frac{58}{100} \quad = \quad \frac{29}{50}$$

1. Use the percent as the numerator.
2. Name the denominator by 100.
3. Reduce to simplest form.

2. Change a Fraction into a Percent

$$\frac{3}{4} \quad \equiv \quad \frac{n}{100} \quad = \quad ?\,\%$$

a. Change fraction into a decimal.

$$4)\overline{3.00}^{\,.75}$$

b. Multiply by 100 to change into a percent.

.75 $.75 \times 100 = 75\%$
$\times\,100$
75.00

3. Changing a Decimal into a Percent

Any decimal can be changed into a percent by multiplying the decimal numeral by 100. Remember to move the decimal point to the right two places and write the percent symbol (%) to indicate that the decimal was multiplied by 100.

.45	=	45%
.376	=	37.6%
.00005	=	.005%
65.00	=	6500%

99: Decimal Resources*

Decimal Abacus	(NASCO)
Decimal Blackjack	(ETA)
Decimal Factory™ Activity Binder	(Creative Publications)
Decimal Factory™ Blocks	(Creative Publications)
Decimal Fraction Dominoes	(Didax)
Decimal Mods™ Sets	(ETA)
Decimal Olympics	(ETA)
Decimal Squares®	(Didax, ETA)
Decimal Squares® Activity Mats	(Didax)
Decimal Squares® Classroom Management Center	(Cuisenaire, ETA, Didax, NASCO)
Decimal Squares® Games	(ETA, NASCO)
Decimal Squares Playing Cards	(Didax)
Decimal Squares® Program	(Didax, Cuisenaire)
Decimal Squares® Starter Set	(Didax, ETA, NASCO, Creative Publications)
Decimal Squares Step-by-Step Teacher's Guide	(Didax)
Decimal Squares Teacher Resource Package	(Didax)
Decimal Squares Transparencies	(Didax)
Factor Football	(ETA)
Focus on Decimals	(ETA)
Math Stick	(Didax)
Overhead Decimal Factory™ Blocks	(Creative Publications)
Overhead Decimal Squares	(Cuisenaire)
Poster Decimal Equivalents of Ruler Fractions	(Dale Seymour)
10-Sided Decimal Dice	(Cuisenaire)
24® Game Platinum Series: Decimal Edition	(Cuisenaire)

©1997 by The Center for Applied Research in Education

---

*See List 5 for addresses.

100: Decimal Activity Books*

Decimal Factory™ Activity Binder	(Creative Publications)
Decimal Mods™ Activity Book	(ETA)
Decimal Squares Activity Mats	(ETA, Didax)
Decimal Squares Step-by-Step Teacher's Guide	(Didax)
Decimal Squares Teacher Resource Package	(Didax)
Decimal Squares® Teacher's Guide	(Cuisenaire)
Exploring Fractions & Decimals with Manipulatives	(NASCO)
Focus on Decimals	(ETA, NASCO)
Get to the Point!: Investigating Decimals	(Creative Publications)
Key to Decimals	(ETA)
Word Problems with Decimals, Proportions, and Percents	(ETA)

*See List 5 for addresses.

SECTION 9

MEASUREMENT

Name _____

Answer the questions, then draw your answer to fit the measurement in the fish tank.

1. Cyndie bought 2 sets of seaweed that were three inches high. She placed them inside her fish tank. She paid 40¢ for the seaweed. How much was 1 set?

_____

_____

2. Winston bought 4 guppies that were one inch long. Each guppy cost 25¢. How much did he pay for the guppies?

_____

_____

3. Mary Ann dropped one large flake of fish food in the tank. The diameter of the flake was 1/2 inch. Draw the flake floating in the tank. How many inches across are four flakes?

_____

_____

101: The English System of Measurement

- *Dry Measures*

2 pints = 1 quart   8 quarts = 1 peck   4 pecks = 1 bushel

- *Liquid Measures*

3 teaspoons = 1 tablespoon   2 tablespoons = 1 fluid ounce
16 tablespoons = 1 cup   8 fluid ounces = 1 cup
2 cups = 1 pint   2 pints = 1 quart
4 quarts = 1 gallon

- *Linear Measures*

12 inches = 1 foot   3 feet = 1 yard
6 feet = 1 fathom   5.5 yards = 1 rod
40 rods = 1 furlong   8 furlongs = 1 mile
5,280 feet = 1 mile   1,760 yards = 1 mile
3 miles = 1 league

- *Square Measures*

144 square inches = 1 square foot   9 square feet = 1 square yard
30.25 square yards = 1 square rod   4,840 square yards = 1 acre
640 acres = 1 square mile

- *Cubic Measures*

1,728 cubic inches = 1 cubic foot   27 cubic feet = 1 cubic yard

- *Weight Measures*

Avoirdupois System: the system for general weighing

437.5 grains = 1 ounce   16 ounces = 1 pound
100 pounds = 1 hundredweight   2,000 pounds = 1 ton

Troy System: for weighing precious metals

480 grains = 1 ounce   12 ounces = 1 pound

(continued)

● *Abbreviations*

acre—A

bushel—b

cubic foot—cu ft

cubic inch—cu in

cubic yard—cu yd

cup—c

fathom—fm

foot—ft

furlong—fur

gallon—gal

grain—gr

hundredweight—cwt

inch—in

mile—mi

ounce—oz

peck—pk

pint—pt

pound—lb, #

rod—rd

square foot—sq ft

square inch—sq in

square mile—sq mi

square yard—sq yd

tablespoon—T, tbsp

teaspoon—t, tsp

ton—T

yard—yd

102: The Metric System of Measurement

The basic unit of linear measurement in the metric system is the *meter*. Originally, the meter was calculated as one ten-millionth of the distance between the North Pole and the equator, through Paris. A more recent definition is 1,650,763.73 wavelengths of orange-red cadmium light waves under specific conditions. The meter is divided into 100 equal parts, or centimeters.

The basic unit of weight or mass is the *gram*. The gram is defined as the weight of one cubic centimeter of pure water under specific conditions. A cubic centimeter is a cube that is one centimeter of length on each side.

The basic unit of volume is the *liter* which is defined as the volume of 1,000 grams (1 kilogram) of pure water under specific conditions. It is easy to see that the metric measures are all related, unlike the U.S. customary system which has no logical relationships between length, weight, and volume.

The other units of measurement in the metric system are related by powers of tens. Their names are composed of the measure (meter, gram, or liter) being used and the prefix relation of the unit to that measure.

Prefix	Common Unit	Exponent	Symbol
kilo	1,000	10^3	k
hecto	100	10^2	h
deka	10	10^1	da
	1	10^0	m, g, L, or *l*
deci	.1	10^{-1}	d
centi	.01	10^{-2}	c
milli	.001	10^{-3}	m

In elementary school, children should only be asked to use the prefixes kilo, deci, centi, and milli.

Measurement	Common Units	Symbol
Length	kilometer	km
	meter	m
	centimeter	cm
	millimeter	mm
Weight	kilogram	kg
	gram	g
	centigram	cg
	milligram	mg
Volume	kiloliter	kl
	liter	L
	centiliter	cl
	milliliter	ml
Temperature	degrees Celsius	°C

103: Common Conversions

1 acre = 43,560 square feet

1 cord (firewood) = 128 cubic feet

1 centimeter = 0.3937 inch

1 cubic centimeter = 0.061 cubic inches

1 cubic foot = 7.48 gallons

1 cubic foot = 283.16 cubic centimeters

1 cubic inch = 0.554 fluid ounce

1 cubic meter = 1.308 cubic yards

1 cubic yard = 0.765 cubic meter

1 foot = 30.48 centimeters

1 foot = 0.304 meter

1 gallon = 3.785 liters

1 gallon = 0.833 British gallon

1 inch = 2.54 centimeters

1 kilogram = 2.205 pounds

1 kilometer = 3,281 feet

1 kilometer = 0.621 mile

1 liter = 1.057 liquid quarts

1 liter = 0.908 dry quart

1 liter = 61.024 cubic inches

1 ounce, fluid = 1.805 cubic inches

1 ounce, fluid = 29.574 milliliters

1 peck = 8.810 liters

1 pint, dry = 0.551 liter

1 pint, liquid = 0.473 liter

1 quart, dry = 1.101 liters

1 quart, liquid = 0.946 liter

1 ton = 0.907 metric ton

1 yard = 0.914 meter

104: The U.S. Monetary System

Coins and bills currently in circulation in the United States are:

penny	$ .01	1¢	1/100 of a dollar
nickel	.05	5¢	1/20 of a dollar
dime	.10	10¢	1/10 of a dollar
quarter	.25	25¢	1/4 of a dollar
half dollar	.50	50¢	1/2 of a dollar
dollar (coin)	1.00	$1	
dollar (bill)	1.00	$1	
two dollars	2.00	$2	
five dollars	5.00	$5	
ten dollars	10.00	$10	
twenty dollars	20.00	$20	
fifty dollars	50.00	$50	
one hundred dollars	$100.00	$100	

Denomination	Portrait on Front	Design on Back
$1	Washington	Great Seal of the U.S.
$2	Jefferson	Declaration of Independence
$5	Lincoln	Lincoln Memorial
$10	Hamilton	U.S. Treasury Building
$20	Jackson	White House
$50	Grant	U.S. Capitol
$100	Franklin	Independence Hall

Bills of higher denominations ($500, $1,000, $5,000, and $10,000) are no longer being printed. As they are returned to Federal Reserve banks, they are taken out of circulation and destroyed. The $100 bill was recently redesigned to increase security from counterfeiting.

The motto "In God We Trust" was first authorized in 1864 and used on the two-cent coin. A law passed in 1955 stipulated that "In God We Trust" shall appear on all U.S. coins and paper currency. In 1956, "In God We Trust" was declared the official motto of the United States.

105: International Currencies

Dollars, francs, and pesos are familiar currencies to many people in the world. There are also several currencies that are not so familiar. However, each currency is recognized in its own country.

Although countries like the United States and Canada use the dollar, the value of the U.S. dollar does not equal the value of the Canadian dollar. Similarly, Mexico, Argentina, and Cuba use the peso, but their value is not necessarily equal to each other. The exchange rate—the value of one currency compared to another currency—fluctuates on almost a daily basis. Many banks handle foreign currencies and can provide up-to-date exchange rates for how many Mexican pesos or Canadian dollars one can get for U.S. dollars.

Country	Currency	Country	Currency
Argentina	peso	Laos	kip
Australia	dollar	Liberia	dollar
Austria	schilling	Macao	pataca
Bahamas	dollar	Mexico	peso
Belgium	franc	Morocco	dirham
Bolivia	peso	Netherlands	guilder
Brazil	cruzeiro	New Zealand	dollar
Cambodia	rial	Nicaragua	cordoba
Canada	dollar	Norway	krone
Chad	franc	Oman	rial-Omani
Chile	peso	Paraguay	guarani
China	renminbi	Peru	sol
Colombia	peso	Poland	zloty
Costa Rica	colon	Portugal	escudo
Cuba	peso	Romania	leu
Czech Republic	koruna	Russia	ruble
Denmark	krone	Saudi Arabia	riyal
Ecuador	sucre	Singapore	dollar
Egypt	pound	South Africa	rand
El Salvador	colon	South Korea	won
Ethiopia	birr	Spain	peseta
Finland	markka	Sweden	krona
France	franc	Switzerland	franc
Germany	deutsche mark	Syria	pound
Greece	drachma	Taiwan	yuan
Guatamala	quetzal	Thailand	baht
Haiti	gourde	Trindad & Tobago	dollar
Honduras	lempira	Turkey	lira
Hong Kong	dollar	United Arab Emirates	dirham
Hungary	forint	United Kingdom	pound
Iceland	krona	United States	dollar
India	rupee	Venezuela	bolivar
Iran	rial	Vietnam	dong
Iraq	dinar	Zambia	kwacha
Israel	shekel		
Italy	lira		
Japan	yen		
Kenya	shilling		

106: Figuring Taxes

While there are many taxes that help support governments and institutions, there are two main types of taxes that most people face: sales tax and income tax.

• *Sales Tax.* A sales tax is a percentage of the price of goods or services added to the price of those goods or services. A sales tax is the primary source of money for state and local governments, and is often used to pay the salaries and expenses of police, firefighters, teachers, and other government workers.

Buying a new pair of shoes where there is an 8% sales tax.
New shoes: $50 × .08 = $4. $50 + $4 = $54 including tax.

Buying a new pair of shoes where there is a 5% sales tax.
New shoes: $50 × .05 = $2.50. $50 + $2.50 = $52.50 including tax.

• *Income Tax.* An income tax is a tax on an individual's salary, or the tax on the profits of a business. It is the federal government's primary source of money for running the country. Several states and large cities also collect income taxes. In many cases, when the individual's salary or business' profit goes up, the tax percentage also goes up.

The federal income tax rate on a salary or profit of $50,000 is approximately 20%. In other words, 20% of the salary or profit must be paid to the government.

$50,000 × .20 = $10,000. The amount of tax collected is $10,000.

This leaves the individual $40,000 left over to live on and buy the things that are needed.

If the individual were to receive a big raise in salary or if the business makes a larger profit, then the tax percentage usually would go up. The federal income tax rate on a salary or profit of $100,000 is approximately 30%.

$100,000 × .30 = $30,000. The amount of tax collected is $30,000.

Even though the salary or profit is twice as much as before, the tax is three times the amount it was before. This is the way most income tax systems operate in the world. Some do not think this is a fair system, while others do. It probably depends on how much money that person makes!

107: Figuring Interest

• Interest Paid

Interest is a payment that is made to someone for the privilege of borrowing money from them. Say, for example, that you borrow $10,000 from a local bank that charges 10% interest and the loan will be paid over a period of five years. The following table shows the amount of interest paid to the bank, plus the repayment of the $10,000 loan.

	Loan Balance	Loan Payment	Interest Payment	Total Payment
	$10,000	-0-	-0-	-0-
End of year 1	8,000	$2,000	$1,000	$3,000
End of year 2	6,000	2,000	800	2,800
End of year 3	4,000	2,000	600	2,600
End of year 4	2,000	2,000	400	2,400
End of year 5	-0-	2,000	200	2,200

The loan is paid off in equal $2,000 payments each year. The interest is calculated as 10% times the balance of the loan at the beginning of the year. In this example, the interest at the end of year 1 is calculated as $10,000 × .10 = $1,000. At the end of year 2, the balance is $8,000 and the interest is $8,000 × .10, or $800.

The total payments made over the five years equal $13,000. When the original $10,000 loan is subtracted from the $13,000, it can be seen that $3,000 interest was paid for the privilege of borrowing $10,000 for five years at 10% interest.

• Interest Earned

On the other hand, you can earn interest by loaning money. The most common way is to deposit money in a savings account in a bank. Since the bank uses the money that is on deposit, the bank pays a fee, or interest, for that privilege. For example, suppose you deposit $10,000 in a bank savings account that pays 5% interest annually. The following table shows the savings account balance, the interest earned, and the total savings.

	Account Balance	Interest Earned	Total Savings
	$10,000	-0-	-0-
End of year 1	10,000	$500	$10,500
End of year 2	10,500	525	11,025
End of year 3	11,205	551	11,576

At the end of year 1, $500 interest is paid. If the interest is left in the account, this amount will also earn interest. This is called compound interest. At the end of year 2, an additional interest of $25 was earned on the $500 interest paid to the account by the bank at the end of year 1. By the end of year 3, $1,576 has been earned through compound interest.

• Rules for Computing Interest

The following rules can be used for finding the interest of any principal for any number of days. Move the decimal point of the calculations two places to the left to express the interest. This is the same as dividing by 100.

(continued)

Interest Rate	*Calculation*
	Multiply the principal:
4%	by the number of days in the contract and divide by 90.
5%	by the number of days and divide by 72.
6%	by the number of days and divide by 60.
8%	by the number of days and divide by 45.
10%	by the number of days and divide by 36.
12%	by the number of days and divide by 30.
18%	by the number of days and divide by 20.

Examples:

- A loan of $1,000 for 180 days at 5% interest.

  $1,000 × 180 ÷ 72 = 2500. Move the decimal 2 places to the left. The interest is $25.00.

- A loan of $2,545.72 for 365 days at 10% interest.

  $2,545.72 × 365 ÷ 36 = 25810.7. Move the decimal point two places to the left. The interest is $258.10.

108: Figuring Profits

Profits are what you make if you are in business and sell products or perform services for more than it costs to make or perform them. If a business does not earn a profit, it will eventually have to close since there will not be enough money to pay the workers or buy supplies.

Suppose you own a shore store. You rent space for your store for $12,000 a year from the owner of the store. You pay your employees $68,000 a year to sell the shoes and you pay $220,000 to your shoe supplier for your stock of shoes. Your costs for the year total $300,000.

Rent	$ 12,000
Wages	68,000
Shoe Stock	220,000
Total Costs	$300,000

If the stock of shoes sells for more than $300,000 then a profit is made. For example, if the stock of shoes sold for $500,000, there would be a $200,000 profit. If they sold for $350,000, there would be a $50,000 profit. However, if they sold for only $200,000, there would be a loss of $100,000. Losses like this put stores out of business.

Why not just raise the price of the shoes so that there would be a profit? Some businesses try, but customers cannot be forced to buy things they feel are too expensive. The price of the shoes can be raised from $75 to $150 a pair, but probably no one would want to buy the shoes. When prices are raised, some buyers are lost. When a lot of buyers are lost, it is not good for profits. Profits may actually decrease after prices are raised.

On the other hand, profits may increase if prices are lowered. If enough people buy the shoes at the new low prices, more customers buying more shoes could make up for what is lost with the lower price on each pair of shoes.

Setting the right price to make a profit is not so easy as it sounds. People cannot be forced to buy a product. If competitors are selling the same product for less money, the customers will buy from the competitors. Lowering prices to the competitors' level may bring in more customers, but the profit may be so small that the business may not survive.

To Make a Gross Profit of:	Add to the Cost of the Product or Service:
50%	100%
40%	66.6%
35%	53.8%
30%	42.85%
25%	33.3%
20%	25%
15%	17.6%
10%	11.11%
5%	5.25%

©1997 by The Center for Applied Research in Education

109: Keeping a Checkbook

keep a balance.

• *Information for the Check Register*

1. Date: Date the check was written.
2. Check Number: The number of the written check.
3. Written to: The name of the person, business, or organization to whom the check was written.
4. Amount: The amount of money for which the check was written.
5. Deposit: The amount of money placed into the checking account.
6. Tax: Mark if the check can be used as documentation for an income tax deduction.
7. Balance: The amount of money left in the account after the check has been deducted.

Date	Check Number	Written To	Amount	Deposit	Tax	Balance
						27.36
7-2				56.47		83.83
7-2	151	Power Electric	12.45			71.38
7-10	152	The Red Cross	25.00		✓	46.38

• *Recording a Deposit*

1. Record the date of the deposit.
2. Record the amount of the deposit.
3. Add the deposit to the balance.

• *Recording a Check*

1. Record the date the check was written.
2. Record the number of the check.
3. Record to whom the check was written.
4. Record the amount of the check.
5. Subtract the amount of the check from the balance.
6. Record a check in the tax box if the check is used as documentation for an income tax deduction.

• *Writing a Check*

1. Date: Write the date the check was written.
2. Pay to the Order of: Write the name of the person, business or organization to whom the check was written.
3. $: Write the amount of money the check was written for in dollars and cents ($12.45).

(continued)

4. Dollars: The amount of money the check was written for in words. Write the dollar value of the check and show the cents as a fraction of 100 (Twelve and 45/100).

5. For: What the check was written for. This is for the benefit of the writer of the check.

6. Signature: Authorizes the bank to pay the money. Do not print.

Juan and Maria Torres   151

July 2 19 97

PAY TO THE
ORDER OF   Power Electric $ 12.45

Twelve and ————— 45/100 Dollars

Hometown Bank

For Switches   Maria Torres

110: Terms in Time

- Sunday, Monday, Tuesday, Wednesday, Thursday, Friday, Saturday
- January, February, March, April, May, June, July, August, September, October, November, December
- Second, Minute, Hour, Day
- Day Before Yesterday, Yesterday, Today, Tomorrow, Day After Tomorrow
- Dawn, Morning, Noon, Afternoon, Evening, Dusk, Night, Midnight
- Summer, Fall, Winter, Spring
- Year, Decade, Century, Millennium
- 60 seconds = 1 minute
- 60 minutes = 1 hour
- 24 hours = 1 day
- 1 day = the period of time for the earth to make one full rotation
- A.M. = from 12:00 midnight until 12:00 noon
- P.M. = from 12:00 noon until 12:00 midnight
- 7 days = 1 week
- 30 or 31 (also 28 or 29) days = 1 month
- 1 month = the period of time for the moon to make one revolution around Earth
- 365 days = 1 common year
- 366 days = 1 leap year
- 365 days, 5 hours, 48 minutes, 46 seconds = 1 solar year
- 1 year = the period of time for Earth to make one revolution around the sun
- 10 years = 1 decade
- 100 years = 1 century
- 10 centuries = 1 millennium
- 1,000 years = 1 millennium

111: 24-Hour Clock

12-Hour Clock		24-Hour Clock
A.M.	1:00	01:00
	2:00	02:00
	3:00	03:00
	4:00	04:00
	5:00	05:00
	6:00	06:00
	7:00	07:00
	8:00	08:00
	9:00	09:00
	10:00	10:00
	11:00	11:00
P.M.	12:00	12:00
	1:00	13:00
	2:00	14:00
	3:00	15:00
	4:00	16:00
	5:00	17:00
	6:00	18:00
	7:00	19:00
	8:00	20:00
	9:00	21:00
	10:00	22:00
	11:00	23:00
	12:00	24:00

The time on a 24-hour clock is always written with four numbers. The first two digits show the hour and the second two digits show the minutes. For the A.M. times, the 12-hour and the 24-hour times look similar. Fifteen minutes after seven in the morning is written 7:15 A.M. (12-hour) and 07:15 (24-hour). No A.M. designation is necessary with the 24-hour time since 07:15 only occurs once each day. Twenty minutes after 3:00 in the afternoon is written 3:20 P.M. (12-hour) and 15:20 (24-hour).

To convert from the 24-hour clock to the 12-hour clock, subtract 12 from the first two digits when they are greater than 12. For example, 17:30 equals 17:30 minus 12 or 5:30 P.M. 22:45 minus 12 equals 10:45 P.M.

(continued)

When it is 12 noon (Eastern Standard Time) in New York, these are the standard 24-hour times in the following cities:

Amsterdam	18:00	Honolulu	7:00
Anchorage	8:00	Jerusalem	19:00
Bangkok	24:00	London	17:00
Buenos Aires	14:00	Melbourne	3:00
Denver	10:00	Moscow	20:00
Hamilton, Bermuda	13:00	Tokyo	2:00

112: Temperatures

The most commonly used temperature scales are the Fahrenheit and Celsius scales. A third, the Kelvin scale, is used mainly in scientific experiments.

To gain a sense comparison between the Fahrenheit and Celsius scales, it is often useful for students to convert from one to the other.

- To convert from degrees Fahrenheit (°F) to degrees Celsius (°C):

$$C = (F - 32) \times 5/9$$

If F = 65° $C = (65 - 32) \times 5/9 = 18.3°C$

- To convert from degrees Celsius to degrees Fahrenheit:

$$F = 9/5 \, C + 32$$

If C = 21° $F = 9/5 \times 21 + 32 = 69.8°F$

- *Absolute Zero:* The theoretical temperature at which a substance would have no molecular motion and no heat. It is equal to 0°Kelvin, which is equal to −459.67°F.

Some Common Temperatures

	Celsius	Fahrenheit
a hot oven	190°	375°
water boils	100°	212°
hot faucet water	60°	140°
a high fever	40°	104°
normal body temperature	37°	98.6°
a hot day	32°	90°
a cool day	10°	50°
a cold day	2°	36°
water freezes	0°	32°

©1997 by The Center for Applied Research in Education

113: Speed, Time, and Distance

• *Speed*

—A ghost crab can move at the speed of 4 meters per second.

—A sloth, one of the slowest moving land animals, travels at 7 feet per minute.

—Sound travels through the air at approximately 1,088 feet per second.

—The speed of light is approximately 186,281 miles per second.

$$\text{Speed} = \frac{\text{Distance}}{\text{Time}}$$

Distance	÷	Time	=	Speed
120 miles		3 hours		40 miles per hour
5 kilometers		2 minutes		2.5 kilometers per minute
3,600 feet		5 seconds		720 feet per second

• *Time*

—Light travels from the sun to the earth in 8 minutes 12 seconds.

—The Concord flies from Washington, D.C. to Paris in 3 hours 33 minutes.

—A train in France runs from Paris to Lyons in 2 hours.

$$\text{Time} = \frac{\text{Distance}}{\text{Speed}}$$

Distance	÷	Speed	=	Time
120 miles		40 miles per hour		3 hours
5 kilometers		2.5 kilometers per minute		2 minutes
3,600 feet		720 feet per second		5 seconds

• *Distance*

—The average distance from the sun to the earth is 92,956,000 miles.

—The air distance between Melbourne, Australia and London, England is 10,508 miles.

—The air distance from Tampa, FL to Seattle, WA is 2,527 miles.

Speed × Time = Distance

Speed	×	Time	=	Distance
40 miles per hour		3 hours		120 miles
2.5 kilometers per hour		2 minutes		5 kilometers
720 feet per second		5 seconds		3,600 feet

114: Air Miles Between Major U.S. Cities

	Atlanta	Baltimore	Boston	Charlotte	Chicago	Cincinnati	Cleveland	Dallas	Denver	Houston	Indianapolis	Kansas City, MO	Las Vegas	Los Angeles
Atlanta	—	576	946	227	597	373	559	707	1208	692	432	681	1747	1934
Baltimore	576	---	370	360	613	430	312	1196	1503	1240	515	961	2106	2317
Boston	946	370	---	727	860	752	558	1543	1766	1603	817	1254	2381	2600
Charlotte	227	360	727	---	589	335	433	913	1348	917	428	799	1917	2113
Chicago	597	613	860	589	---	254	312	790	907	932	167	407	1521	1740
Cincinnati	373	430	752	335	254	---	226	793	1081	879	98	533	1678	1888
Cleveland	559	312	558	433	312	226	---	1010	1217	1104	266	696	1829	2046
Dallas	707	1196	1543	913	790	793	1010	---	664	222	746	448	1081	1248
Denver	1208	1503	1766	1348	907	1081	1217	664	---	875	989	552	616	839
Houston	692	1240	1603	917	932	879	1104	222	875	---	854	643	1229	1372
Indianapolis	432	515	817	428	167	98	266	746	989	854	---	446	1591	1803
Kansas City, MO	681	961	1254	799	407	533	696	448	552	643	446	---	1145	1357
Las Vegas	1747	2106	2381	1917	1521	1678	1829	1081	616	1229	1591	1145	---	227
Los Angeles	1934	2317	2600	2113	1740	1888	2046	1248	839	1372	1803	1357	227	---
Miami	595	946	1258	650	1188	948	1083	1096	1716	959	1021	1239	2175	2330
Milwaukee	669	641	860	651	74	318	331	843	908	994	237	438	1524	1745
Minneapolis	906	936	1124	980	334	596	624	850	693	1046	503	404	1300	1526
Nashville	214	587	942	329	401	230	453	610	1023	663	249	480	1587	1785
New York	755	179	191	537	721	579	410	1363	1627	1416	654	1098	2237	2453
Oklahoma City	761	1180	1505	941	694	756	954	185	500	407	689	306	986	1175
Philadelphia	672	96	274	453	675	513	365	1289	1575	1336	593	1040	2183	2396
Phoenix	1587	1999	2300	1774	1445	1569	1742	893	589	1015	1489	1046	255	358
Pittsburgh	526	210	496	366	404	256	104	1049	1302	1124	325	769	1910	2124
St. Louis	484	737	1046	575	256	308	492	537	781	677	229	229	1372	1581
Salt Lake City	1589	1864	2105	1727	1257	1449	1569	1010	381	1204	1355	928	368	583
San Diego	1891	2295	2588	2077	1729	1865	2031	1196	840	1308	1783	1337	258	101
San Francisco	2141	2456	2703	2298	1853	2036	2164	1493	956	1647	1944	1507	419	355
Seattle	2182	2334	2495	2279	1730	1964	2023	1681	1020	1885	1866	1501	869	959
Tampa	410	841	1183	508	1006	776	932	911	1520	791	841	1040	1991	2153
Washington, DC	540	37	406	325	591	400	297	1161	1476	1204	487	932	2077	2288

(continued)

Miami	Milwaukee	Minneapolis	Nashville	New York	Oklahoma City	Philadelphia	Phoenix	Pittsburgh	St. Louis	Salt Lake City	San Diego	San Francisco	Seattle	Tampa	Washington, DC
595	669	906	214	755	761	672	1587	526	484	1589	1891	2141	2182	410	540
946	641	936	587	179	1180	96	1999	210	737	1864	2295	2456	2334	841	37
1258	860	1124	942	191	1505	274	2300	496	1046	2105	2588	2703	2495	1183	406
650	651	930	329	537	941	453	1774	366	575	1727	2077	2298	2279	508	325
1188	74	344	401	721	694	675	1445	404	256	1257	1729	1853	1730	1006	591
948	318	596	230	579	756	513	1569	256	308	1449	1865	2036	1964	778	400
1083	331	624	453	410	954	365	1742	104	492	1569	2031	2164	2023	932	297
1096	843	850	610	1363	185	1289	893	1049	537	1010	1196	1493	1681	911	1161
1716	908	693	1023	1627	500	1575	589	1302	781	381	840	956	1020	1520	1476
959	994	1046	663	1416	407	1336	1015	1124	677	1204	1308	1647	1885	791	1204
1021	237	503	249	654	689	593	1489	325	229	1355	1783	1944	1866	841	487
1239	438	404	480	1098	306	1040	1046	769	229	928	1337	1507	1501	1040	932
2175	1524	1300	1587	2337	986	2183	255	1910	1372	368	258	419	869	1991	2077
2330	1745	1526	1785	2453	1175	2396	358	2124	1581	583	101	355	959	2153	2288
---	1259	1501	807	1092	1223	1017	1972	1013	1068	2088	2267	2589	2725	199	920
1259	---	297	475	733	736	695	1460	430	317	1246	1739	1844	1694	1078	623
1501	297	---	695	1016	694	985	1276	726	448	991	1532	1587	1398	1311	919
807	475	695	---	758	615	681	1448	462	271	1403	1751	1969	1978	616	552
1092	733	1016	758	---	1335	84	2143	329	882	1977	2435	2574	2408	1003	215
1223	736	694	615	1335	---	1268	833	1010	462	865	1136	1386	1521	1030	1147
1017	695	985	681	84	1268	---	2082	274	820	1932	2376	2526	2383	923	133
1972	1460	1276	1448	2143	833	2082	---	1814	1262	507	304	657	1109	1795	1967
1013	430	726	462	329	1010	274	1814	---	553	1659	2106	2253	2124	874	194
1068	317	448	271	882	462	820	1262	553	---	1156	1557	1736	1710	874	707
2088	1246	991	1403	1977	865	1932	507	1659	1156	---	626	598	691	1894	1839
2267	1739	1532	1751	2435	1136	2376	304	2106	1557	626	---	456	1053	2094	2264
2589	1844	1587	1969	2574	1386	2526	657	2253	1736	598	456	---	671	2403	2430
2725	1694	1398	1978	2408	1520	2383	1109	2124	1710	691	1053	671	---	2527	2317
199	1078	1311	616	1003	1030	923	1795	874	874	1894	2094	2403	2527	---	811
920	623	919	552	215	1147	133	1967	194	707	1839	2264	2430	2317	811	---

PROBABILITY
AND STATISTICS

What is the probability of tossing 5 pennies and have none of them land on a line?

_____

115: Probability

Probability is the numerical measure of the number of times something can occur over the number of events that could possibly occur. Probability is expressed as a ratio.

$$\frac{\text{The number of ways that an event can occur}}{\text{The number of possible events}} = \text{The probability of a particular event occurring}$$

• *Coins*

1. Tossing 1 coin.

$$\frac{\text{Ways the event (head or tail) can occur}}{\text{Total possible events}} = \frac{1}{2}$$

The probability of tossing a coin and correctly calling head or tail is 1 time out of every 2 events.

2. Tossing 2 coins.

4 Possible Outcomes	*1st Coin*	*2nd Coin*
	Head	Head
	Head	Tail
	Tail	Head
	Tail	Tail

    The probability of tossing 2 heads is 1 out of 4 times (1/4).
    The probability of tossing 1 head and 1 tail (no order) is 2 out of 4 times (2/4).
    The probability of tossing 2 tails is 1 out of 4 times (1/4).

3. Tossing 3 coins.

8 Possible Outcomes	*1st Coin*	*2nd Coin*	*3rd Coin*
	Head	Head	Head
	Head	Head	Tail
	Head	Tail	Head
	Head	Tail	Tail
	Tail	Head	Head
	Tail	Head	Tail
	Tail	Tail	Head
	Tail	Tail	Tail

    The probability of tossing 3 heads is 1/8.
    The probability of tossing 2 heads and 1 tail (no order) is 3/8.
    The probability of tossing 1 head and 2 tails (no order) is 3/8.
    The probability of tossing 3 tails is 1/8.

(continued)

- *Pascal's Triangle*

  Blaise Pascal, a 17th-century French mathematician, spent time exploring the mathematics of gambling (which is based on probability) and developed a way of representing the probability of events occurring. The pattern of the triangle develops by adding two adjacent numbers and producing a number below. The three numbers form a triangle.

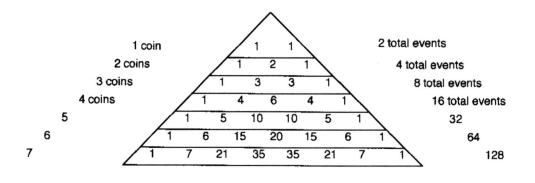

116: Independent Events with Cards, Dice, Spinners, and Marbles

• *Cards*

A standard deck of playing cards contains four suits (clubs, spades, hearts, and diamonds) and 13 individual cards (ace, 2, 3, 4, 5, 6, 7, 8, 9, 10, jack, queen, king) in each suit for a total of 52 cards.

The probability of drawing a particular suit from a deck of cards—for instance, a club—is:

$$\frac{13 \text{ cards of each suit}}{52 \text{ cards total}} = \frac{13}{52} \text{ or } \frac{1}{4}$$

The probability of drawing a particular card from a deck—for instance, a queen—is:

$$\frac{4 \text{ queens in the deck}}{52 \text{ cards total}} = \frac{4}{52} \text{ or } \frac{1}{13}$$

The probability of drawing a specific card from a deck—for instance, a queen of clubs—is:

$$\frac{1 \text{ queen of clubs in the deck}}{52 \text{ cards total}} = \frac{1}{52}$$

• *Dice*

A standard die has six sides representing the values from 1 through 6. The probability of rolling a specific number—for instance, 4—on a die is the number of ways the event can occur (1) over the total possible events (6), or 1/6. If two dice are tossed, the possibilities are 6 events on one die and 6 events on the other. When multiplied, there are 36 total possible events.

©1997 by The Center for Applied Research in Education

243

(continued)

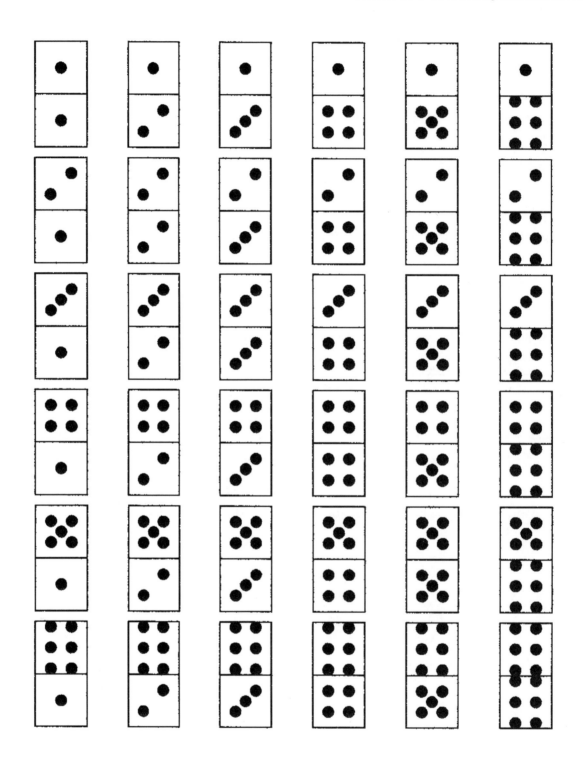

The probability of tossing a sum of 2 is 1/36.

The probability of tossing a sum of 3 is 2/36 or 1/18.

(continued)

The probability of tossing a sum of 4 is 3/36 or 1/12.
The probability of tossing a sum of 5 is 4/36 or 1/9.
The probability of tossing a sum of 6 is 5/36.
The probability of tossing a sum of 7 is 6/36 or 1/6.
The probability of tossing a sum of 8 is 5/36.
The probability of tossing a sum of 9 is 4/36 or 1/9.
The probability of tossing a sum of 10 is 3/36 or 1/12.
The probability of tossing a sum of 11 is 2/36 or 1/18.
The probability of tossing a sum of 12 is 1/36.

• *Spinners*

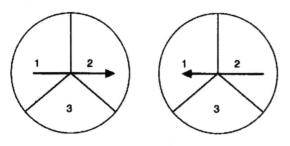

There are three possible events for spinner A (1, 2, 3) and three possible events for spinner B. The probability of a number appearing on spinner A is 1/3, which is also the same for spinner B. Spinning both spinners yields a total of nine possible events (3 events x 3 events). The nine events are;

Spinner A lands on	1 1 1 2 2 2 3 3 3
while	
Spinner B lands on	1 2 3 1 2 3 1 2 3

The probability of spinning the two spinners and obtaining a specific sum is:

Sum	Probability	Possible Events
2	1/9	1 and 1
3	2/9	1 and 2; 2 and 1
4	3/9	1 and 3; 2 and 2; 3 and 1
5	2/9	2 and 3; 3 and 2
6	1/9	3 and 3

• *Marbles*

Six marbles in a jar: 3 blue, 2 red, and 1 green.

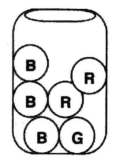

1. 1 Pick

    The probability of picking a blue marble from the jar is 3/6 or 1/2.

(continued)

The probability of picking a red marble from the jar is 2/6 or 1/3.

The probability of picking a green marble from the jar is 1/6.

2. **2 Picks Without Replacement**

   The probability of picking a blue marble from the jar and, without replacing it, picking another blue marble is:

$$3/6 \times 2/5 = 6/30 \text{ or } 1/5$$

   There are 3 blue marbles out of 6 total marbles. After picking one marble, it is assumed that there are 2 blue marbles of the remaining 5 marbles.

3. **3 Picks Without Replacement**

   The probability of picking a blue marble from the jar and, without replacing it, picking another blue marble and, without replacing it, picking another blue marble is:

$$3/6 \times 2/5 \times 1/4 = 6/120 \text{ or } 1/20$$

   The probability of picking a red marble from the jar and, without replacing it, picking a blue marble and, without replacing it, picking a green marble is:

$$2/6 \times 3/5 \times 1/4 = 6/120 \text{ or } 1/20$$

117: Simple Statistics

- *Inferential Statistics:* Inferential statistics, or hypothesis testing, is concerned with making probability statements or making formal statistical inferences. It involves making a prediction that would apply to a large group on the basis of a small sample. If the results of some study indicated that there exists a significant difference between a control group and an experimental group in a small sample, the investigator can show that the probability of finding a certain result is a certain critical level. This is usually written as $P < .05$ or $P < .01$. The investigator can either accept or reject the hypothesis on this information. Therefore, the investigator is making an "inference" about the data that was collected.

- *Samples/Populations:* Inferential statistics are concerned with populations and samples.

  Populations have parameters. Parameters are characteristics of populations.

  The mean for a population is a parameter signified as a μ.

  The standard deviation is a parameter signified as a σ.

  Samples are small subset groups taken from a population and must be random.

  Statistics is a characteristic of a sample.

  The sample for normal distributions has three statistical characteristics:

  Mean

  Median

  Mode

  Mean: The mean is the average or normal data for a given situation. The mean is calculated by dividing the sum of the measure by the number of measures.

  $$\frac{\Sigma N}{N} = \text{the mean}$$

  Median: When data is arranged in order of size, the median is the middle measure. Half the data lies at or above the median and half lies below. At times the median will not be one of the data, but will be a point between two data. For example, the number of students in the four first-grade classes at Math Elementary are 21, 22, 23, and 23. The median, or middle measure, is a point midway between 22 and 23 or 22.5.

  If the data above had been 21, 22, 23, and 25, the median would still be 22.5. The median is a reliable measure when the data has extremely large or small ranges.

  Mode: The mode is the most frequently occurring data. In the given set of data: *22, 23, 22, 22, 25, 23, 26, 22, 24,* the mode is 22. 22 occurs 4 times in the set.

  The range for the above given data is 22 to 26.

- *Normal Distributions*

  Normal distribution (bell-shaped curve) says that from any population, if you draw samples of size N, then the distribution of *means* from those samples is:

247

(continued)

©1997 by The Center for Applied Research in Education

a. approximately normally distributed
b. it has a mean
c. it has a standard deviation

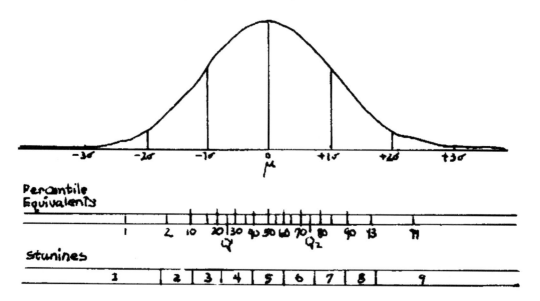

* *Statistical Forms*

  Statistical forms have a set of variables that can be organized in two ways:

  1. Discrete—Qualitative
      a. Unordered categories (sex, M, F, hair color)
      b. Rating Scales (SA A UD SD)
      c. Rank (1, 2, 3; first second; according to height, etc.)

  2. Continuous Scale—Quantitative

      6   6.4   7
      •   •   •   •   •   •   •   •   •   •   •

      A continuous scale is a unit of measurement that can be subdivided without limits.

      I.Q. Scores

      •   •   •   •   •   •   •   •   •   •
      99   99.5   100   100.5 101   101.5 102   102.5 103   103.5

118: Stem-and-Leaf Plots

Stem-and-leaf plots are a newer form of graphs in which the recorded data shows the shape of the entire set. Consider the data representing the number of cans of food collected by each class during the holiday canned food drive: 46, 78, 36, 28, 97, 74, 56, 68, 67, 83, 75, 84, 68, 91, 88, 78, 46, 65, 49, and 68. The data is unorganized and it would be difficult to make any quick determinations about the central tendencies.

Since the data is limited to two-digit numbers, construction of the graph begins by listing the tens place which includes the data (20 through 90) which forms the stem.

STEM

20
30
40
50
60
70
80
90

The next step is to record the ones place digit next to the appropriate tens place digit forming the leaves.

STEM	LEAVES	STEM	LEAVES
20	8	20	8
30	6	30	6
40	6 6 9	40	6 6 9
50	6	50	6
60	8 7 8 5 8	60	5 7 8 8 8
70	8 4 5 8	70	4 5 8 8
80	3 4 8	80	3 4 8
90	7 1	90	1 7

To provide additional information, the graph can be quickly rewritten ordering each leaf from least to most. In this form it is easy to identify the median (the middle score) as 68, the mode (the most frequent score) also as 68, and the mean (average) as somewhere in the 60s.

Stem-and-leaf plots are not limited to two-digit data. If the data is recorded in the hundreds (378, 236, 499, 396, 405, 259, 214, 461, and 324), the stem would be the hundreds place followed by two-digit leaves.

STEM	LEAVES
2	14, 36, 59
3	24, 78, 96
4	05, 61, 99

Stem-and-leaf plots are an excellent way of visually comparing two distinct sets of data.

119: Picture Graphs

Picture graphs use pictures or drawings to represent the data that is being graphed. Young children can make drawings or can use actual pictures to construct the graphs.

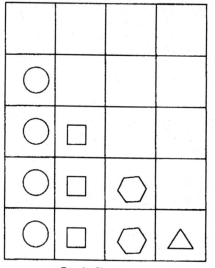

Favorite Shapes

The most favorite shape was the circle and the least favorite was the triangle. More students preferred the square as their favorite shape than those who favored hexagons or the triangle.

As students develop their skills with picture graphs, they can begin to explore the concept of each picture being equal to more than one datum.

Monday

Tuesday

Wednesday

Thursday

Bicycles Ridden to School for a Four-Day Period
(Each picture equals 50 bicycles)

On Monday 200 bicycles were ridden to school.
On Tuesday 125 bicycles were ridden to school.
On Wednesday 100 bicycles were ridden to school.
On Thursday 250 bicycles were ridden to school.

©1997 by The Center for Applied Research in Education

120: Histogram

A histogram, often referred to as a bar graph, displays data using consecutive intervals along a numeric scale. The scale can be changed to fit the data being displayed and the intervals should always be the same size with no gaps. Histograms cn be drawn horizontally or vertically; however, the variable should be displayed on the horizontal axis. Histograms are best suited for discrete (data which can be counted) data.

Histogram of the Number of Members in the Family of a Third-Grade Classroom at Math Elementary School

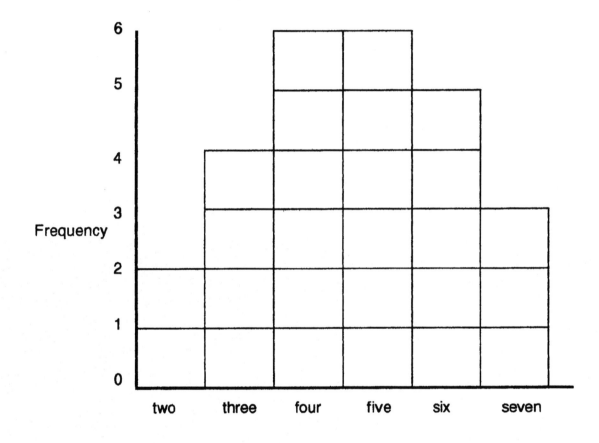

Number of Members in the Family

121: Frequency Polygon

A frequency polygon, often referred to as a line graph, is best suited for displaying continuous (data that is measured) data. Points are plotted to show two related pieces of data and then a line is drawn connecting consecutive points. The lines and points show any changes in the data, usually over a period of time. The data are displayed using consecutive intervals along a numeric scale. The intervals should always be the same size with no gaps, and the scale can be constructed to fit the data.

Frequency of the Growth of a Plant Over the Period of a Week

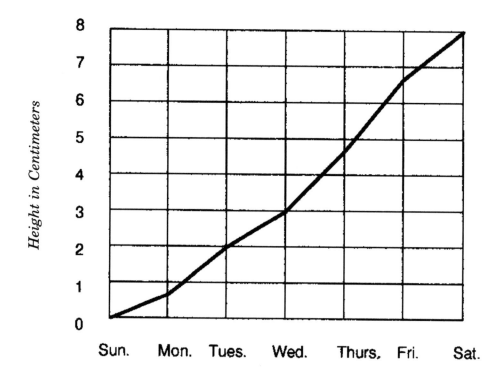

Days of the Week

122: Circle Graphs

Circle graphs use sectors of a circle to represent percentages of the data being shown. Circle graphs are easy to read and interpret since the relative value of each sector can be seen at a glance. However, knowledge of percentages and angular measurement is essential, which make circle graphs the most difficult for students to construct.

• *Construction of Circle Graphs*

1. *Data*

   Favorite Lunch Choices

Hamburger	343
Hot Dog	481
Pizza	686
Sandwich	171
Salad	34
Total	1715

2. *Percentages*

   Calculate the percentage of the total for each set of data by dividing the data by the total and multiplying by 100.

   $343 / 1715 \times 100 = 20\%$

   $481 / 1715 \times 100 = 28\%$

   $686 / 1715 \times 100 = 40\%$

   $171 / 1715 \times 100 = 10\%$

   $34 / 1715 \times 100 = 2\%$

3. *Degrees*

   Calculate the number of degrees of the circle for each sector by dividing each percentage by 100 and multiplying that total times 360°.

   $20\% / 100 = .20 \times 360° = 72°$

   $28\% / 100 = .28 \times 360° = 100.8°$

   $40\% / 100 = .40 \times 360° = 144°$

   $10\% / 100 = .10 \times 360° = 36°$

   $2\% / 100 = .02 \times 360° = 7.2°$

(continued)

Use a protractor to divide the circle into the corresponding sectors.

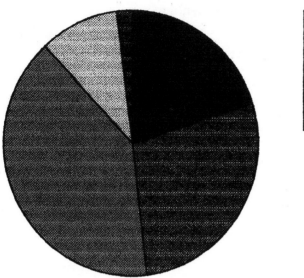

■	Hamburger
▨	Hot Dog
▧	Pizza
▥	Sandwich
■	Salad

123: Probability and Statistics Resources*

Bean Counters	(ETA)
Binostat	(ETA)
Color Cube	(Didax)
Color Spinners	(NASCO, Cuisenaire, Didax, ETA, Creative Publications)
Dice	(Dale Seymour, Cuisenaire, ETA Creative Publications, Didax)
Dice Kit	(ETA)
Dime Materials Probability Kits	(Didax)
Giant Foam Dice	(ETA)
Manipulite® Basic Fraction Pieces	(ETA)
Manipulite® Dice	(ETA)
Manipulite® Two-Color Counters	(ETA)
Number Probability Spinners	(NASCO, Cuisenaire, Didax, ETA, Creative Publications)
Overhead Dot Dice	(Creative Publications)
Overhead Number Probability Spinners	(NASCO, ETA)
Overhead Playing Cards	(ETA)
Oversized Playing Cards	(ETA)
Polyhedra Dice	(Didax, Creative Publications Cuisenaire)
Poster: A Sample of Cats	(Dale Seymour)
Probability Kit	(Dale Seymour, NASCO, Didax, ETA)
Probability Model Cards	(Dale Seymour)
Probability Tool Kit	(Dale Seymour, ETA)
Quadice Probability Set	(NASCO)
Round Two-Color Counters	(ETA)
Statistic and Probability Kit	(ETA)

---

*See List 5 for addresses.

124: Probability and Statistics Activity Books*

Box Cars and One-Eyed Jacks™	(ETA, Cuisenaire)
Data and Chance Activity Books	(NASCO)
Data, Chance, and Probability Activity Books	(Cuisenaire, ETA, Didax, NASCO)
Hands on Statistics, Probability, and Graphing	(NASCO)
In All Probability	(NASCO, ETA, Creative Publications)
Math by All Means: Probability	(Creative Publications, ETA)
NASCO Data & Chance Kit	(NASCO)
Math Discoveries about Data and Chance	(NASCO)
Math Games and Activities with Cards	(ETA)
Probability	(Cuisenaire)
Probability Activities	(ETA)
Probability Jobcards®	(Creative Publications)
Probability Model Masters	(Dale Seymour, ETA)
Problem Solving with Polyhedra Dice	(ETA, Cuisenaire)
Quadice Book	(NASCO)
Statistics: Middles, Means, and In-Betweens	(Creative Publications, Dale Seymour)
Statistics: Prediction and Sampling	(Creative Publications, Dale Seymour)
Statistics: The Shape of the Data	(Creative Publications, Dale Seymour)
The Math Machine: Polyhedra Dice Games	(ETA)
What Are My Chances?	(Creative Publications, Dale Seymour)

©1997 by The Center for Applied Research in Education

---

*See List 5 for addresses.

SECTION 11

ALGEBRAIC THINKING

Name _____

1. Color all of the circles yellow.
2. Color all of the triangles red.
3. Color all of the hexagons blue.

125: Equations

- *Equation:* An equation is a statement of equality between two mathematical expressions. Each expression is called a member of the equation. The left, or first, member is equal to the right, or second, member of the equation.

  When solving an equation, you are "undoing" those operations that have been performed on a variable in order to determine what the value of the variable is.

  An equation is like a beam balance with both sides weighing the same. If you do something on one side of the point of the balance, then you must do the same thing on the other side in order to maintain the balance.

- *Properties of Equality*

  1. The Addition Property

  If you add any quantity to one member of the equation, you must add the same quantity to the other member in order to maintain the balance or equality.

  if a = b, then a + c = b + c

  2. The Multiplication Property

  If you multiply one member of the equation by a value, you must also multiply the other member of the equation by the same value to maintain the equality or balance.

  if a = b, then ac = bc

- *One-Step Operations*

  1. One-Step Equation for Addition

  n + 6 = 15

  n is the variable

  6 is the number added to the variable

  To find the number for the variable, you need to subtract the number that is given in the equation.

  n + 6 = 15

  n + 6 − 6 = 15 − 6

  n = 9

  In the elementary classroom this operation can be shown using beans.

  n + 6 = 15

  n + 6 − 6 = 15 − 6

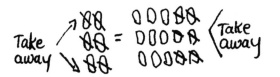

  If you take away 6 beans from the left of the = sign, then you need to take away 6 beans from the right of the = sign.

(continued)

n = 9

9 beans remain on the right of the = sign.

2. One-Step Equation for Subtraction

n − 5 = 8

n − 5 + 5 = 8 + 5

n = 13

Using beans, you need to add 5 beans to the left of the = sign; then you need to add 5 beans to the right of the = sign.

If the negative number is on the left side of the = sign, then it changes to a positive number on the right side of the = sign.

n − 5 = 8

n − 5 + 5 = 8 + 5

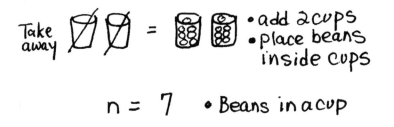

n = 13

3. One-Step Equation for Multiplication

If the problem is 2n = 14, the variable has been multiplied by 2. In order to "undo" this multiplication, you need to divide by 2. If you divide one member of the equation by 2, then you must also divide the other member by 2.

2n = 14

2 n ÷ 2 = 14 ÷ 2

n = 7

Using beans and cups:

Take
away   ▢ ▢ = 🮽 🮽 • add 2 cups
                • place beans
                      inside cups

n = 7   • Beans in a cup

4. One-Step Equation for Division

In the equation n/4 = 5, the variable has been divided by 4. To "undo" this division, you must use multiplication, since multiplication is the inverse of division. In other words, multiplication "undoes" what division does.

(continued)

If you multiply one member of the equation by 4, you must also multiply the other member by 4.

n/4 = 5

n/4 × 4 = 5 × 4

n = 20

126: Logic:
Learning to Read Mathematics

- *Verbal Language Compound Statements*

  Compound Statements are made by joining two simple statements with a connector.
  1. This is the way we speak in everyday language.
     The sky is clear.
     The grass is green.

  2. Each sentence has a noun phrase and a verb phrase.
     or

  3. Each sentence has a pattern such as NV (noun/verb) or NVN (noun/verb noun).

  4. Connectors are: *and, or, if, then* for next.
     n | v | c | n | v
     The sky is clear and it is cold.

  5. Mathematics also has compound statements.
     2 < 3 and 3 < 4
     2 < π or 3 < π
     If 7 > 6, then 8 > 6

  6. Statements used to form a compound statement are called components ✓ of the compound statement.

- *Conjunction Statements:* The symbol ^ is used as a connector or connection in the statement. It means "and."
  (2 < 3) ^ (4 < 1)

  1. Is this a true or false statement? (false)
  2. The statement is false because one of the components is false.
     (6 < 10) ^ (4 < 9)

  3. This statement is true because both components are true.
  4. In mathematics the letters P and Q are used to represent the components.
  5. A Truth Table is used to determine possible combinations of true and false statements.

     T = True   F = False

  Truth Table

P	Q	$P \wedge Q$
T	T	T
T	F	F
F	T	F
F	F	F

©1997 by The Center for Applied Research in Education

- *Disjunctive Statements:* A compound statement formed by joining two simple statements with the connector "or" is called a disjunction.

  "or" in mathematics is written as "v"

1. It means *either* or *both* of the statements are true.
2. Each of the following or both are true.

$$\overset{T}{(4 < 5 + 2)} \text{ v } \overset{T}{(8 > 7)} \qquad T$$

$$\overset{T}{(7 > 3)} \text{ v } \overset{F}{(5 = 8 - 4)} \qquad T$$

$$\overset{F}{(6 < 2)} \text{ v } \overset{T}{(3^3 = 9)} \qquad T$$

3. Both statements here are false.

$$\overset{F}{(5 > 12 - 2)} \text{ v } \overset{F}{(9 = 3 \times 4)} \quad F$$

Truth Table for Disjunctive Statements

P	Q	P v Q
T	T	T
T	F	T
F	T	T
F	F	F

- *Conditional Statements:* If P, then Q

  Symbol is P → Q

  It is cloudy → it is raining.

1. The first component is called the *antecedent. It is cloudy.*
2. The second component is called the *consequent. It is raining.*
3. To see whether or not "if /then" statements are true, think of them as promises. If the promise is broken, then the statement is false.

   Example: If it snows, then I will build a snowman.
4. If all the conditions are met, the following Truth Table applies:

(continued)

Truth Table for Conditional Statements

P	Q	P → Q	
T	T	T	
T	F	F	If p is true and q is false:
			If it does snow, then I won't build a snowman.
F	T	T	If p is false and q is true:
			If it doesn't snow, I will build a snowman.
F	F	T	If p and q are false:
			If it doesn't snow, I will not build a snowman.

- *Negations or Denial:* Negating a statement and using *not.*

  Symbol   ~   means *not* or implies a negative.

       ~   (It is snowing.)

  $3 \nless 2$ can be written $\sim (3 < 2)$

  Truth Table for Negations

P	~P
T	F
F	T

- *Qualifiers*
1. Along with connector we have words called *qualifiers.*

   $$X > 5 = X < 9$$
2. The symbol "X" represents a specific number.
3. Whatever X is makes the statement true or false.

   Example: If X equals 4, this makes a specific statement and the statement becomes false.
4. However, X used as a qualifier means "for some X" when placed in front of a sentence.

   For some X, $X > 5 = X < 9$

   This is read as: Some numbers are greater than 5 and less than 9.
5. Qualifiers are:

   Some

   All

   None

- *Arguments:* The main business of logic is judging the validity of arguments.
  1. An argument is a chain of reasoning.
  2. Statements in an argument are called *premises.*

(continued)

3. The final statement is called a *conclusion*.
4. *Arguments* are either *valid* or *invalid*.

Example: If it is snowing, then it is cold.

It is snowing.

∴ It is cold.

P > Q

P_____

∴ Q

Truth Tables for Arguments

P Q	P > P	Q
T T	T T	T
T F	F T	F
F T	T F	T
F F	T F	T

If both premises are true, a false conclusion means the argument is invalid.

If it is raining, then the humidity is high.

The humidity is high.

It is raining.

127: Vectors in Elementary Mathematics

In real life we deal with more than one variable at a time. For example, two families:
Smith Family Jones Family
<pre>   Need to keep track of: </pre> *number of children*
how long they have been married
telephone numbers
occupations

Now consider this life situation and look at two variables for Johnny Smith and Mary Jones:

<blockquote>Variable #1: How much money they earned in one day.
Variable #2: How many hours they help at home.</blockquote>

When we are considering several variables simultaneously, we say that we are dealing with a *VECTOR*.

The *NUMBER OF DIMENSIONS* in a Vector is the number of different variables we are considering at *ONE AND THE SAME TIME*.

In Johnny and Mary we are looking at a two-dimensional vector.

The *FIRST VECTOR* is the number of hours Johnny is working more than Mary or Mary is working more than Johnny.

The *SECOND VECTOR* is how much money they earned.

Hours Worked Per Day

	Day 1	Day 2	Day 3
Mary	3	3	2
Johnny	5	4	1

Money in Their Pockets

Mary	6	3	1
Johnny	3	4	4

At the end of three days, we can sum up the hours worked per day and how much each earned.

An easier way to write this is:

Variable #1: {2 J, 1 J, 1 M}
Variable #2: {3 M, 1 J, 3 J}

• You can add more vectors to the Johnny and Mary list:

<blockquote>Vector 1: Money earned

Vector 2: Hours worked

Vector 3: Earning tallies for completing tasks

Vector 4: Jogging miles per day</blockquote>

©1997 by The Center for Applied Research in Education

(continued)

How to keep count:

Johnny		Day 1	Day 2	Sums
	V1	2	3	5
	V2	3	4	7
	V3	2	1	3
	V4	5	2	7
Mary	V1	3	6	9
	V2	2	2	4
	V3	1	5	6
	V4	3	1	4

What is the relationship between Johnny and Mary on all the vectors?

Day 1 {1 M, 1 J, 1 J, 2 J}

Day 2 {3 M, 2 J, 4 M, 1 J}

Sums {4 M, 3 J, 3 M, 3 J}

- You can consider a 3-dimensional vector.
  For example:
  Start at 0, a point that has a relationship with other points.

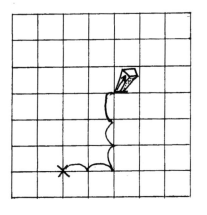

Vector 1: Now go 2 blocks east

Vector 2: then go 3 blocks north

Vector 3: and then climb to the top floor of a 2-story building.

Vector Directions

Vector 1 = E-W direction

Vector 2 = N-S direction

Vector 3 = Up/down direction

Vectors can be tied to space as well as numbers.

128: Vectors:
Sailing Activity

The following activity will help introduce vectors in the elementary classroom. This activity was developed by MINNEMAST (Minnesota Mathematics and Science Project) in 1976.

1. On a grid, mark five small dots wherever you like.

    Each dot represents a boat.

    Make a sailing path for each boat.

    Label your five marks A, B, C, D, E.

    Rule for your moves are either:

    right   left

    $\rightarrow$ $\leftarrow$

    up   down

    $\uparrow$ $\downarrow$

    Example:

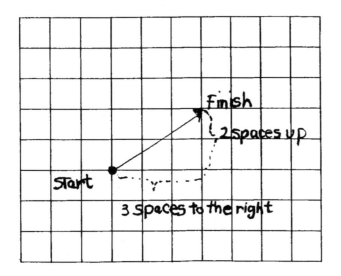

2. Study these paths that show how far a sailboat traveled in 1 hour.

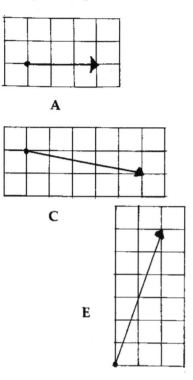

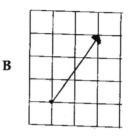

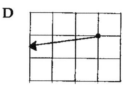

Activity:

1. Using a red pencil, show A travel 5 hours.
2. Using a blue pencil, show B travel 2 hours.
3. Using a green pencil, show C travel 3 hours.
4. Using a purple pencil, show D travel 1 hour.
5. Using an orange pencil, show E travel 2 1/2 hours.

3. Suppose these are your paths for three days.

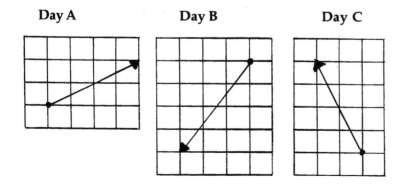

Day A   **Day B**   **Day C**

(continued)

On your grid, chart the sailing paths for each 3-day voyage. Begin at point A and chart the path, followed by path B and then by path C.

Here is what your sailing path would look like.

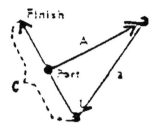

Complete the following using colored pencils to chart each sailing path.

Color	*3-Day Voyage*
red	A, B, C
blue	A, C, B
green	B, A, C
orange	B, C, A
purple	C, A, B
brown	C, B, A

4. *Understanding more about vectors:*

When you sail from one point to another, you change positions. This change is called a VECTOR. We sometimes draw arrows to illustrate changes (vectors). The arrows are not vectors. They are only pictures of vectors (changes).

You can name your vectors: Danna's vector or Sonia's vector, or whatever!

Your starting point is the beginning state.

The move you make is called the operator.

Where you end up is called the new state.

Operator

Beginning State   **New State**

Here the operator is called X.

The starting point is named A.

The ending point is named A_1.

(continued)

5. *Describing your vectors:*

Here is a picture of a move or change called a vector.
We call it vector X.
The name for vector X is

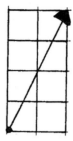

2 Right	2 R
4 Up	4 U

Vector X will move point A to point A_1.
It will also move A_1 to A_2, etc.

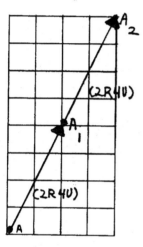

- Use the vectors you drew from your first five dots and extend them.
- Every time you move a point, draw an arrow to show that move.
- Write the name of the move next to each arrow you drew.
- Write the names of your vectors like this:

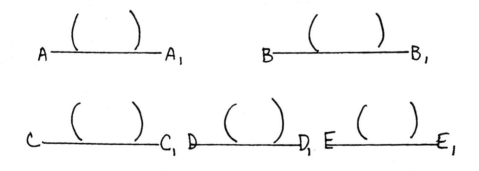

(continued)

6. *Adding vectors:*

Name the moves in this picture.

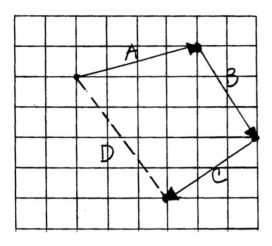

A = (,)
B = (,)
C = (,)
D = (,)

On a grid pick a starting point and draw the moves represented by the three names in the sentence below. Finish the sentence.

$$\frac{2R}{4D} \; + \; \frac{3L}{2D} \; + \; \frac{4R}{5U} \; = \; (\quad)$$

7. Write the name of the missing move or vector.

$$\frac{4R}{2D} \; + \; (\quad) \; = \; \frac{2R}{2U}$$

You can think of it this way:

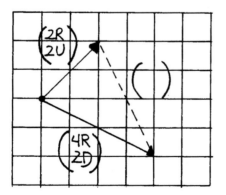

(continued)

Try to answer these problems:

$$\frac{2L}{4U} \quad + \quad \frac{3R}{1D} \quad = \quad (\quad) \qquad\qquad \frac{3R}{2U} \quad + \quad (\quad) \quad = \quad \frac{6R}{4D}$$

8. Study the path this boat sailed. There are 5 vectors.

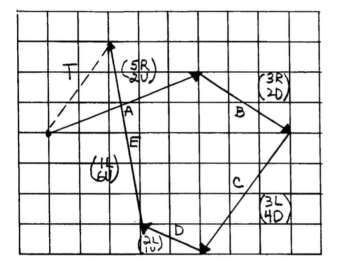

The dotted arrow T shows the one move that will give the same result as
A + B + C + D + E = T.

Without using any grid, write the vector for move X.

A		B		C		D		E		X
$\frac{5R}{2U}$	+	$\frac{3R}{2D}$	+	$\frac{3L}{4D}$	+	$\frac{2L}{1U}$	+	$\frac{1L}{6U}$	=	( )

9. Here is a quick way to find answers to an unknown vector.

$$\frac{4R}{2U} \quad + \quad \frac{6L}{4D} \quad + \quad \frac{2L}{1U} \quad + \quad \frac{5R}{1D} \quad = \quad (\quad)$$

Identify a starting state. (Do I go R or L? U or D?)
Do the operations.
Where do you end?

(continued)

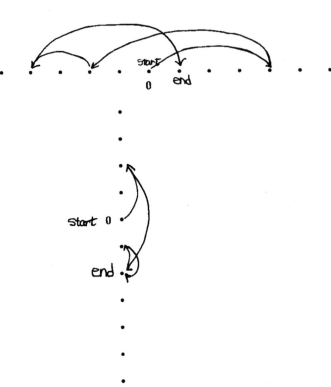

10.   Solve these problems.

$$\begin{pmatrix} 3R \\ 4U \end{pmatrix} + \begin{pmatrix} \quad \end{pmatrix} = \begin{pmatrix} 0 \\ 0 \end{pmatrix}$$

$$\begin{pmatrix} 3 \text{ boys} \\ 2 \text{ men} \end{pmatrix} + \begin{pmatrix} 2 \text{ girls} \\ 4 \text{ women} \end{pmatrix} = \begin{pmatrix} \quad \end{pmatrix}$$

$$\begin{pmatrix} 17\,\text{L} \\ 12\,\text{U} \end{pmatrix} + \begin{pmatrix} \quad \end{pmatrix} = \begin{pmatrix} 0 \\ 0 \end{pmatrix}$$

$$\begin{pmatrix} 6 \text{ girls} \\ 5 \text{ men} \end{pmatrix} + \begin{pmatrix} 3 \text{ girls} \\ 4 \text{ men} \end{pmatrix} = \begin{pmatrix} \quad \end{pmatrix}$$

$$\begin{pmatrix} \overleftarrow{6} \\ 4\downarrow \end{pmatrix} + \begin{pmatrix} \overrightarrow{4} \\ 5\downarrow \end{pmatrix} + \begin{pmatrix} \overleftarrow{3} \\ 9\uparrow \end{pmatrix} = \begin{pmatrix} \quad \end{pmatrix}$$

$$\begin{pmatrix} 6 \text{ girls} \\ 5 \text{ men} \end{pmatrix} + \begin{pmatrix} 4 \text{ boys} \\ 6 \text{ women} \end{pmatrix} = \begin{pmatrix} \quad \end{pmatrix}$$

$$\begin{pmatrix} 6 \text{ moos} \\ 2 \text{ Swizz} \end{pmatrix} + \begin{pmatrix} 3 \text{ goos} \\ 4 \text{ Phizz} \end{pmatrix} = \begin{pmatrix} \quad \end{pmatrix}$$

(continued)

11. Stretching the paths:

Trip A is stretched to the size of Trip B. Write the names of the two trips.

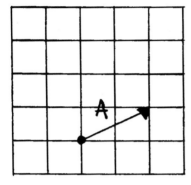   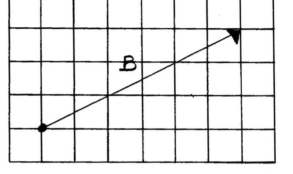

Name is (   )   Name is (   )

It takes _____ A trips to make one B trip.

Make these paths on your grid paper by stretching.

$$2\begin{pmatrix} 3\,R \\ 2\,D \end{pmatrix} \qquad 4\begin{pmatrix} 3\,L \\ 2\,D \end{pmatrix} \qquad 2\begin{pmatrix} 5R \\ 4D \end{pmatrix}$$

12. Make a multiplication machine:

$$10\begin{pmatrix} 1\,R \\ 1\,U \end{pmatrix} \quad 10\begin{pmatrix} 1\,R \\ 2U \end{pmatrix} \quad 10\begin{pmatrix} 1\,R \\ 3U \end{pmatrix} \quad 10\begin{pmatrix} 1\,R \\ 4U \end{pmatrix} \quad 10\begin{pmatrix} 1\,R \\ 5U \end{pmatrix}$$

$$10\begin{pmatrix} 1\,R \\ 6U \end{pmatrix} \quad 10\begin{pmatrix} 1\,R \\ 7U \end{pmatrix} \quad 10\begin{pmatrix} 1\,R \\ 8U \end{pmatrix} \quad 10\begin{pmatrix} 1\,R \\ 9U \end{pmatrix}$$

Stretch each vector ten times.

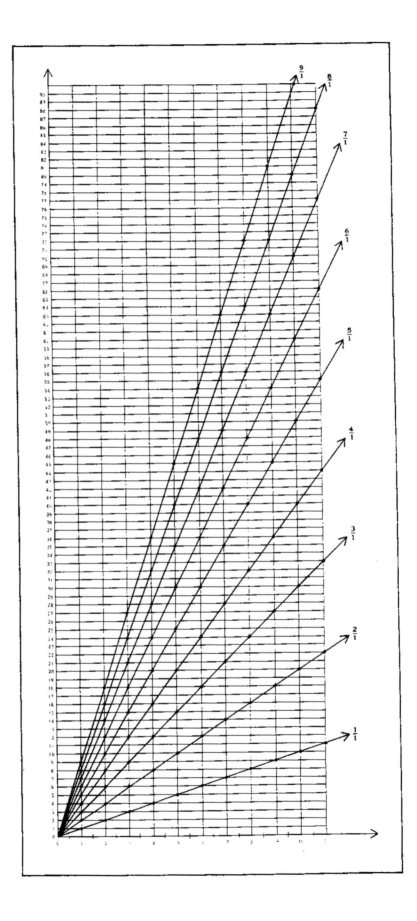

130: Multiplying Mixed Numbers

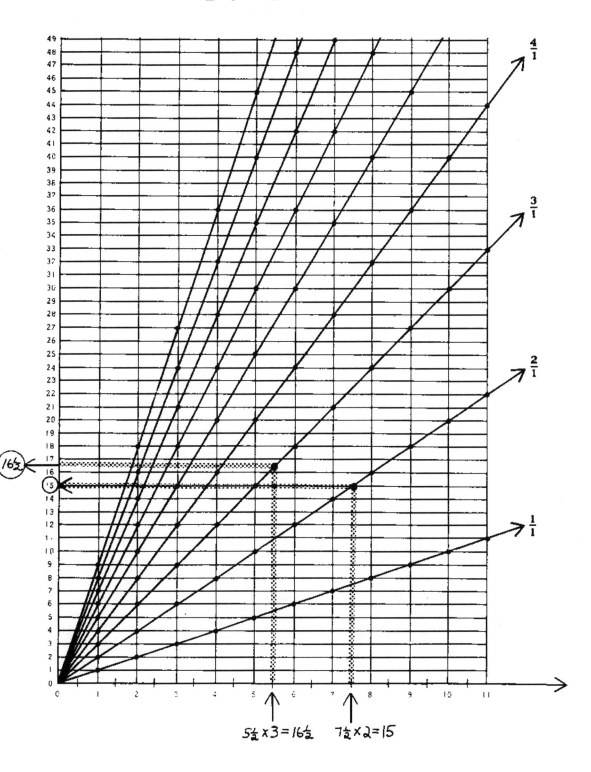

$5\frac{1}{2} \times 3 = 16\frac{1}{2}$ $7\frac{1}{2} \times 2 = 15$

277

131: Dividing on a Grid

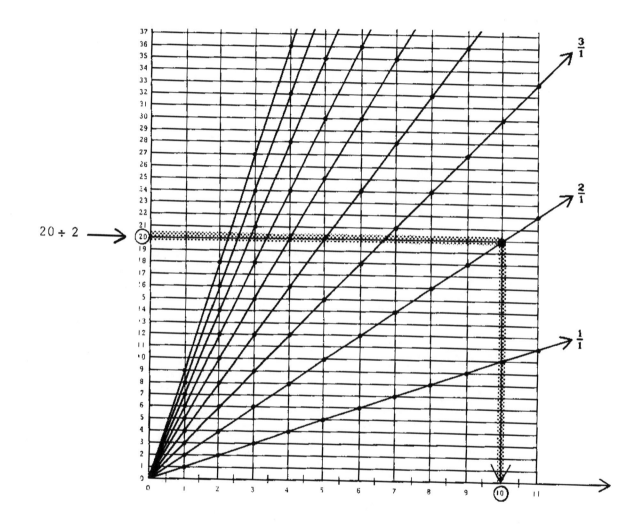

PROBLEM SOLVING

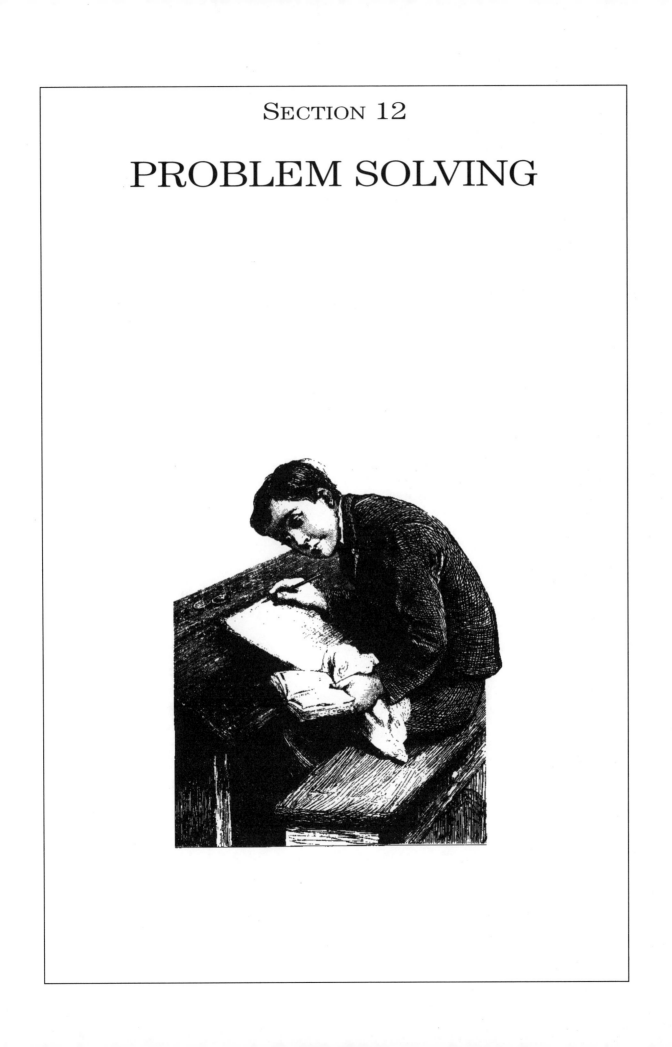

Mars Munchie Mania

You are on Mars with your lunch bag.
This is what you brought for the trip.

    2 peanut butter sandwiches

    1 chili dog

    2 apples

    1 banana

    1 orange drink

    1 milk

    2 bags of potato chips

1. How many items are in your lunch bag all together?

2. If a Mars Mouse eats one bag of potato chips and you eat one peanut butter sandwich, how many items are left in the bag?

3. Three Mars Creatures become your friends. If each of you give each other a hug, how many hugs are given?

4. Make a drawing ordering your three new friends and you according to height.

132: Developing a Problem-Solving Heuristic

A sequence for developing a student's ability to solve word and other mathematical problems requires the student to have some understanding of how to *structure* his or her thinking in order to solve the problem. This structuring of one's thinking is called a *heuristic*. There are several heuristics available to the elementary teacher.

The heuristic is not to be confused with the strategy for solving. The strategy for solving the problem is the plan you use as to how you work the problem out. The strategy is part of the heuristic. Traditionally in the elementary classroom there are nine strategies taught to children. The nine are presented at the end of this list.

- A *traditional heuristic* was developed by George Polya:

1. *Getting to know the problem.* Seeing what is given and understanding what is asked.
2. *Devising a plan to solve the problem.* Figuring out what to do.
3. *Carrying out the plan.* Doing it.
4. *Looking back.* Evaluating the situation.

- Here is another way of interpreting this heuristic, which is helpful for students in grades 4 through 8:

1. *Main idea:* Determine what the problem is about.
2. *Question:* Look for what is being asked.
3. *Important facts:* Note the important facts in the problem that must be used to solve the problem. Discard any useless information.
4. *Relationship sentence:* State verbally who is to solve the problem.
5. *Equation:* The important facts are rewritten in equation form based upon the relationship sentence.
6. *Estimation:* Estimate the answer before computing the equation.
7. *Computation:* Compute the equation and compare to the estimation.
8. *Answer sentence:* Verbally state the computed answer.
9. *Check:* Verify the answer.

- This simplified version of the heuristic is helpful for students in grades 1 through 3:

1. *READ the problem:* Read it more than once, if needed.
2. *WRITE the problem:* Write the problem in your own words.
3. *CIRCLE the facts:* Circle all the facts in the problem.
4. *Select a STRATEGY for solving the problem:* Select one of the nine strategies to organize your thinking in solving the problem.
5. *ESTIMATE the answer:* Write down an estimation of what you think the answer might be.
6. *EQUATION:* Write out the equation in the language of mathematics.
7. *SOLVE the problem:* Compute the answer.
8. *ANSWER:* Label your answer by writing the answer in sentence form.
9. *LOOKING BACK:* Check your answer. Is it correct?

(continued)

- A teacher may wish to print out the following for students in order to help them remember the heuristic (plan) and the strategies (options for solving).

Steps to Solve a Problem

1. Read the problem.
2. Write the problem in your own words.
3. Decide on a strategy of action.
4. Estimate the answer.
5. Write the equation.
6. Solve the problem by computing.
7. Label your answer.
8. Check your answer.

   or

1. Read the problem.	(1. Getting to know the problem.)
2. Decide on a strategy.	(2. Devising a plan to solve the problem.)
3. Estimate/compute.	(3. Carrying out the plan.)
4. Verify by checking answer.	(4. Looking back.)

Strategies for Solving Problems

1. Act it out.
2. Draw a picture.
3. Guess and check.
4. Look for a pattern.
5. Make a chart or table.
6. Make a list.
7. Make a model.
8. Work backwards.
9. Write a number sentence.

133: Problems for Strategy 1: Act It Out

1. There are eight people in a room. Each person shakes hands with each of the other people. How many handshakes are there? (*56*)

2. Every person in your class is on line to buy lunch. The first person buys chocolate milk. The second person buys white milk. Continue the pattern until everyone in your class has milk. How many people have bought chocolate milk? (*Answer will vary with size of class.*)

3. Melinda Millionaire had a spare million dollars and decided to give it away to one of her 12 loving relatives. The decision was a most difficult one that left Melinda totally stressed out. One day she had an idea! She decided that all 12 of her loving relatives will line up in a straight line in front of her. The first person in line will get a candy, but no money. She decided that she would skip three relatives and the next relative will get a candy, but no money. She said she would continue this pattern of skipping three relatives and giving the next relative a candy until there is only one relative left without a candy. That relative will receive the million dollars. Where would *you stand* in line to receive the million dollars?

4. Great-grandma lives by herself. The doorbell rings and in comes her daughter (grandma). They hug each other. The doorbell rings again and in comes Grandma's daughter and son-in-law (Jesse and Juanita). Jesse and Juanita each hug Grandma and Great-grandma. Then Jose and Maria the grandchildren come in. They hug everyone. How many hugs are given all together? (*38*)

5. Put ten pennies in a row on your table. Now replace every other coin with a nickel. Next replace every third coin with a dime. What is the value of the ten coins on the table?

6. Gloria put ten checkers into two stacks. One stack has four more checkers than the other stack. How many checkers are in each stack?

7. Floppy the rabbit is taller than Mopsy the rabbit. Topsy is shorter than Mopsy. Arrange the three rabbits in order of size with the shortest first.

8. Carl is on the lunch line. There are four children in front of him and six children behind him. How many children are standing in the lunch line?

134: Problems for Strategy 2:
Draw a Picture

1. A cricket and a grasshopper were hopping on a stairway that had 12 steps. The cricket landed on every second step, and the grasshopper landed on every third step. On which step did they both land?

2. How many lines are there in a tic-tac-toe grid? How many squares?

3. In an office, there are two square windows. Each window is 4 feet high, yet one window has an area twice that of the other window. Explain how this could take place.

4. Joey found 8 buttons. There are 26 holes in all. How many buttons had 4 holes? How many buttons had 2 holes?

5. A rectangular garden 40m long and 30m wide is to be fenced with fence posts at each corner. All the other posts will be 5m apart. How many posts will be needed to fence in the garden?

6. Antelope Hill, Buffalo Corner, Coyote Canyon, and Dry Gulch lie along a straight road in the order named. The distance from Antelope Hill to Dry Gulch is 100 miles. The distance from Buffalo Corner to Coyote Canyon is 30 miles. The distance from Buffalo Corner to Dry Gulch is 60 miles. How far is it from Antelope Hill to Buffalo Corner?

7. You have the following choices of ice cream cone combinations. You have a choice of a sugar cone or a plain cone. How many different ice cream cones can you order? ($2 \times 4 \times 3 \times 2 = 48$)

Ice Cream Flavors	Toppings	Sprinkles
Chocolate	Hot fudge	Nuts
Strawberry	Caramel	Candies
Pumpkin	Marshmallow	
Coconut		

8. How many triangles can you draw inside an equilateral triangle?

9. There are 11 wheels on some bicycles and tricycles. How many of each are there?

10. Hassan has Spelling before Art in his classroom. He has Math right after Art. Which subject does he have first?

©1997 by The Center for Applied Research in Education

135: Problems for Strategy 3: Guess and Check

1. Given the sequence of numbers, 2, 3, 5, 8, . . ., explain why the next number might be 12 or 13, or 2 or 5.

2. Which of the four numbers in the array does not belong? Why?

   23 / 20

   25 / 15

3. Jeremy worked a math problem and got 16 as his answer. However, in the last step he multiplied by 2 instead of dividing by 2. What should have been the correct answer?

4. The answer is 25. What is the question?

5. I am thinking of two 2-digit numbers. They have the same digits, only reversed. The difference between the numbers is 54, while the sum of the digits of each number is 10. Find the two numbers.

6. Gladys, Jeanette, Jesse, and Randy went fishing. Gladys caught 16 fish, Jeanette caught 13 fish, Jesse caught 17 fish, and Randy caught 14 fish. How many more fish did Jesse and Randy catch than Gladys and Jeanette?

7. Mary Ann has 18 cents. She has a total of 10 coins. Which coins does she have?

8. How many shoes long is your friend?

9. What is the circumference of a basketball? Cut a string the length you think will fit around the basketball. Check to verify your cut.

10. Here is a table showing the runs scored by two teams in three baseball games played against each other. If this scoring pattern continues, what will be the score in the 5th game they play?

Game	1	2	3	4	5
Jays	2	4	6		
Eagles	5	6	7		

11. The 3-digit number 53A is exactly divisible by 6. Find the value of A.

12. How many breaths do you take in 1 minute? in 1 hour?

136: Problems for Strategy 4:
Look for a Pattern

1. A train can travel 10 miles in 4 minutes. How far will it travel in 14 minutes? (*35 miles*)

2. A rabbit can run 10 feet in the time that a dog can run 7 feet. How far will the rabbit run in the time that the dog runs 21 feet? (*30 feet*)

3. Find the three consecutive numbers that add up to 24.

    $1 + 2 + 3 = 6$ $2 + 3 + 4 = 9$ $3 + 4 + 5 = 12$

4. How many 2's must you multiply together to reach a 3-digit number?

5. Find the next set of numbers in this sequence of numbers: 1, 2, 3, 5, 8, 13, ____, ____, ____.

6. Using 2 numbers, how many different ways are there to add to 10? 11? 12?

7. Sonia's puppy, Jiggs, weighed 1 pound when he was born. If he gained 1 pound each week, how much would he weigh in 8 weeks? 3 months? 9 months? 1 year?

8. Renee picks up 1 soda can on Monday, 3 on Tuesday, 5 on Wednesday, and 7 on Thursday. If she continues to increase the number she picks up on Friday, Saturday, and Sunday, she will have 49 on Monday. How many will she pick up on Friday, Saturday, and Sunday?

9. You have cubes that are red and cubes that are black. What color will the 16th cube be if you lay them down in this pattern?

    R B R B B R B R

10. A hallway of rooms on the left are numbered 21, 23, 25. What will the next room number be? What is the number of the 5th door on the left after room number 25?

11. The houses on Imperial Way all have even numbers. The first house is number 2. The second house is number 4. The third house is number 6. What is the number of the 10th, 15th, and 23rd house on Imperial Way?

12. How many 2-digit numerals can be made using 1 and 2? How many 3-digit numerals can be made with 1, 2, and 3? How many 4-digit numerals can be made using 1, 2, 3, and 4? etc.

©1997 by The Center for Applied Research in Education

137: Problems for Strategy 5:
Make a Chart or Table

1. A woman has some cows and chickens. Together there are 54 legs. How many are cows and how many are chickens? What are all the possibilities?

2. What is the greatest number of coins you can use to make 35¢? What is the smallest number of coins you can use? In how many different ways can you make 35¢?

3. I am taking these people to dinner: myself, my mother, my sister's 2 sons and their wives, and each son's 2 children. How many reservations should I make?

4. Three students, Steve, Jennifer, and Lenny, have raised a total of 30 chickens, 18 of which are roosters. Steve has 6 hens and Jennifer has the same number of roosters. Jennifer has 2 more chickens than Steve, who has 8 chickens. Lenny has 8 more roosters than hens and the same number of hens as Steve has roosters. How many roosters do Steve and Lenny each have?

5. You can buy a crayon for 1¢. Each extra crayon costs 2¢. How much will you pay for 8 crayons?

6. Bill has three quarters and four nickels. A baseball card costs 20¢. How many baseball cards can Bill buy?

7. A chicken can lay about 7 eggs each week. How many eggs can you expect 8 chickens to lay in 4 weeks?

8. How many 10¢ packages of gum can you buy if you have two quarters, 1 dime, two nickels, and four pennies?

9. How many different ways can you make change for 30¢ using quarters, dimes, and nickels?

10. Classify the number of corners, edges, and sides of the following nine solids shapes: triangle-based pyramid, square-based pyramid, cube, square prism, rectangular prism, triangular prism, cylinder, cone, sphere.

11. Make a chart of the kinds of shoes the children wear in your class: sneakers, sandals, leather ties, etc.

12. Make a chart showing the number of children in your class who are wearing glasses and have brown hair.

138: Problems for Strategy 6: Make a List

1. Margaret is having lunch. She eats a lot of sandwiches. She makes sandwiches with white bread and rye bread. She uses either cheese, jelly, or lunch meat, no tomatoes. How many different sandwiches can she make for her lunch?

2. Find all of the two-digit numbers in which the sum of the two digits is 10.

   For example: 19, 28, etc.

3. At which step do you not go over 100?

Step 1	2	3	4
1	2	3	4
+1	+2	+3	+4
2	4	6	8

4. A special plant doubles its height each day. On Monday it was 2 inches tall. On Tuesday, it reached 4 inches tall. How tall will it be on Friday?

5. The roller coaster at the amusement park takes a new group of 15 people every 10 minutes. There are 70 people who want to ride. It is now 2:00 P.M. At what time will the 50th person complete the ride?

6. Steve has two children. The product of their ages is 24. The sum of their ages is 10. Find the ages of the children.

7. Kim has a package of 48 stickers. She wants to arrange them in rows, so that each row has the same number of stickers. How can she arrange them so that the number of stickers in each row is an odd number?

8. Wayne has five coins: quarters, nickels, and dimes. The total value of the coins is 50¢. How many of each coin does Wayne have?

9. There were 8 girls and 16 boys at a fourth-grade party committee meeting. Every few minutes, one boy and one girl left the meeting to go back to the classroom. How many of these boy-and-girl "pairs" must leave the meeting so that there will be exactly five times as many boys as girls left sitting at the meeting?

10. The bakery had a bake sale with this sign:

    Donuts   7¢

    Cookies   5¢

    LIMIT: 3 per customer

    If you had 20¢, how many different combinations of donuts and cookies could you buy?

©1997 by The Center for Applied Research in Education

139: Problems for Strategy 7: Make a Model

1. How many squares are on a checkerboard?

2. Make a small birdhouse from a milk carton. Find the following answers to these measurement questions using the measurements of your birdhouse.

   a. What is the height?

   b. What is the length?

   c. What is the width?

   d. What is the perimeter of the birdhouse?

   e. What is the area of one side?

   f. What is the area of the floor?

   g. What is the area of the roof?

   h. What is the volume?

   i. What is the name of the solid shape it represents?

   j. How many different figures form the birdhouse? Name each.

   k. How many birds can live in your birdhouse?

3. Draw a floor plan or a bird's-eye view of the ideal classroom you would like to be in. What would you study in that classroom? Give the measurements of the room and the objects in the room.

4. Make a cube using toothpicks and white glue.

5. Make a paper airplane and toss it into the air. Measure the length it will fly. Make a line graph to show the length of the time it stayed in the air and how far it traveled each time.

6. How many green triangle pattern blocks does it take to make 4 yellow hexagon pattern blocks?

7. Twelve couples have been invited to a party. The couples will be seated at a series of small square card tables placed end to end so as to form one large long table. How many of these small tables are needed to seat all 24 people?

8. How would you make 7 quarts if you have two buckets, where one bucket holds 8 quarts and the other holds 3 quarts?

9. How many different ways can you stack 6 cubes?

10. How many reflection lines of symmetry are there in a snowflake?

140: Problems for Strategy 8:
Work Backwards

1. Add 5 to the mystery number. Then subtract 7. The result is 23. What is the mystery number?

2. Tracy asked her dad how old he was. He told her, "If I add 10 to my age and double the result, I will get 84." How old is Tracy's dad?

3. A boy ate 100 peanuts in five days. Each day he ate six more than on the previous day. How many did he eat on each day of the five days?

4. Jan scored 20 on the target-throwing darts. How many darts were in each zone/ring? Make your own target zones. What are the possibilities?

5. Janet gave away half of her candy, dividing the candy equally among Jill, David, and Tai. Tai took her share of the candy and shared the candy equally among herself and four of her friends. Each friend ended up with 4 pieces of candy. How many pieces of candy did Janet have to share? (*120*)

6. A grocery stockman decided to stack his apples in a triangle shape by placing a row of apples on a stand. The next row up, he placed one less apple on top of the first row. If he used a total of 15 apples, how many rows are in the triangular-shaped stack? (*5*)

7. Cami starts the week with a dollar. School lunch costs 20 cents. Will she spend the dollar in the week?

8. Sammy rode his bicycle 100 miles during summer vacation. He covered 10 miles each day. How many days did it take him to cover 100 miles?

9. Otto mowed one lawn a day for 5 days. He earned $60. How much did Otto earn each day?

10. Helen ate 16 cookies in 4 days. Each day she ate 2 more than on the previous day. How many cookies did she eat on each of the four days?

©1997 by The Center for Applied Research in Education

141: Problems for Strategy 9:
Write a Number Sentence

1. If apples are worth 2 oranges, how many oranges are 24 apples worth?

2. There are 48 children in two classrooms. One classroom has 15 boys in it. There are 10 boys in the other classroom. How many girls are there in both classrooms?

3. I have nine bills in my wallet. Five of them are $1 and the rest of them are $5. How much money do I have in my wallet?

4. How many eyes are there in a class of 20?

5. Two smiles are worth 1 sticker. How many stickers are 16 smiles worth?

6. A squirrel gathered 5 nuts from each tree. She went to 4 trees. How many nuts did she gather?

7. You can buy 5 inches of string candy for 3 cents. How many inches of string candy can you buy for 12 cents?

8. You want to share your midget cars with your friends. If you have 56 cars, how many cars can you share with 7 friends?

9. A dime is worth 2 nickels. How many nickels in 5 dimes?

10. You have $5.00 to buy a $3.49 cassette tape and a 39¢ candy bar. How much change will you have after your purchases?

11. Mother gave you $20.00 for your allowance to last you 4 weeks. How much can you evenly spend each week so it will last you 4 weeks?

12. You have a case of 24 soda cans. You want to give 1/4 of the cans to your friend Celeste to take on a picnic. How many cans of soda will you give her?

13. You have 4 feet of ribbon. You want to cut it in half and give it to Camille so she can tie up her hair. How many inches of ribbon will you give her if you cut the ribbon in half?

14. Thomas has new puppies at his house. He has 4 white, 3 black, and 2 spotted puppies. How many puppies does he have at his house?

SECTION 13

TECHNOLOGY

Name _____

Can you identify the different parts of the computer? If you need help, the names are on the bottom of this sheet.

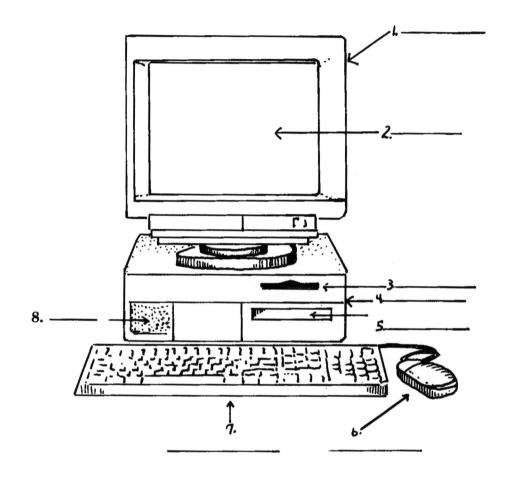

©1997 by The Center for Applied Research in Education

| Keyboard | Disk Drive | Mouse | Hard Drive |
| CD-ROM Drive | Screen | Speaker | Monitor |

142: Computer Math Programs for Grades K-12

Multi-Vendor Educational Resource Vendors

- Educational Resources, 800-624-2926
- Learning Services, 800-877-9378

A+Advanced Learning Systems

Math I-VIII (3-8)

Addison Wesley

Adventures in Flight (4-6)
Real World Math CD (4-6)

Aims Multimedia

The Children's Encyclopedia of Mathematics Fraction Series (3-8)

Attainment

Show Me Math Series (1-up)
Dollars and Cents Series (1-up)

Barnum

The Quarter Mile (K-9)
The Quarter Mile Whole Numbers! (K-6)
The Quarter Mile Fractions! (4-7)
The Quarter Mile Decimals & Percents! (4-7)
The Quarter Mile Integers and Equations! (5-9)
The Quarter Mile Estimation & Math Tricks! (3-9)

Broderbund 1-800-521-6263

Janis Discovers Math (K-2)
Geometry (9-up)
Math Workshop (PreK-2)
Math Workshop CD (K-8)
Logical Journey of the Zoombinis (K-8)
Tabletop Jr. (K-6)

Computer Curriculum Corp., 800-455-7910

Math Concepts and Skills (K-8)
Math Processor (4-10)

Creative Wonders Electronic Arts, 800-245-4525

Counting on Frank: A Real Math Adventure (3-6)
Sesame Street Numbers (PreK-K)

Curriculum Associates, Inc., 800-225-0248

Math Problem Solver Series (3-8)

Davidson and Associates, Inc., 1-800-545-7677

Rodio Addition (PreK-3)
Math Blaster Jr. (PreK-2)
Math Blaster 1: In Search of Sept (1-6)
Math Blaster: Secrets of the Lost City (3-8)
Math Blaster Mystery: The Great Brain Robbery (5-adult)
The Cruncher (3-adult)
Money Town (K-2)
Fisher Price 1-2-3's (PreK-1)
Math Dodger (2-12)
What's My Angle? (8-up)

use manipulatives.

Decision Development Corporation

Math Series (3-8)

EA Kids

Counting on Frank: A Real Live Math (3-6)

Edmark Corporation, 800-320-8380

Thinking Things Collection 1 (PreK-4)
Thinking Things Collection 2 (1-6)
Thinking Things Collection 3 (3-8)
Millie's Math House (PreK-2)

(continued)

Trudy's Time & Place House (PreK-2)

Educational Activities

The Math Map Trip (4-8)

Educational Pub Concepts

Basic Mathematical Concepts (K-8)

Edunetics Corp, 1-800-969-2602 or 1-800-290-3958

Rediscover Mathematics and Science (3-5)
Mathematical Concepts On-Line Series CD (3-5)

EPC

Basic Mathematical Concepts (K-8)
Math Computation 1 (1-5)
Basic Mathematical Facts (1-8)
Math Worksheet Generator (1-5)
Fraction Worksheet Generator (4-up)

Gamco

Discover Time (K-6)
Money Challenge (1-5)
Touchdown Math Series (2-12)
Paws and Pyramids (5-10)
Sphinx's Secret: A Perimeter, Area & Volume Game (4-8)
Whole Numbers, Decimals & Fractions Series (1-12)
Addition & Subtraction Defenders (K-6)
On Target Multiply & Divide (2-8)
Number Facts Fire Zapper (K-8)
Perimeter, Area and Volume (5-10)
Word Problems Square Off (3-8)
Money (1-6)
Telling Time (K-5)
Geo-Pool and Geo-Billards (5-up)
Sphinx's Secret (5-10)

(continued)

Great Wave Software, 800-423-1144

Number Maze (K-6)
Decimal & Fraction Maze (3-8)
Kids Math (PreK-3)

Greene & Assoc.

Folding Boxes

Hartley

Math Skills Collection CD (4-6)

Houghton

Geometry Concepts (7-12)

Intellimation

Geometry: Area & Perimeter (K-12)

IPS

Exam in a Can-Geometry (K-12)

Jostens, 800-422-4339

World of Math: Decimals & Percents (4-6)
World of Math: Measurements & Representation of Data (4-6)
World of Math: Shapes & Figures (4-6)
World of Math: Whole Numbers & Fractions (4-6)
ActionMATH (K-3)

Jostens Home Learning

Classroom Grade Level Math Programs (K-8)
Geometry (8-12)

Key Curriculum Press

Geometer's Sketchpad (6-12)

(continued)

Lawrence Productions

Mystery Math Island (3-8)

Math Dodger (3-up)

Mathology: The Greek Legend Math Adventure (3-up)

Legacy

Magic Bear's Masterpieces (5-9)

Mutanoid Math and Word Challenge (2-up)

Magic Bear's Masterpieces (PreK-4)

Logo Computer Systems, Inc.

Math Links (4-8)

Turtle Math (3-6)

Magic Quest

Math Ace (3-12)

Maxis, 800-996-2947

Widget Workshop (3-9)

MECC, 800-685-6322

Tessel mania (3-12)

Math Munchers Deluxe (3-6)

Number Munchers (3-12)

Fraction Munchers (3-12)

Troggle Trouble Math (1-6)

Math Keys (K-6) *(Houghton Mifflin also)*

DinoPark Tycoon (3-12)

The Secret Island of Dr. Quandary (3-12)

Money Works (1-4)

Clock Works (1-3)

Fraction Concepts, Inc. (3-5)

Fraction Practice Unlimited (4-6)

Quilting Bee (Apple) (K-2)

(continued)

Flip Flop (Apple) (1-2)
Sum Stories (Apple) (K-2)
The Geometric Golfer (7-12)
Graphing (1-5)

Micrograms

Numberball (3-8)
Pondering Problems (2-5)
Fearless Lou's Burning Fuse (3-8)
Dancing Dinos (1-3)
Mathosaurus (K-2)

Microlab/Microlearn

Geometry Planely Simple (6-10)

Mindplay

Fraction-Oids Series (3-8)

National School Products

Reading and Making Graphs (4-12)
GeoArt (4-9)

Nordic

Turbo Math Facts 3.0 (K-6)
Clock Shop (K-6)
Coin Critters (K-6)
The Math Majors (K-6)

Optimum Resource

Stickeybear Math 1 (1-4)
Stickeybear Math 2 (1-up)
Stickeybear's Math Town (K-5)
Stickeybear Shapes (K-3)
First Steps Counting & Thinking Games (PreK-3)

(continued)

Orange Cherry

Action Fraction FunHouse (3-6)

Math Arcade Games (2-5)

Math Word Problems (2-6)

Talking Using Money and Making Change (2-4)

Talking Clock (PreK-2)

Power Industries

M*A*T*H Circus (K-8)

Putnam New Media

Anno's Learning Games—Primary (K-5)

Queue

Mastering Math CD (3-9)

Mastering Math II (5-12)

Intermediate Math (3-9)

Sanctuary Woods, 800-943-3664

Math Ace (3-12)

Math Ace Grand Prix (3-12)

NFL Math (2-6)

Bit Bot's Math Voyage (K-3)

Real World Math Adventures in Flight (1-6)

Real World Math (4-6)

Travelrama (1-8)

Addison Wesley's Real World Math (3-6)

Scholastic

Math Shop Jr. (1-4)

Math Shop (4-8)

Math Shop Spotlights: Fractions & Decimals (4-8)

Math Shop Spotlights: Weights & Measures (4-8)

(continued)

Scott Foresman

GeoExplorer (K-12)

Sierra-on-line, Inc.

Early Math (shapes) (PreK-2)

Simon & Schuster Interactive

Nick Jr.-Play Math CD (PreK-2)

Soleil Software, Inc., 415-494-0114

Zurk's Alaskatrek (K-4)

Steck-Vaughn Publishing Co., 800-531-5015

Time Town (PreK-3)

Sunburst, 800-321-7511

Blockers and Finder (2-up)
The Factory (4-8)
The Geometric preSupposer (5-adult)
Elastic Lines (4-8)
The Nature Park Adventure (2-3)
Getting Ready to Read & Add (PreK-1)
Teddy's Playground (K-4)
Challenge Math (2-6)
Memory Package (K-adult)
Memory Building Blocks (K-adult)
Shape up (K-8)
Graphers (K-4)
Hop to It ! (K-3)
Sidewalk Sneakers (K-5)
Number Connections (K-3)
Balancing Bear (K-4)
Teasers by Tobbs: Numbers & Operations (2-6)
Bounce! (K-8)

(continued)

Safari Search (3-8)

The Pond (2-6)

The King's Rule (4-8)

Divide and Conquer (4-8)

The Incredible Laboratory (3-adult)

How the West Was One + Three X Four (4-8)

Puzzle Tanks (3-8)

Maya Math (4-8)

Maps and Navigation (4-8)

What Do You Do With a Broken Calculator? (4-adult)

Quadrominoes (4-8)

Building Perspective (4-adult)

Muppet Math (K-3)

Muppetville (PreK-1)

Muppets on Stage (PreK-1)

Hello Kitty Big Fun Deluxe (PreK-3)

Hot Dog Stand Deluxe (5-adult)

Geometry Inventor (6-12)

Tenth Planet, 800-546-2317

Tenth Planet explores:

    Primary Math (K-3)

    Beginning Level Geometry

    Level 1 Geometry

    Level 2 Geometry

Terrapin

Crystal Rain Forest (3-8)

Logo Plus 2.0 (3-10)

Theatrix

Snootz Math Trek (1-5)

The Learning Company, 800-852-2255

Math Rabbit (K-2)

(continued)

Treasure Galaxy (1-3)
Treasure Math Storm (1-3)
Super Solvers Outnumbered (3-5)
Operation Neptune (5-up)
Operation Neptune (6-8)

Tom Snyder, 800-877-9378

The Graph Club (K-3)

Ventura Educational Systems, 800-336-1022

Graph Power (K-8)
Geometry ToolKit (K-8)
Probability Kit (K-8)
Balancing Act (K-8)
Hands on Math (K-7)
Hands-on Math Vol. 1 (K-8)
Hands-on Math Vol. 2 (K-8)
Hands-on Math Vol. 3 (K-8)
Handi-Art for the Creative Teacher (K-8)
Coordinate Geometry (7-adult)
Geometry Concepts (7-12)

Virtual Entertainment, 671-449-7567

Milkcap Mazes (K-4)

Visions Technology in Education

Math Companion (K-8)

Voyager

The Human Calculator (4-adult)
Mastering Math (4-12)
I Know Math Disc (4-adult)
Countdown CD (PreK-5)

(continued)

Wasatch Education Systems, 800-877-2849

Wasatch Math Construction Tools: Counters (PreK-4)
Wasatch Math Construction Tools: Fraction Pieces (3-6)
Wasatch Math Construction Tools: Money (1-6)
Wasatch Math Construction Tools: Number Blocks (PreK-6)

SPECIAL NEEDS SOFTWARE

Attainment

Show Me Math: Addition
Show Me Math: Multiplication
Show Me Math: Division
Dollars and Cents Series I-III

Don Johnston

Big: Calc

MATH EDUCATION LASERDISCS

Cornet

Math for Beginners (3-6)
Mathematics for Primary Series (K-6)

Learning 2000

Problem Solving (4-12)

Optical Data

Windows on Math (Primary)

Tom Snyder

Fizz and Martina at Blues Falls High (K-6)
Problem Solving with Addition & Subtraction (4-12)
Problem Solving with Multiplication & Division (4-12)
Problem Solving with Tables, Graphs, and Statistics (4-12)

143: How to Use the Internet

What is the Internet?

It consists of a network of computers connected worldwide that share information in all types of media and communicate directly with each other.

What can I do with the Internet?

Using the Internet tools, e-mail, Telnet, Gopher, FTP and WWW, you can communicate by voice, text, or video anywhere in the world; locate and research archived or current information; and transfer files containing text or graphics.

What is needed to begin?

- a computer
- a modem
- a phone line
- communication software
- Internet account

Where do I get an account?

- University, college, or local school
- Freenets are found locally through the library, university, or state systems
- Department of Education in your state might provide accounts for teachers
- Local Internet providers may be found in local phonebooks
- Commercial providers: CompuServe, AmericaOnline, Prodigy, etc.

How do I begin using the Internet in my classroom?

- Enter the local number of your Internet provider and the settings for data bits, parity, stop bits, speed, and terminal emulation into your communication package.
- Your provider should provide you with instructions for logging on to the system. Every system is unique.
- You will need to remember your user name, password, and your unique Internet address.
- Create an Acceptable Use Policy for each user in your classroom. The contract among the teacher, parent, and student should establish use policies, unacceptable uses and consequences, and signatures of all parties.

Where do I start once I am connected?

- Use e-mail to join listservs or to send messages to individuals.
- Use FTP (File Transfer Protocol) to download or capture files on software.
- Use Gopher to view archived data in a menu-based format.

(continued)

- Use Telnet to log on to a remote computer and use that system's files and software. Most Telnet sites require that you have a registered user name in order for you to access their system.
- Use WWW (World Wide Web) to search and locate worldwide graphics, text, and audio in a hypertext format with a browser software program.

List of WWW browsers

Text Only

   LYNX—available by Telneting to ukanais.cc.ukans.edu

Text, Graphics, and Sound

   Mosaic—available by FTP to ftp.ncsa.uiuc.edu
   Netscape—available by FTP to ftp.netscape.com

144: World Wide Web (WWW) Sites

. . . ducation at math matiqes
http://www.halcyon.com/cairns/math.html

ASk Professor Math
e-mail>maths@sbu.edu
request for 6-9

BEATCALC: Mental Math Exercises
beatcalc@aol.com "subscribe GEATCALC (firstname)(lastname)"
discussion group

Blue Dog Math
http://fedida.ini.cmu.edu:5550/bdf.html

Calculator Mathematics
http://www.su.edu/west/CALCMATH.html

Chocolate Chip Math
http://unite.tisl.ukans.edu/explorer/RMath31.html
fractions/problem solving

Computer Curriculum Corporation
http://www.cccnet.com.
interactive curriculum on line

Cornell Theory Center Math/Science Gateway
http://www.tc.cornell.edu/Edu/MathSciGateway/

Currency Exchange
gopher.caticuf.csufresno.edu

DVS's list of K-12 Math Education Sites
http://mile.math.ucsb.edu/~vanslyke/math-ed.html

Educational Sites Page
http://www.escape.ca/%7Eeriksdale/edusites.html

Eisenhower National Clearinghouse
http://www.enc.org/

Electronic Games for Ed in Math & Science
http://www.cs.ubc.ca/next/egems/home.html

Geometry Center
http://www.geom.umn.edu/

Geometry Forum
http://forum.swartmore.edu/

©1997 by The Center for Applied Research in Education

(continued)

GEOmetry LABoratory
http://cabsparc.larc.nasa.gov

Group Math Game
http://www.classroom.net/addsub.htm

Houghton Mifflin Education Place (Math Center)
http://www.hmco.com/school/
resources

K-12 Explorer
http://unite.ukans.edu
lesson plans

K-12 Mathematics Lessons & Software Database
http://www.nste.uiuc.edu/mathed/queryform.html

K-9 Math/Science
http://204.161.33.221/AIMS.html

K12 Geometry Forum
http://forum.swarthmore.edu/k12/K12.html

Los Almos National Lab
http://www.lanl.gov/Public/welcome.html

MacVerter
ftp.wentworth.com
shareware

Math & Science Education
http://www.lib.umich.edu/chouse/inter/45.html

Math Brainteasers
http://gnn.com/gnn/meta/edu/curr/math/index.html

Math Centers
http://www.mste.uiuc.edu/centers/directory.html

Math Central
http:/www.math.uregina.ca/Math-Central/

Math Curriculum & Projects
http://www.hub.terc.edu/gn/hub/math-cur.html

Math Ed: Mathematics Resources
http://www-hpcc.astro.washington.edu/scied/math.html

(continued)

Math for K-3
http://www.dpi.state.nc.us/Curriculum/Mathematics/grade1.html

Math Form
http://forum.swarthmore.edu

Math Magic
http://foruml.swarthmore.edu/mathmagic/what.html

Math Reserouces
http://www.telport.com/%7Evincer/math.html

Math Shareware
http://www.bookstore.arizona.educ/www/software.html
shareware and demos

Mathematical Sciences Education Board (MSEB)
http://www.nas.edu/mseb/mseb.html

Mathematics Learning Forums
http://www.edc.org/cct/mlf/MLF.html
Internet seminars for elementary and middle school teachers

Mathematics Resource Page
http://www.deakin.edu.au/~adag
information for teachers and students in primary schools

Mathematics Tools
http://ion.rice.edu'msci/math/math.html

MATHMOL
http://www.nyu.-edu/pages/-mathmol
molecular modeling

MECC Home Page
http://www.mecc.com/
math demos

Mega Math—Los Alamos National Lab
http://www.cs.uidaho.edu/-casey931/mega-math/
lesson plans

Mega Mathematics
http://www.c3.lanl.gov/meg-math/

MegaMath
http://www.c3.lanl.gov/mega-math/welcome.html

(continued)

NCTM Web Page
http://www.nctm.org

National Teachers Enhancement Network
http://www.nomtana.edu/~wwwxs/index.html#topics

Schell Centre for Mathematical Education
http://acorn.educ.nottingham.ac.uk/ShellCent/PubList/
resources from United Kingdom

Science & Math
http://www.halcyon.com/eairns/science.html

Science & Math Initiatives (SAMI)
http://www.c3.lanl.gov:6060/SAMI-home

Science & Math Initatives (SAMI)
http://www.c3.lanl.gov/%7Ejspeck/SAME-home.html

Submit Problems
e-mail>farris@tusuvm.us.twsu.edu
submit problems

Texas Instruments
http://www.ti.com/

Usenet Newsgroup
K 12.ed math
discussion group

Wild Geometry
http://www.geom.umn.edu/apps/gallery.html

145: Search Engines

SEARCH TOOLS

Infoseek WWW Search
http://home,netscape,com/home/internet-search.html

Lycos WWW Search
http://lycos.cs.cmu.edu/

WebCrawler WWW Search
http://webcrawler.com/

W3 Search Engines
http://cuiwww.unige.ch/meta-index.html

WWW SEARCH ENGINES

Yahoo
http://www.yahoo.com

Alta Vista
http:/altavista.digital.com

*NetSearch
http://home.mcom/home/internet-search.html

OpenText Index
http://www.opentext.com:8080

Surf-N-Search
http://www.infohiway.com/index.html

*WWW Meta-Indexes
http://lcweb.loc.gov/global/metaindex.html

---

*Complete list of ALL WWW Search Engines

(continued)

DE-ISOLATING THE TEACHER

Wentworth's Jump to Newsgroups
http://www.wentworth.com/classroom/edulinks.htm

News:misc.education
News:misc.education

Web Forums
http://www.mightymedia.com/talk/working.htm

Ask Eric
http://ericir.syr.edu

The Teacher Lounge
http://www.wentworth.com/classroom/TeachL.htm

EdLinks
http://www.marshall.edu/~jmullens/edlinks.html

Doc's Education Resource Page
http://www.pixi.com/~cram/

General Resources
http://www.pixi.com/~cram/general.html

Global School House: Projects
http://gsn.org/

Index on Funding Agencies
http://www.cs.virginia.edu/~seas/resdev/sponsors.html

ADMINISTRATION POWER

Reinventing Schools: The Technology Is Now
http://www.nas.edu/nap/online/techgap/welcome.html

Reinventing Schools: Index Map
http://www.nas.edu/nap/online/techgap/index.html

Reinventing: A New Model for Education
http://www.nas.edu/nap/online/techgap/newmodel.html

Apple Education
http://www.info.apple.com/education/

(continued)

Acot
http://www.info.apple.com/education/acot8.html

Larry S. Anderson's Home Page
http://www.2.msstate.edu/~lsa1/

National Center for Technology Planning
http://www2.msstate.edu/~lsa1/nctp/index.html

U.S. Department of Education
http://www.edgov/

Money Matters
http://www.edgov/money.html

Funding Opportunities
gopher://gopher.ed.gov/11/announce/competitions

Web66: International WWW School Registry
http://Web66.coled.umn.edu/schools.html

ASCD's Web Search Engine
http://www.ascd.org/wwwwais.html

Curriculum Integration Academy for Elementary Schools
http://odie.ascd.org/aspen.html

Information Technology for Science Education by Keith Mitchell
http://atlantic.austin.apple.com/people.pages/kmitchell/ITSE.html

The following are additional sites that will be valuable resources:

APPLE SITES

Apple Computer
http://www.apple.com/

Apple Support
http://www.info.apple.com/

Apple Software Updates
http://www.support.apple.com/

Claris Corporation
http://www.claris.com/

(continued)

The Apple Virtual Campus H.E.
http://www.info.apple.com/hed/

Apple Education (K-12)
http://www.info.apple.com/education/

Developer Support
http://www.info.apple.com/dev/developerservices.html

ATG
http://www.atg.apple.com/

QuickTime Support
http://quicktime.apple.com/

E-world Web Page
http://www.eworld.com/education/resources/

Apple Business Systems
http://abs.apple.com/

Apple Personal Pages
http://atlantis.austin.apple.com/people.pages/people.pages.html

MULTIMEDIA CONNECTION

RealAudio Homepage
http://www.RealAudio.com/index.html

NetPhone Home Page
http://www.emagic.com/

OTHER

Ceneca Communications (Pagemill)
http://www.ceneca.com/

SECTION 14

REPRODUCIBLE
PATTERNS

Name _____

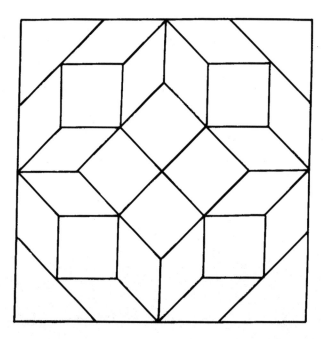

1. How many different shapes can you find on this pattern?

  _____

2. Color the pattern to create a colorful design.

146: Grids

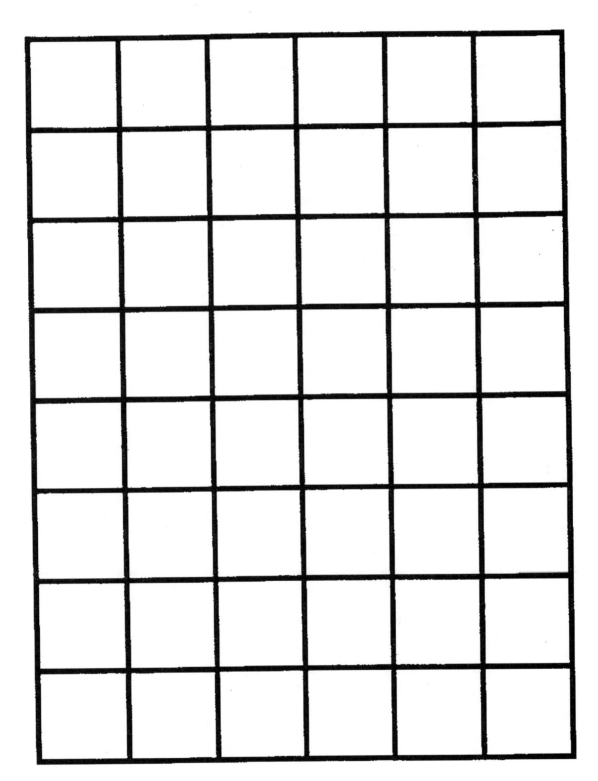

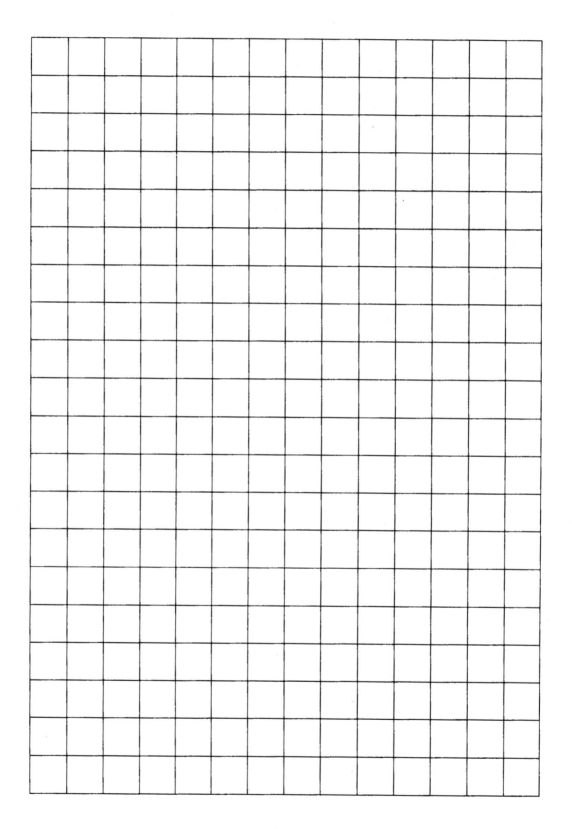

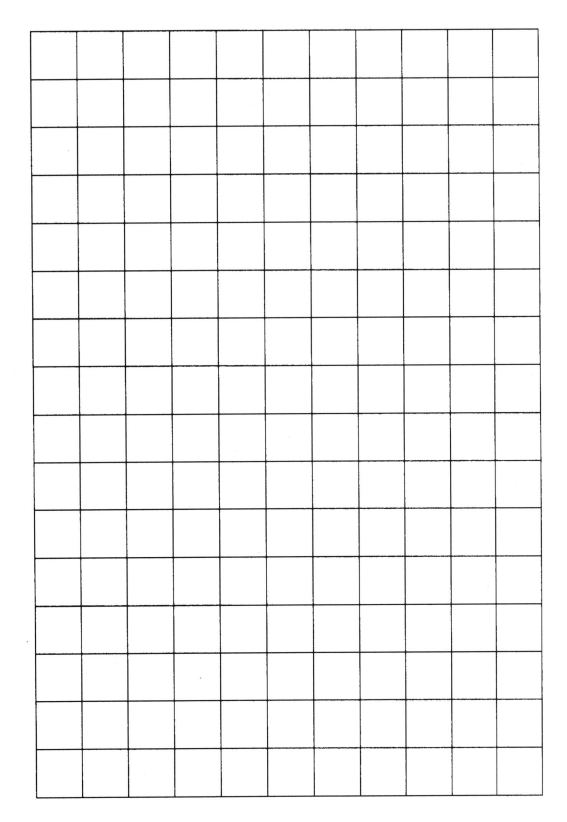

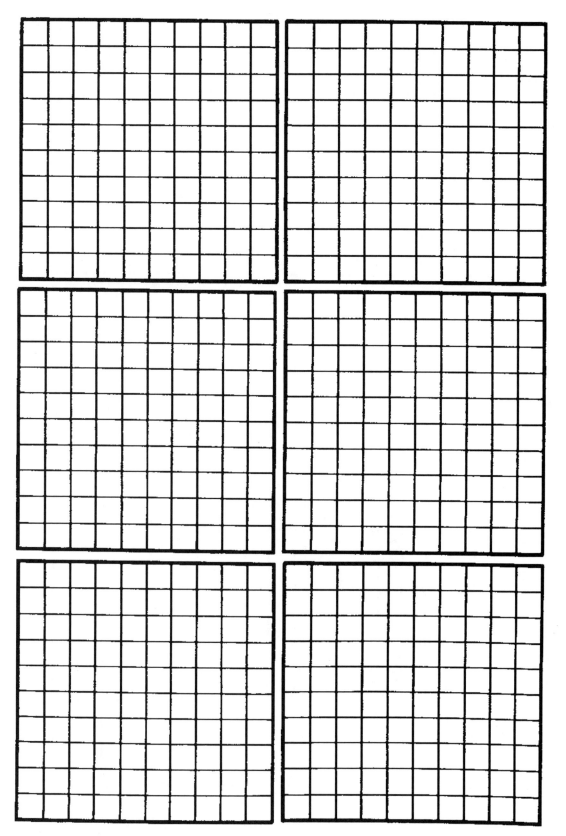

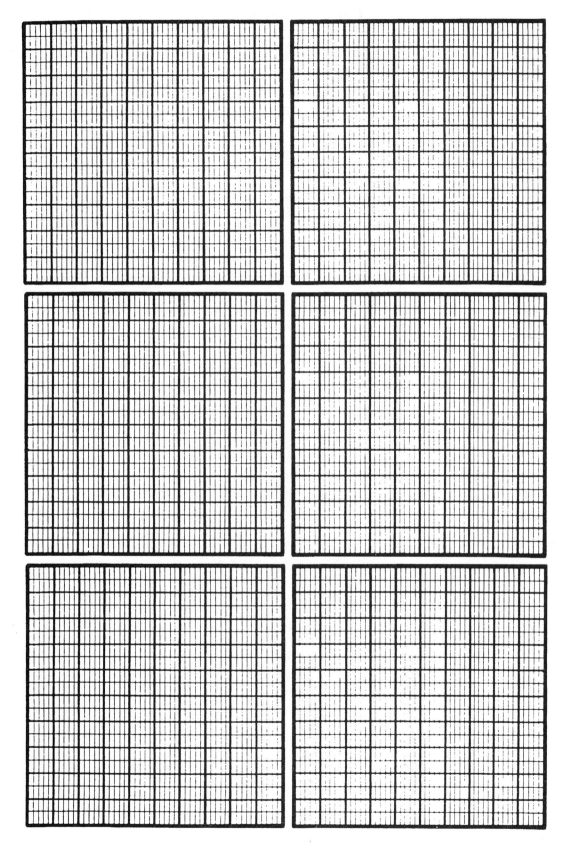

Decimal Squares

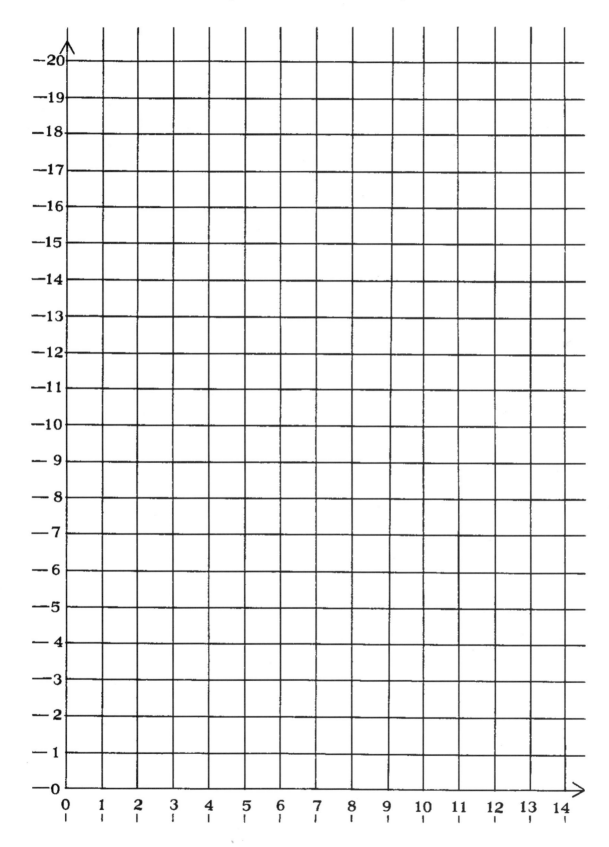

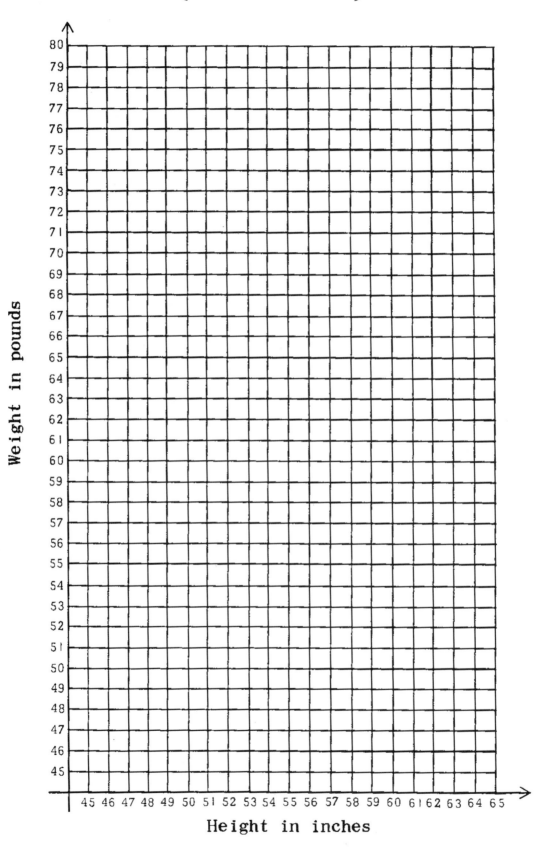

Weight in pounds

Height in inches

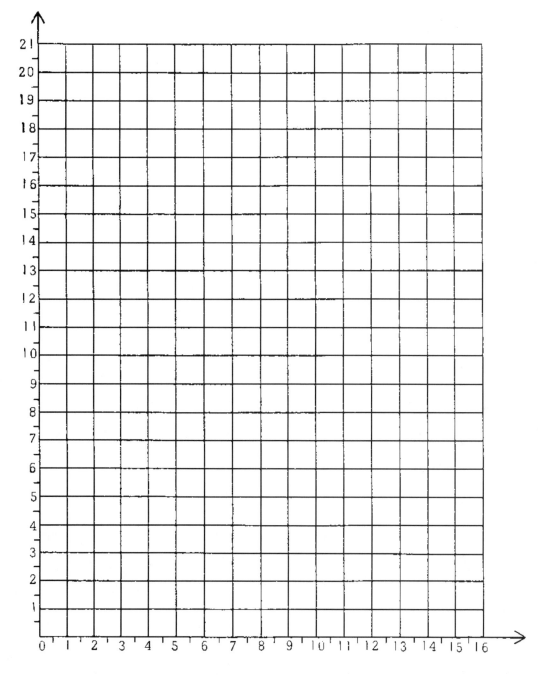

Time (hours)

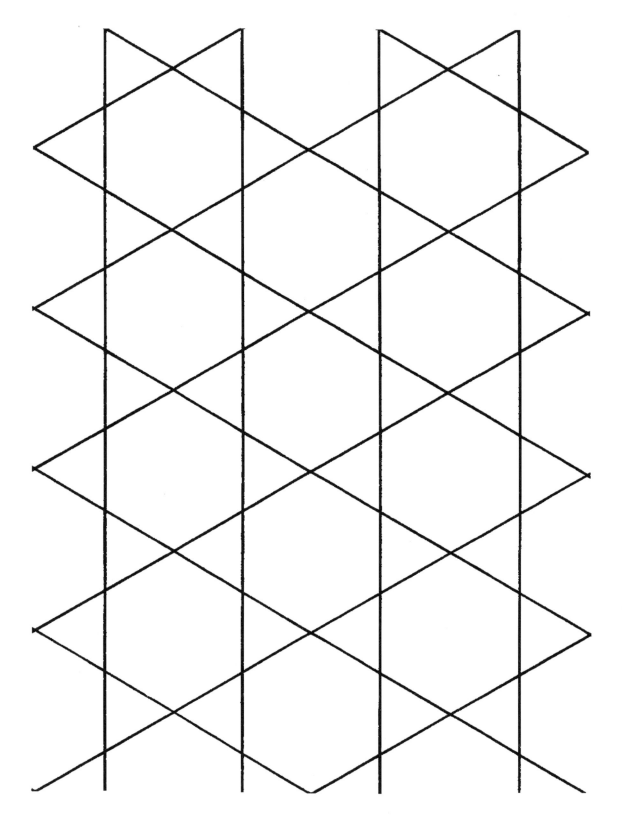

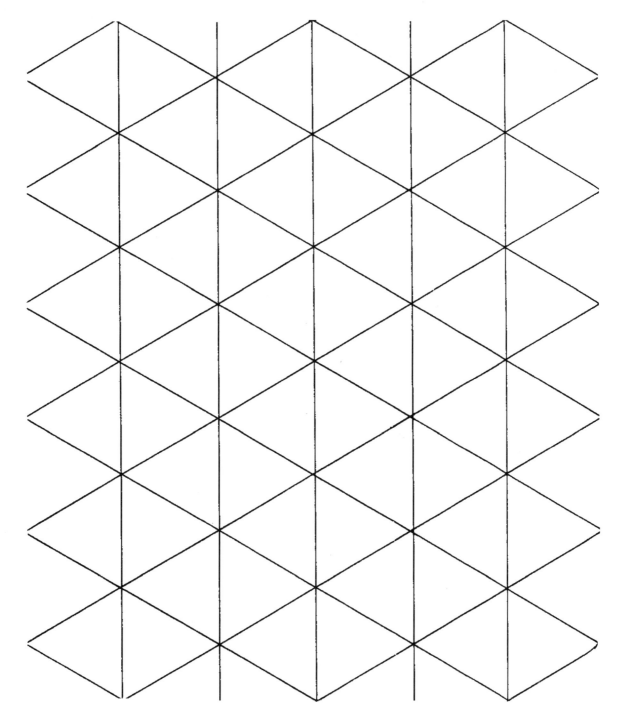

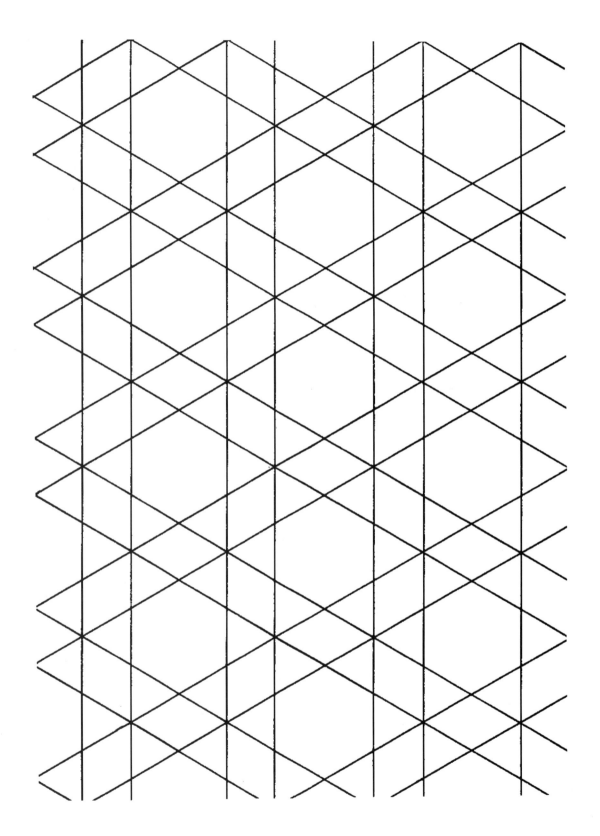

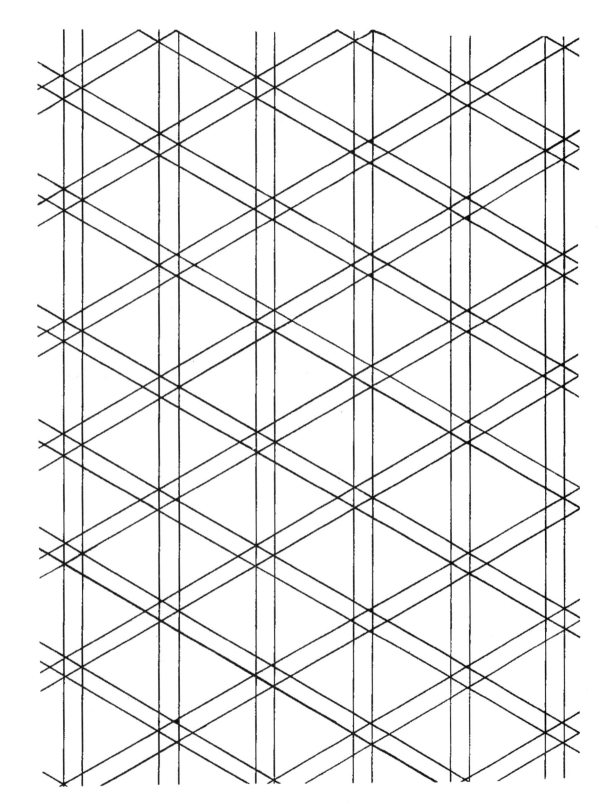

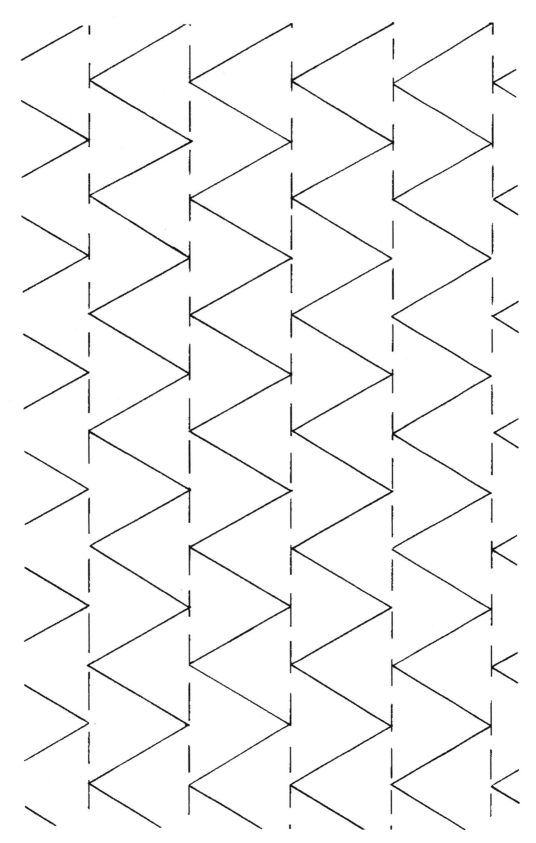

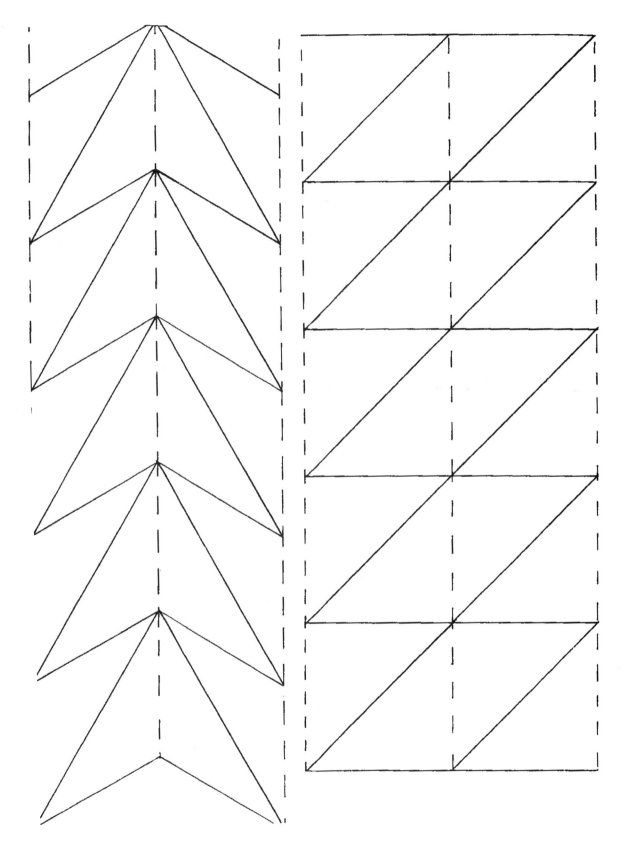

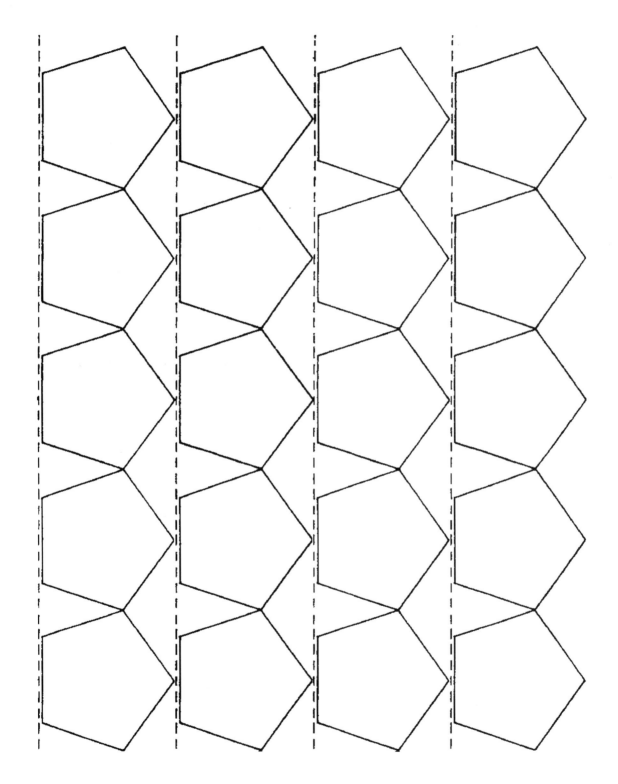

Tetrahedron

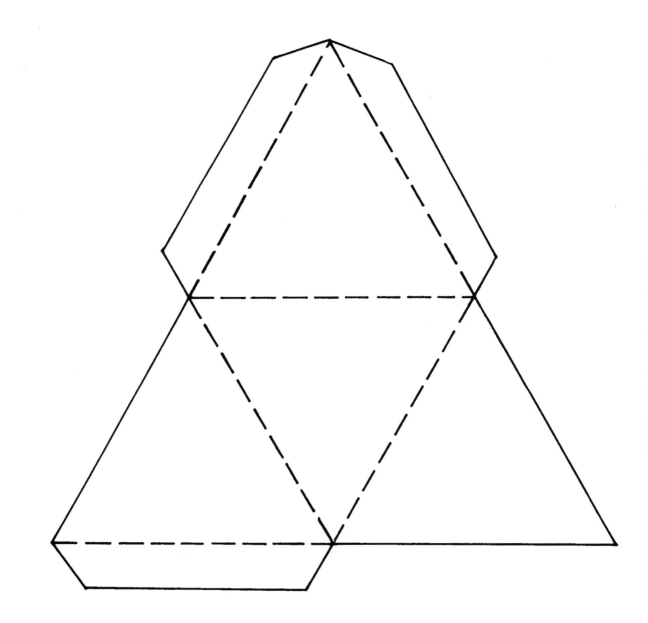

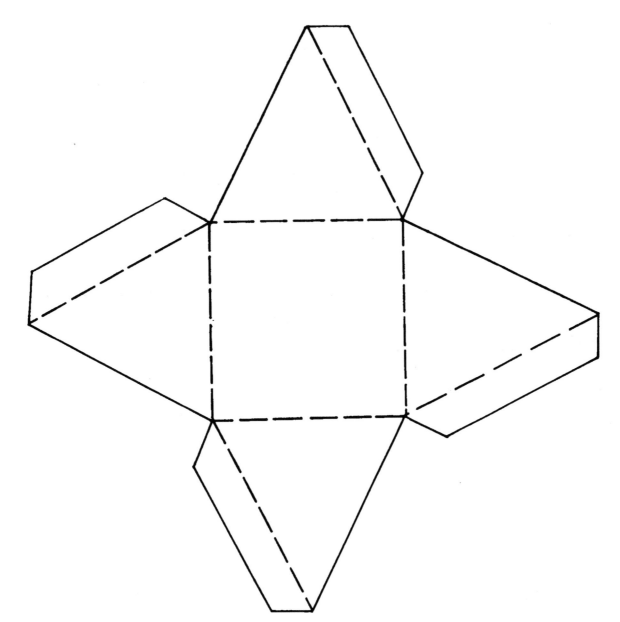

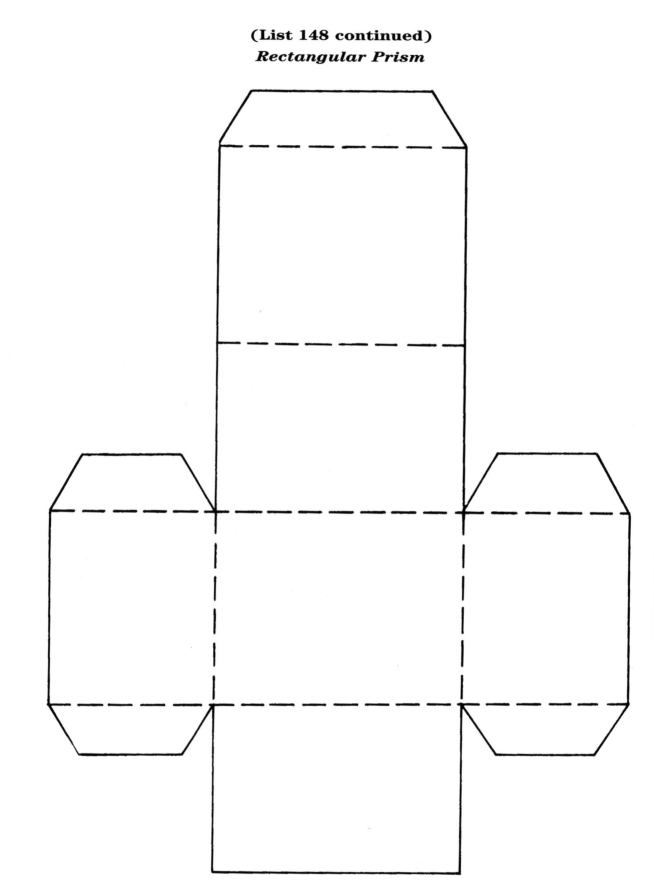

Hexahedron

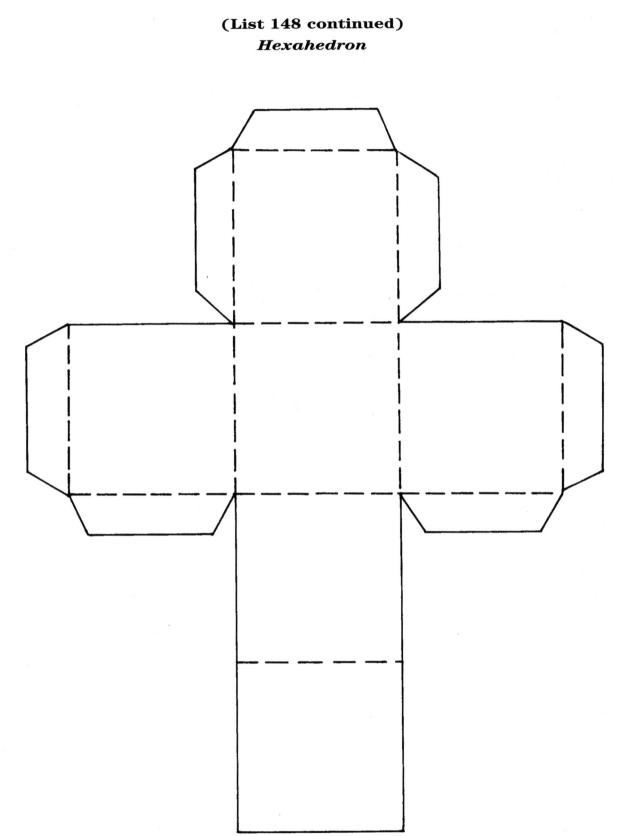

Octahedron

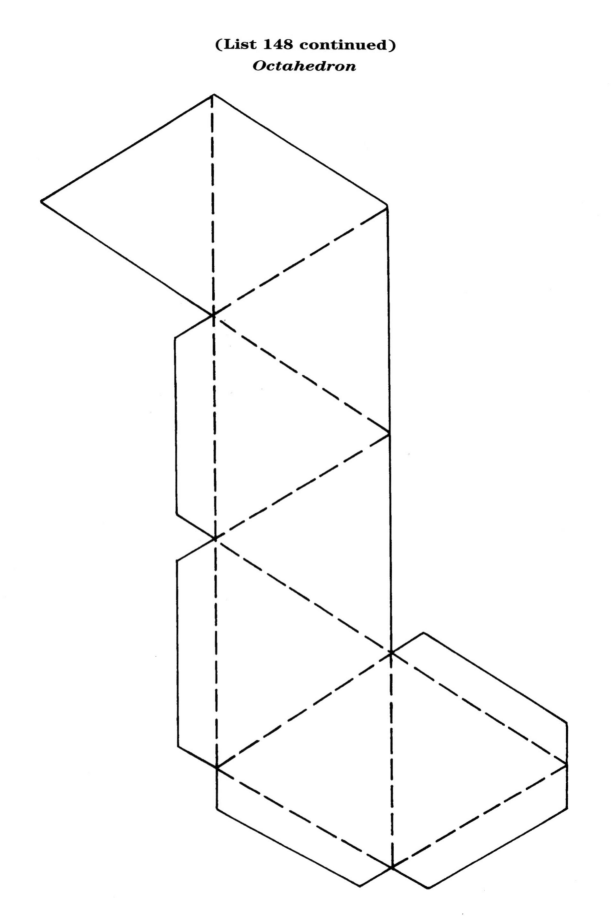

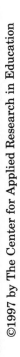

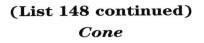

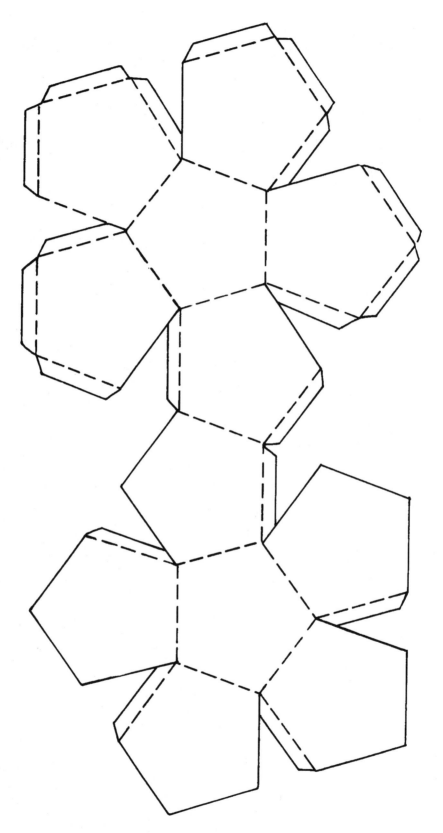

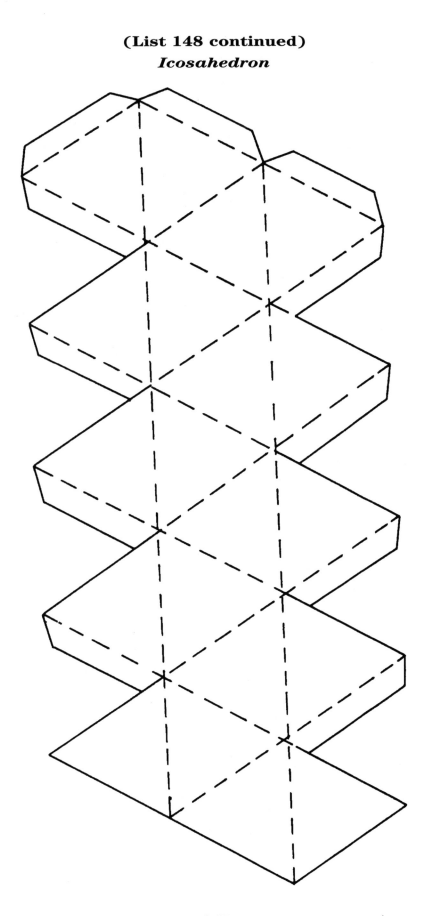

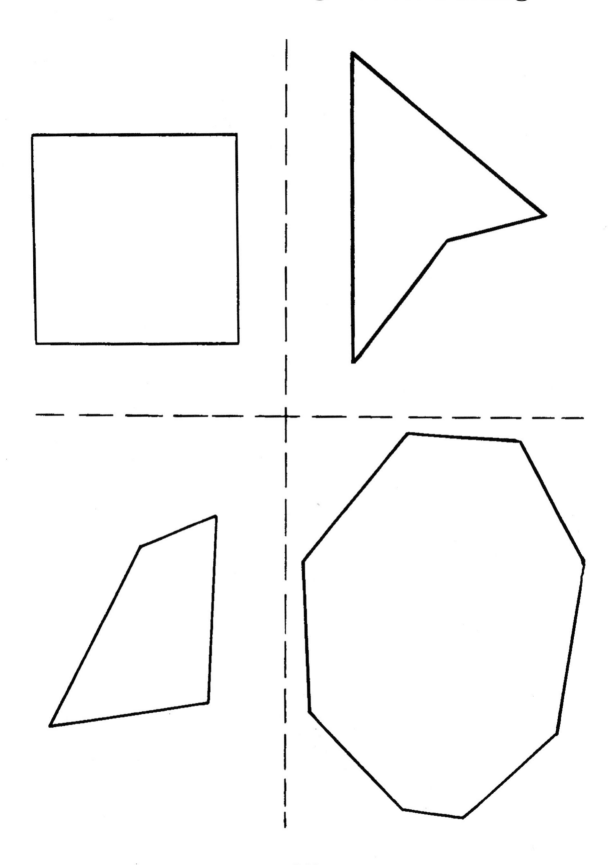

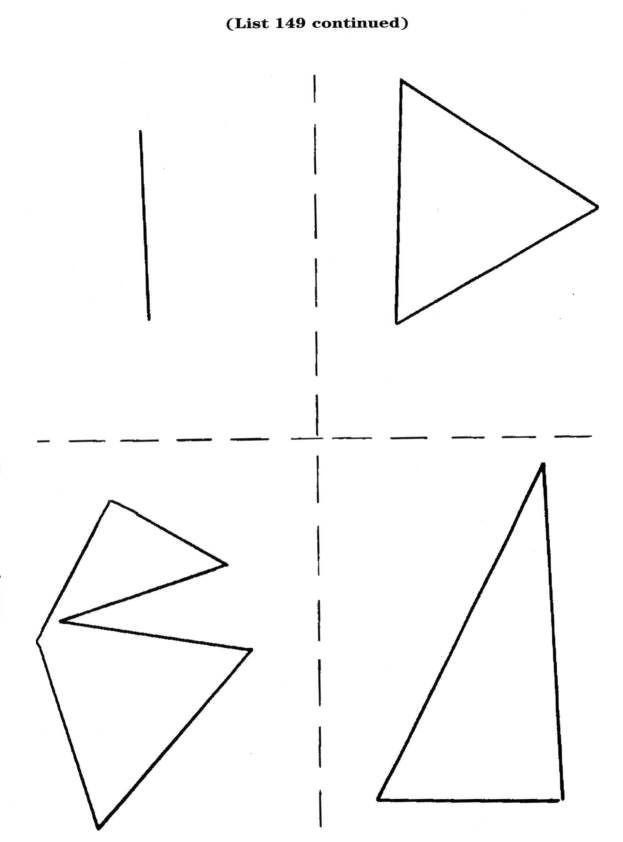

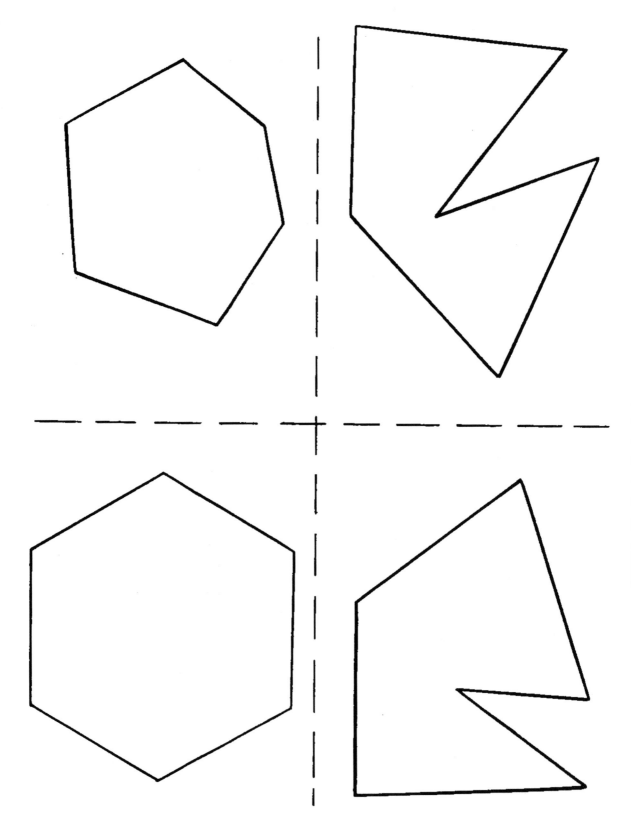

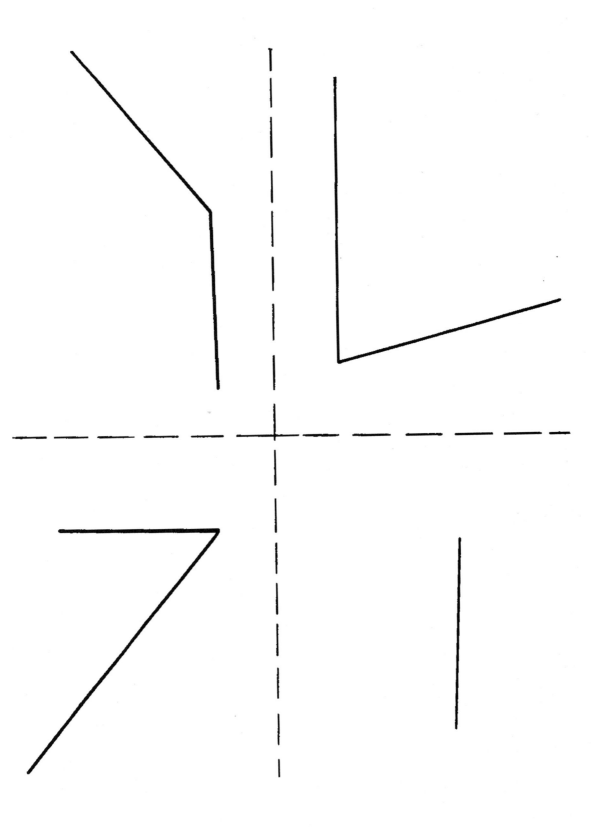

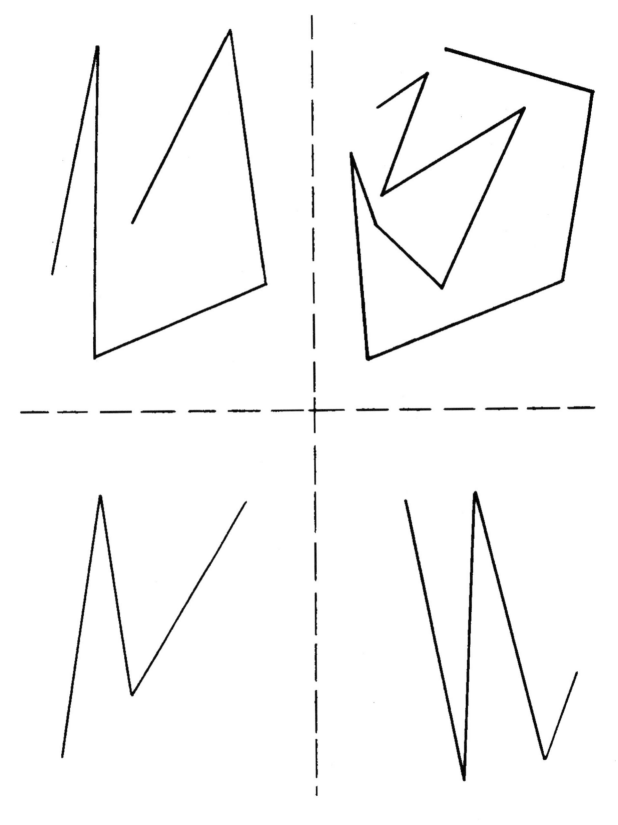

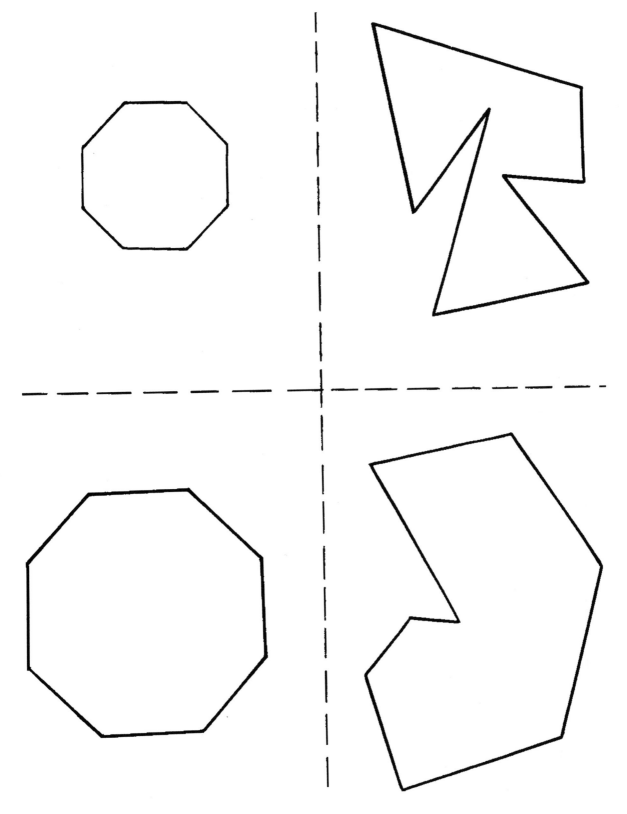

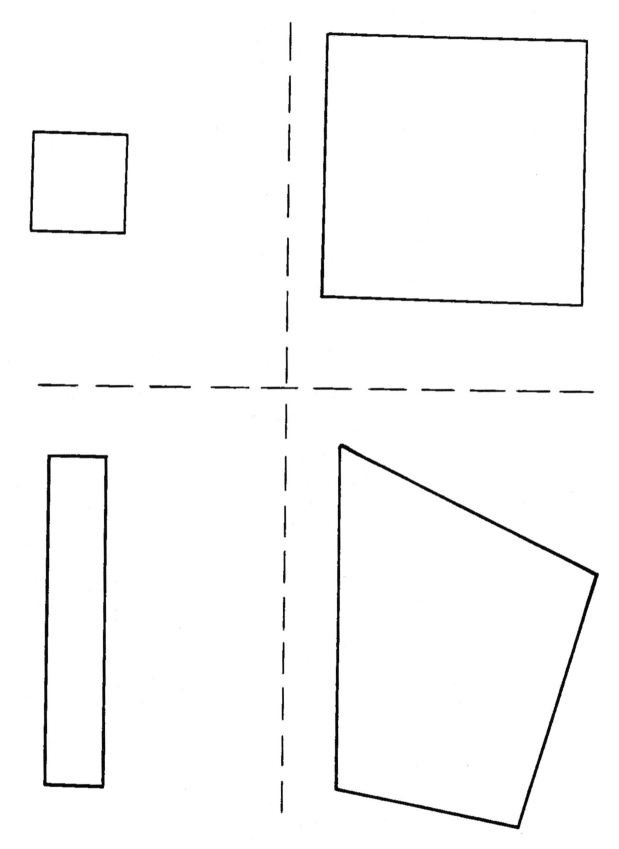

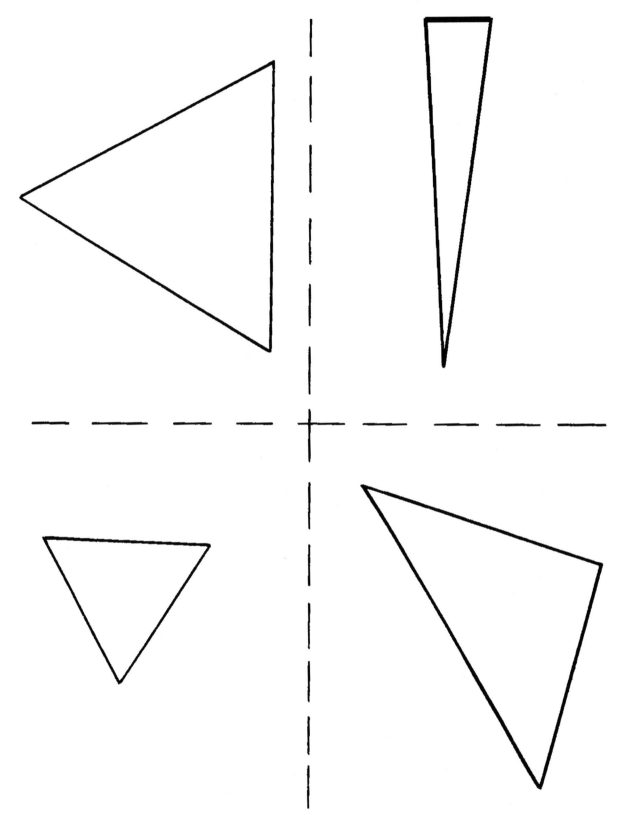

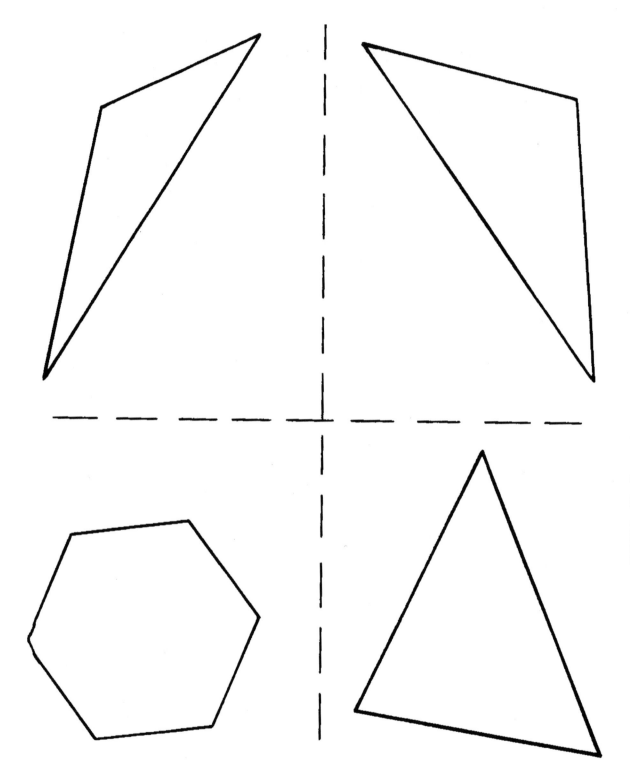

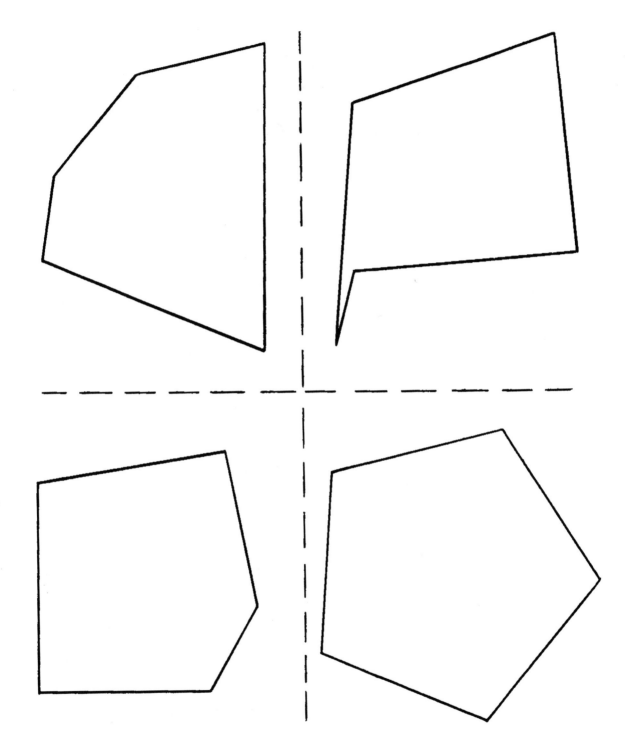

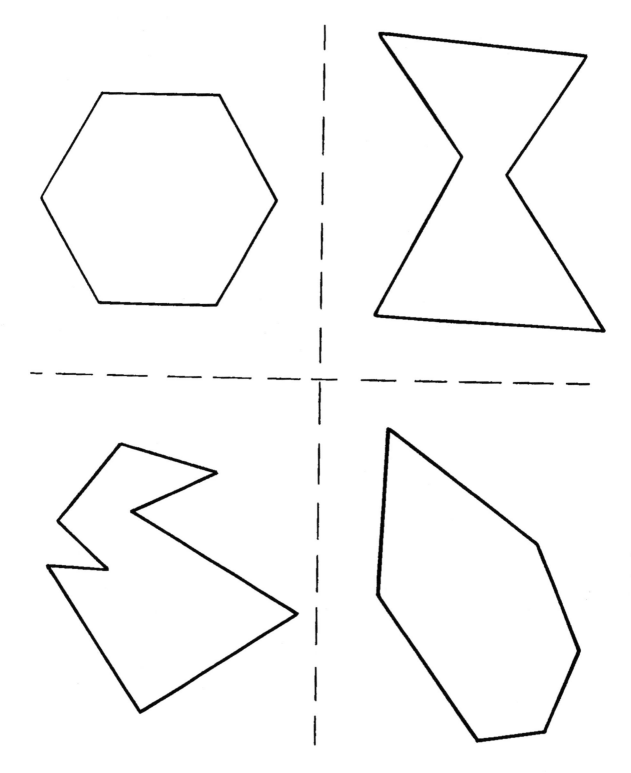

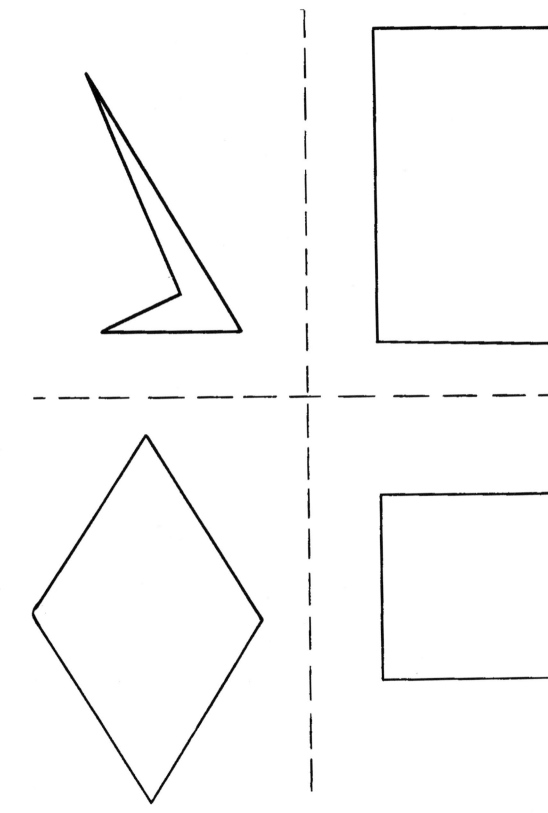

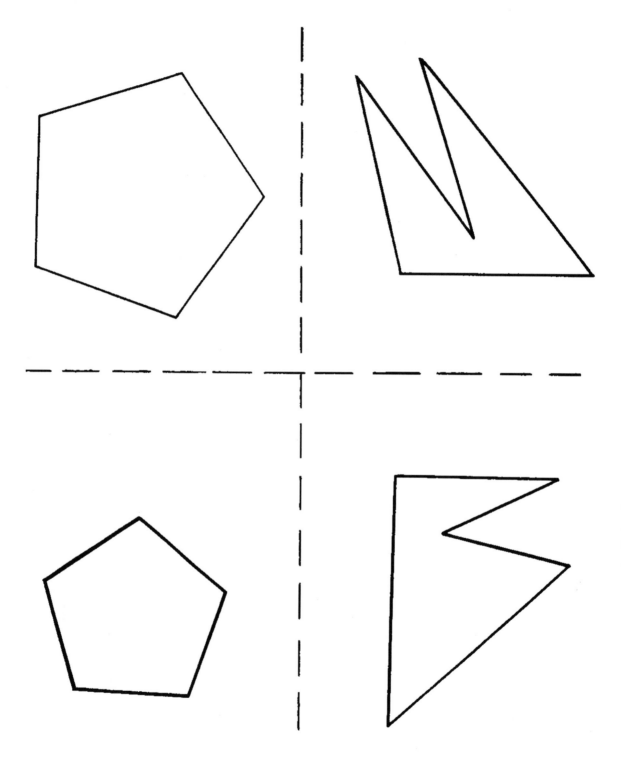

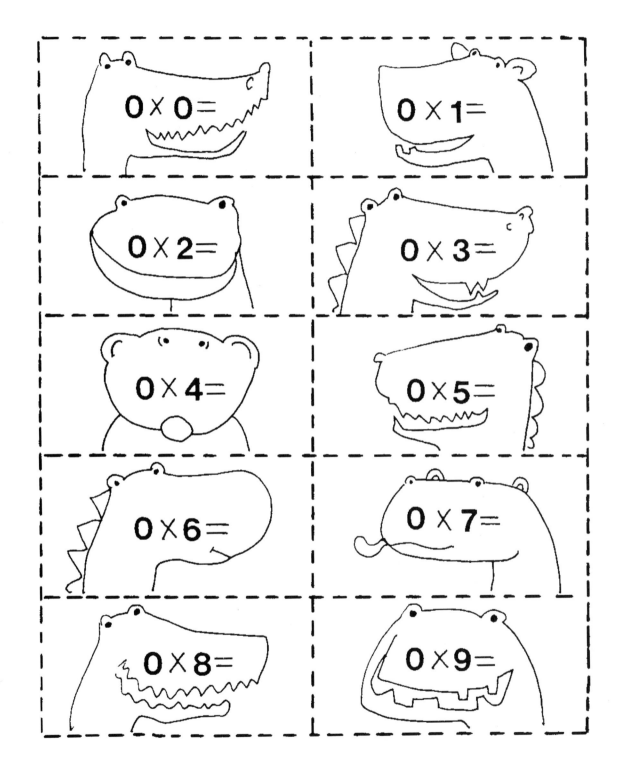

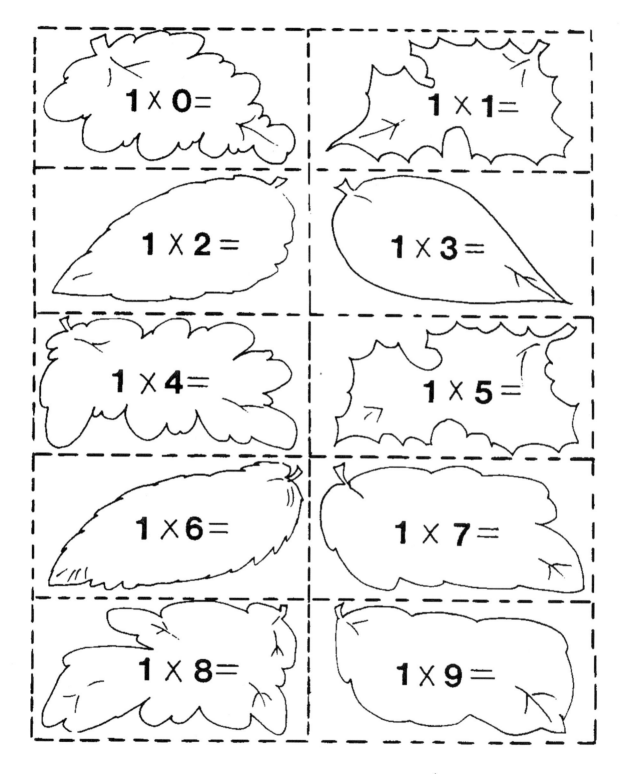

1 × 0 =

1 × 1 =

1 × 2 =

1 × 3 =

1 × 4 =

1 × 5 =

1 × 6 =

1 × 7 =

1 × 8 =

1 × 9 =

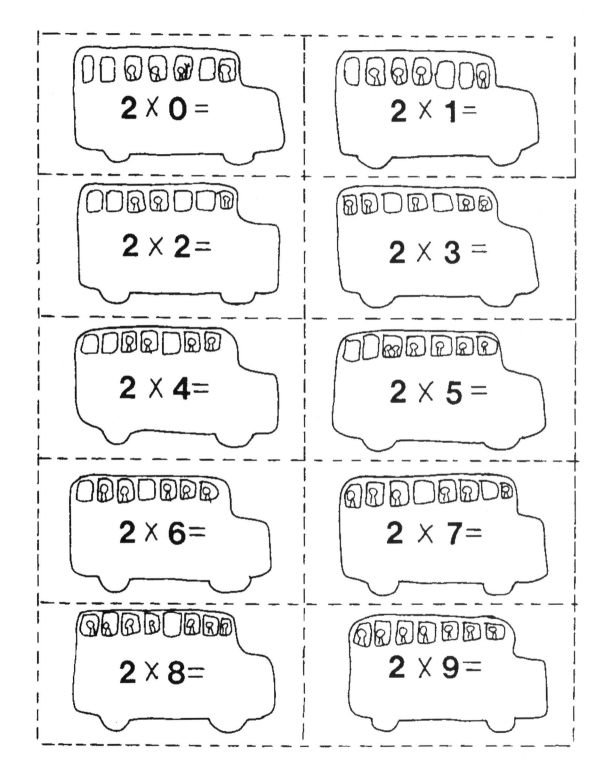

2 × 0 =

2 × 1 =

2 × 2 =

2 × 3 =

2 × 4 =

2 × 5 =

2 × 6 =

2 × 7 =

2 × 8 =

2 × 9 =

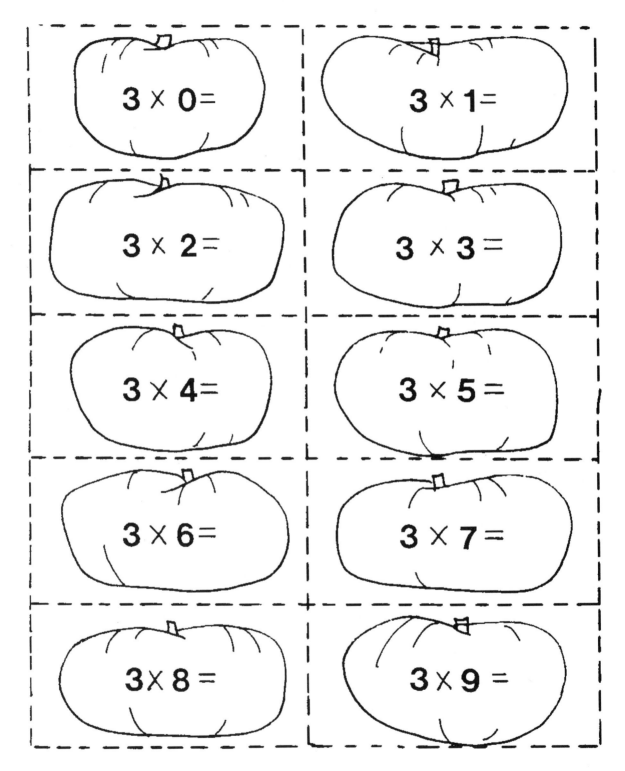

3 × 0 =

3 × 1 =

3 × 2 =

3 × 3 =

3 × 4 =

3 × 5 =

3 × 6 =

3 × 7 =

3 × 8 =

3 × 9 =

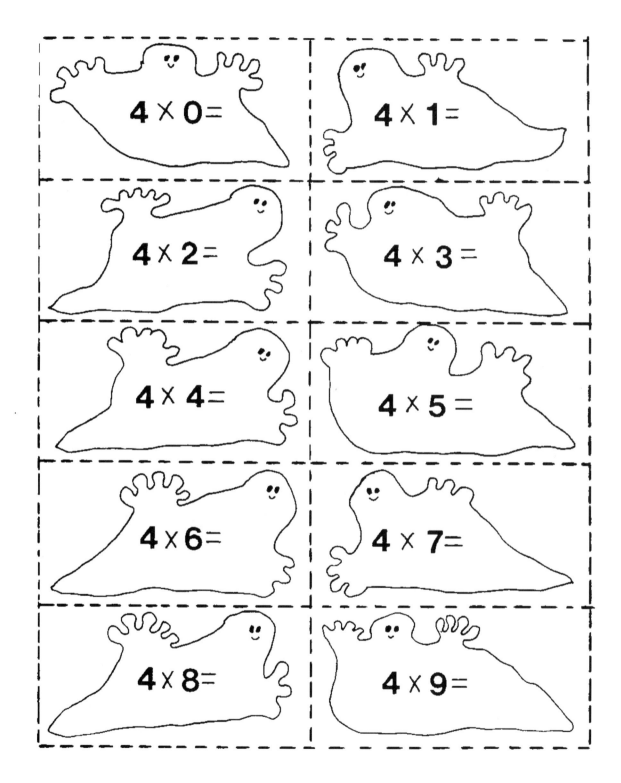

4 × 0 =

4 × 1 =

4 × 2 =

4 × 3 =

4 × 4 =

4 × 5 =

4 × 6 =

4 × 7 =

4 × 8 =

4 × 9 =

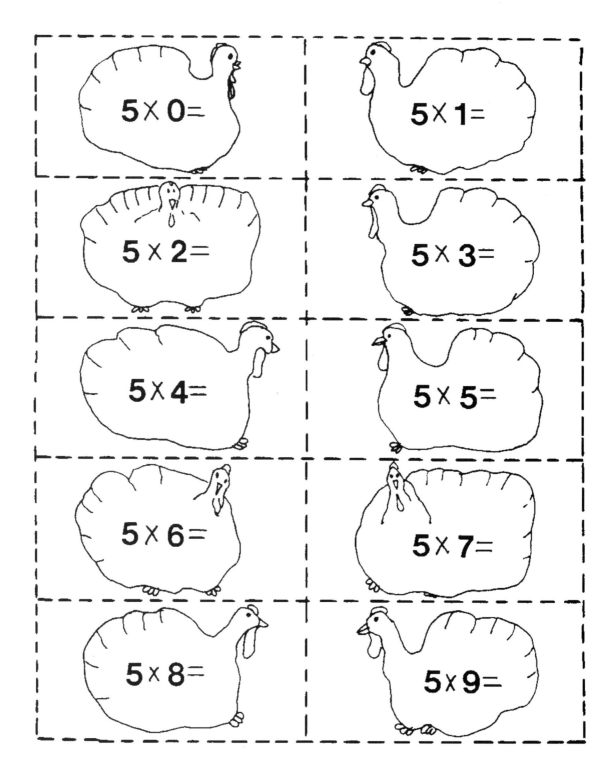

©1997 by The Center for Applied Research in Education

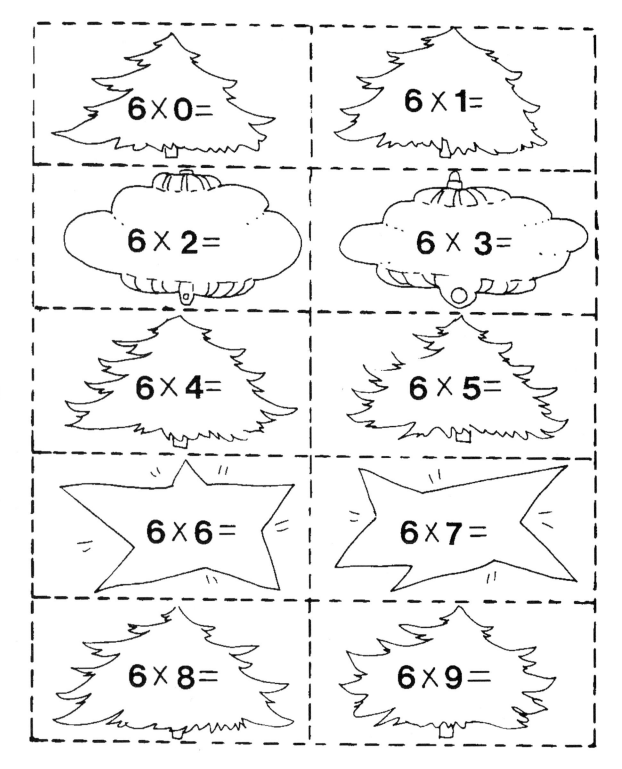

$6 \times 0 =$

$6 \times 1 =$

$6 \times 2 =$

$6 \times 3 =$

$6 \times 4 =$

$6 \times 5 =$

$6 \times 6 =$

$6 \times 7 =$

$6 \times 8 =$

$6 \times 9 =$

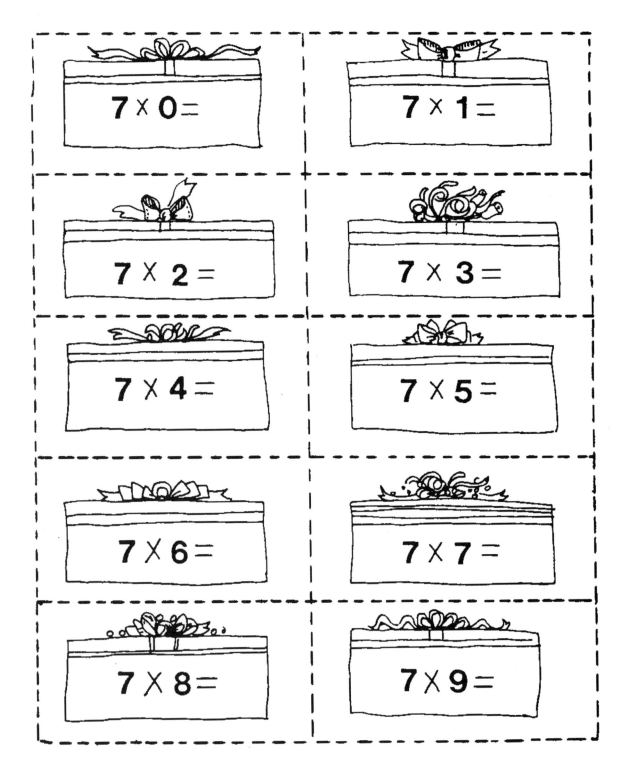

7 × 0 =

7 × 1 =

7 × 2 =

7 × 3 =

7 × 4 =

7 × 5 =

7 × 6 =

7 × 7 =

7 × 8 =

7 × 9 =

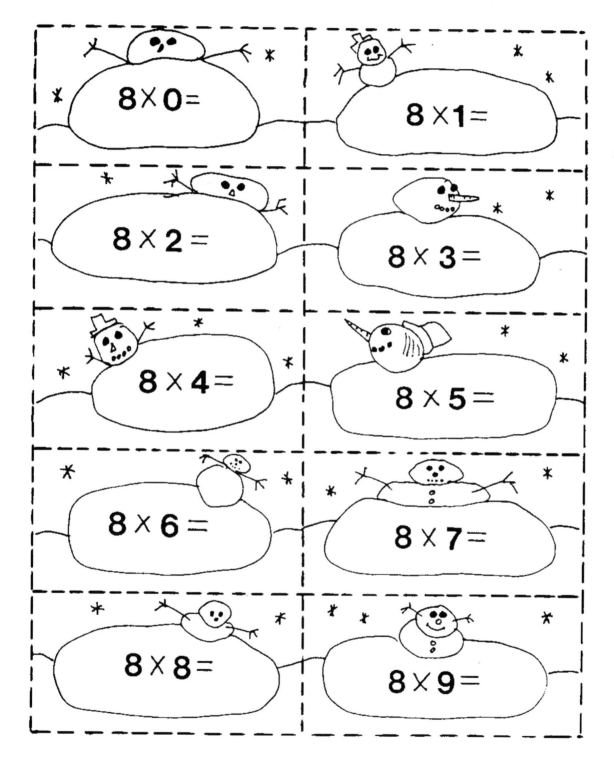

8×0=

8×1=

8×2=

8×3=

8×4=

8×5=

8×6=

8×7=

8×8=

8×9=

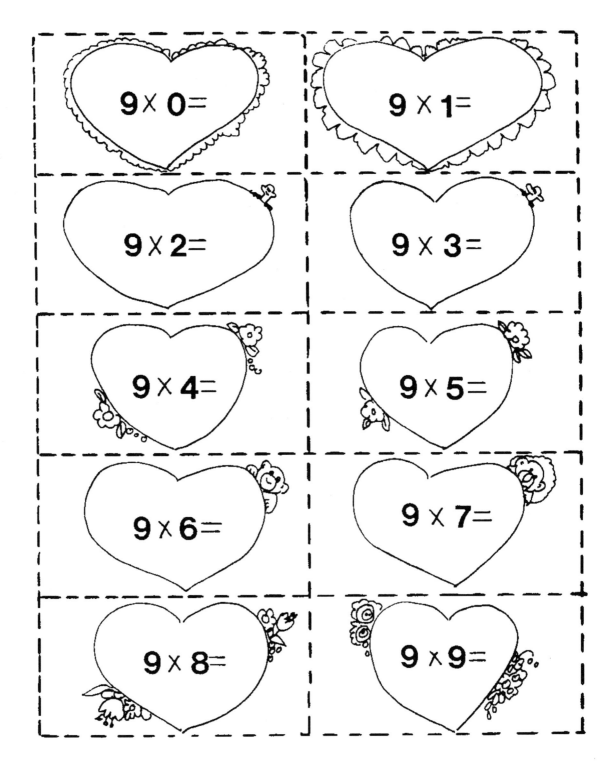

151: Number Lines and Numbers

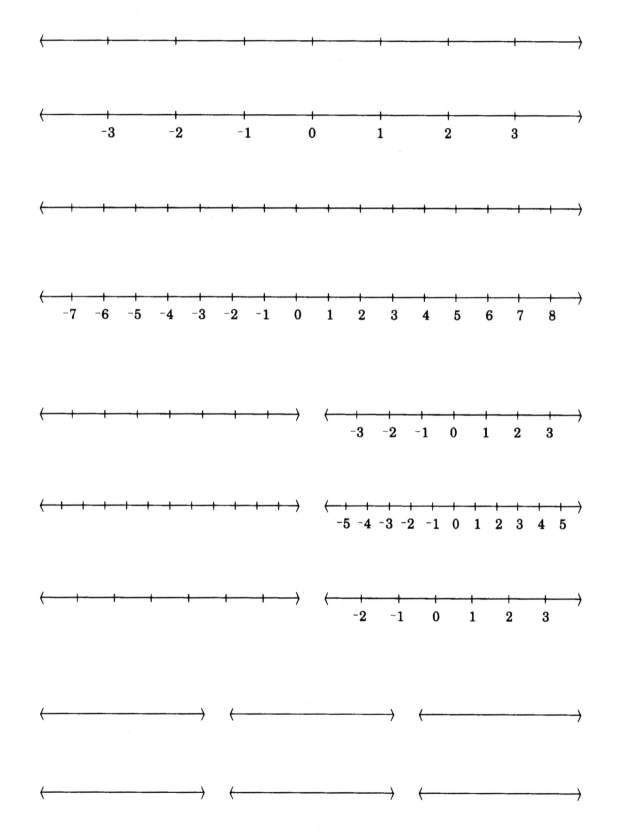

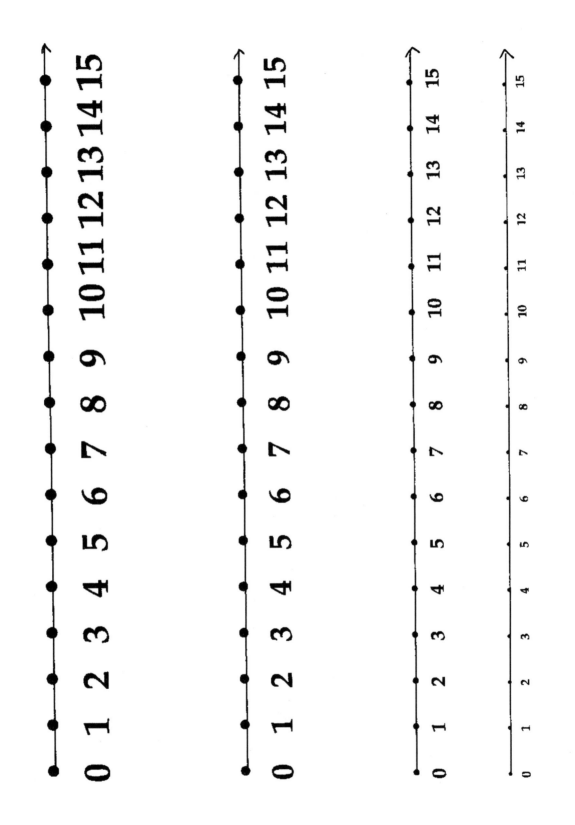

(List 151 continued)

Fraction Number Line

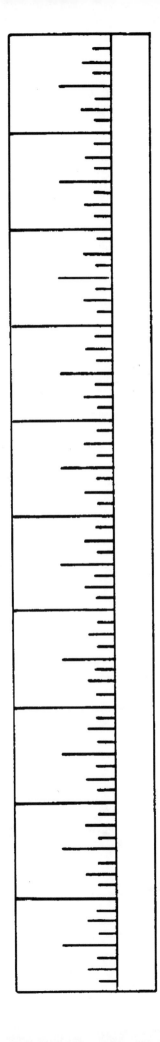

Protractors

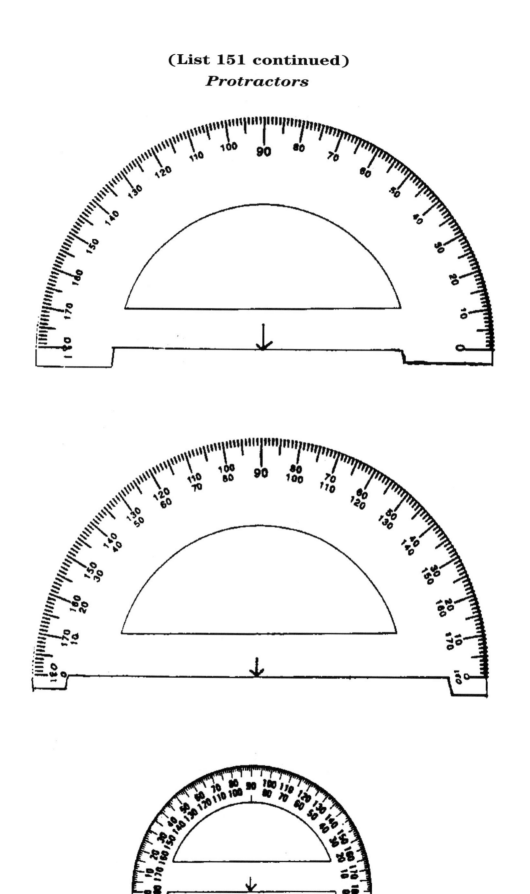

Reproduce and provide students with sets to cut out. These can be used to name sets that children identify.

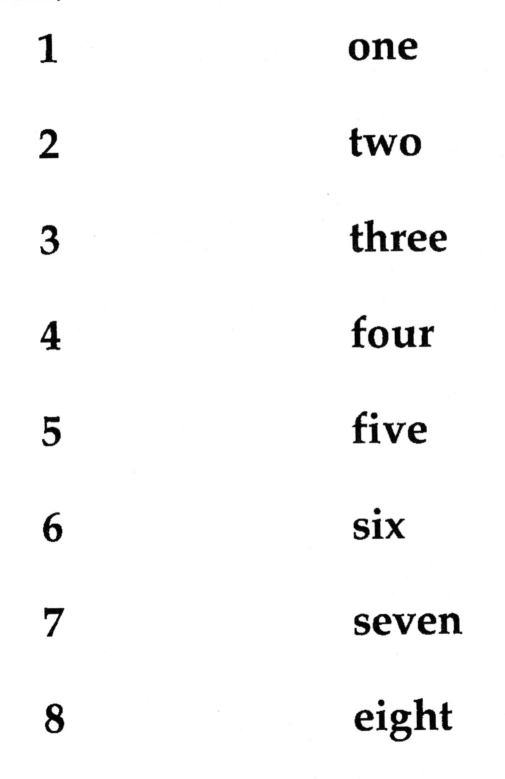

1	one
2	two
3	three
4	four
5	five
6	six
7	seven
8	eight

9	nine
10	ten
11	eleven
12	twelve
13	thirteen
14	fourteen
15	fifteen
16	sixteen
17	seventeen
18	eighteen

19	nineteen
20	twenty
21	twenty-one
22	twenty-two
23	twenty-three
24	twenty-four
25	twenty-five
26	twenty-six
27	twenty-seven

Expanded Notation Numbers

Instructions: Reproduce sheet 4 times. Laminate the sheets and cut out four sets of numbers. Place thousands in one pile, hundreds in second pile, tens in a third pile, and ones in fourth pile.

Game: This game is for 2 to 4 players. One child randomly calls out a number, such as 645. (Or a teacher may have a set of numbers from 1 to 9999 cut into pieces in a box where a child may pick a number.) All players must make the number using the laminated pieces by finding the correct set of three numbers to form 645 (600 + 40 + 5). The winner is the first child to lay down the pieces correctly. A point is earned for each correct answer over a period of 10 minutes.

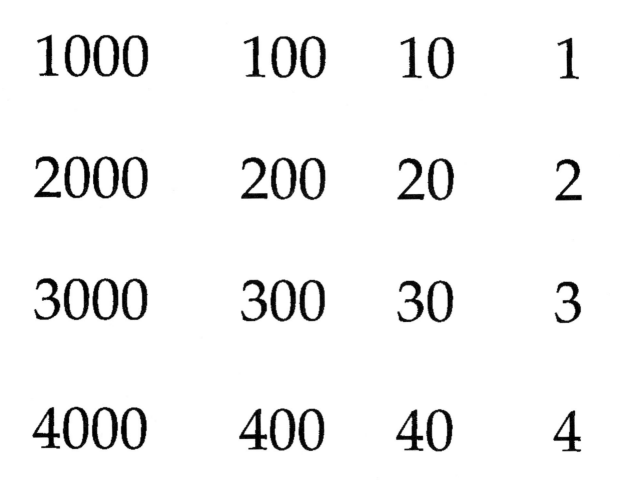

1000	100	10	1
2000	200	20	2
3000	300	30	3
4000	400	40	4

5000	500	50	5
6000	600	60	6
7000	700	70	7
8000	800	80	8
9000	900	90	9

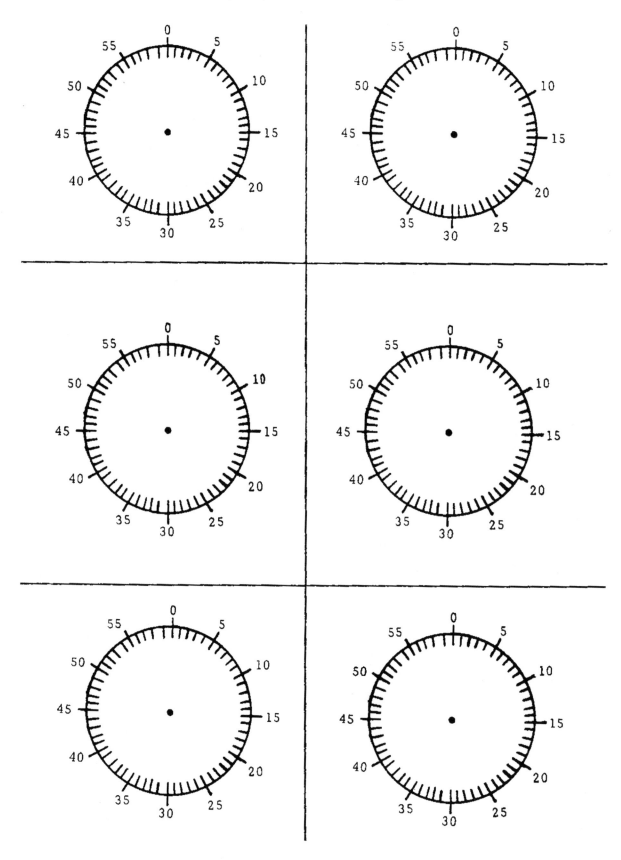

Binary Number Guessing Game

Preparation:

On a set of eight index cards reproduce the set of number in the clusters shown. Either copy the page and cut and paste the numbers *or* print them as shown. Do not write the Card # value on the front side where the cluster of numbers are to be shown. On the *back of each card* write the title such as Card #1, Card # 2, Card #4, Card #8, etc.

Rules:

Instruct the child to think of a number from 1 to 64 and keep it a secret. Then ask the child if the secret number appears on Card #1. If the child responds "yes," then you remember 1. If the child responds "no," then you remember 0. Go to the next card, Card #2. Ask again. If the child responds "yes," add 2 to the number you are remembering. If you had "yes" for 1 and now "yes" for 2, then you remember 3. If you have "no," then you add 0 to the figure you remembered from Card #1. Show the next card, Card #4. If the child responds "yes," then add 4; if "no," add 0. Continue to Card #8 (add 8 or 0), Card #16 (add 16 or 0), and finally Card #32 (add 32 or 0).

Example:

1. Have a child think of a secret number from 1 to 64.
2. Suppose a child thinks of the number 27.
3. Ask the child if the number is on the first card labeled Card #1. The child responds "yes," so remember 1.
4. Ask if the number appears on the second card, Card #2. The child responds "yes," so add 2 to 1 and remember 3.
5. Show Card #4. The child responds "no," so add 0 to 3 and remember 3.
6. Show Card #8. The child responds "yes," so add 8 to 3 and remember 11.
7. Show Card #16. The child responds "yes," so add 16 to 11 and remember 27.
8. Show Card #32. The child responds "no," so the secret number is 0 plus 27, or 27.

Base 2	2	2	2	2	2	2
Base 10	32	16	8	4	2	1
	"no	yes	yes	no	yes	yes"
			OR			
Base 2	0	1	1	0	1	1

Binary Number Guessing Game Cards

Card #1 (2)

1	3	5	7	9	11
13	15	17	19	21	23
25	27	29	31	33	35
37	39	41	43	45	47
49	51	53	55	57	59
		61	63		

Card #2 (2)

2	3	6	7	10	11
14	15	18	19	22	23
26	27	30	31	34	35
38	39	42	43	46	47
50	51	54	55	58	59
		62	63		

Card # 4 (2)

4	5	6	7	12	13
14	15	20	21	22	23
28	29	30	31	36	37
38	39	44	45	46	47
52	53	54	55	60	61
		62	63		

Card #8 (2)

8	9	10	11	12	13
14	15	24	25	26	27
28	29	30	31	40	41
42	43	44	45	46	47
56	57	58	59	60	61
		62	63		

Card #16 (2)

16	17	18	19	20	21
22	23	24	25	26	27
28	29	30	31	48	49
50	51	52	53	54	55
56	57	58	59	60	61
		62	63		

Card # 32 (2)

32	33	34	35	36	37
38	39	40	41	42	43
44	45	46	47	48	49
50	51	52	53	54	55
56	57	58	59	60	61
		62	63		

152: Tangrams, Pattern Blocks, Pentominoes, and Rods

Tangram

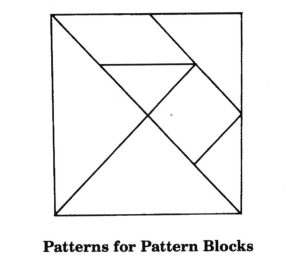

Patterns for Pattern Blocks

Patterns for Cuisenaire Rods®

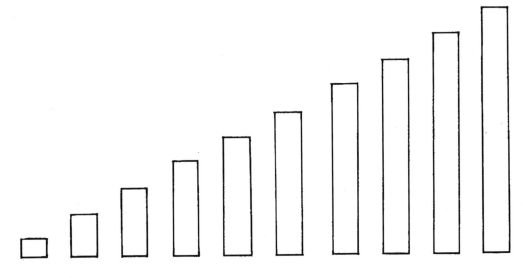

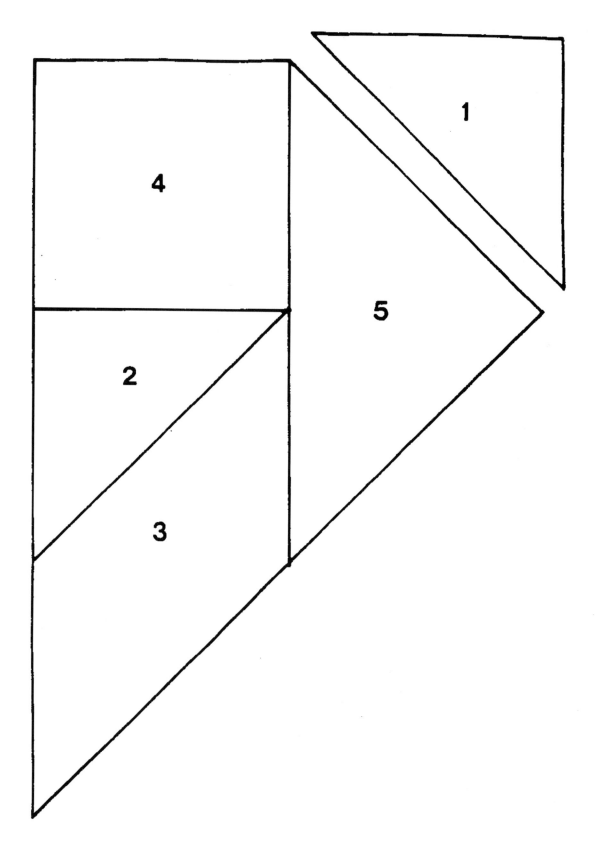

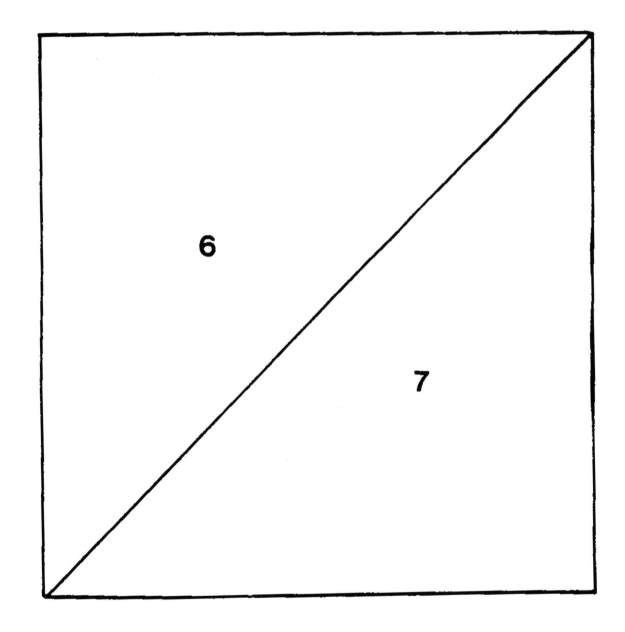

153: Fraction Strips and Circles

Fraction Strips

1											

| $\frac{1}{2}$ | | | | | | $\frac{1}{2}$ | | | | | |

| $\frac{1}{3}$ | | | | $\frac{1}{3}$ | | | | $\frac{1}{3}$ | | | |

| $\frac{1}{4}$ | | | $\frac{1}{4}$ | | | $\frac{1}{4}$ | | | $\frac{1}{4}$ | | |

| $\frac{1}{5}$ | | $\frac{1}{5}$ | | $\frac{1}{5}$ | | $\frac{1}{5}$ | | $\frac{1}{5}$ | | | |

| $\frac{1}{6}$ | | $\frac{1}{6}$ | | $\frac{1}{6}$ | | $\frac{1}{6}$ | | $\frac{1}{6}$ | | $\frac{1}{6}$ | |

| $\frac{1}{8}$ | $\frac{1}{8}$ | $\frac{1}{8}$ | $\frac{1}{8}$ | $\frac{1}{8}$ | $\frac{1}{8}$ | $\frac{1}{8}$ | $\frac{1}{8}$ | | | | |

| $\frac{1}{9}$ | $\frac{1}{9}$ | $\frac{1}{9}$ | $\frac{1}{9}$ | $\frac{1}{9}$ | $\frac{1}{9}$ | $\frac{1}{9}$ | $\frac{1}{9}$ | $\frac{1}{9}$ | | | |

| $\frac{1}{10}$ | $\frac{1}{10}$ | $\frac{1}{10}$ | $\frac{1}{10}$ | $\frac{1}{10}$ | $\frac{1}{10}$ | $\frac{1}{10}$ | $\frac{1}{10}$ | $\frac{1}{10}$ | $\frac{1}{10}$ | | |

| $\frac{1}{12}$ | $\frac{1}{12}$ | $\frac{1}{12}$ | $\frac{1}{12}$ | $\frac{1}{12}$ | $\frac{1}{12}$ | $\frac{1}{12}$ | $\frac{1}{12}$ | $\frac{1}{12}$ | $\frac{1}{12}$ | $\frac{1}{12}$ | $\frac{1}{12}$ |

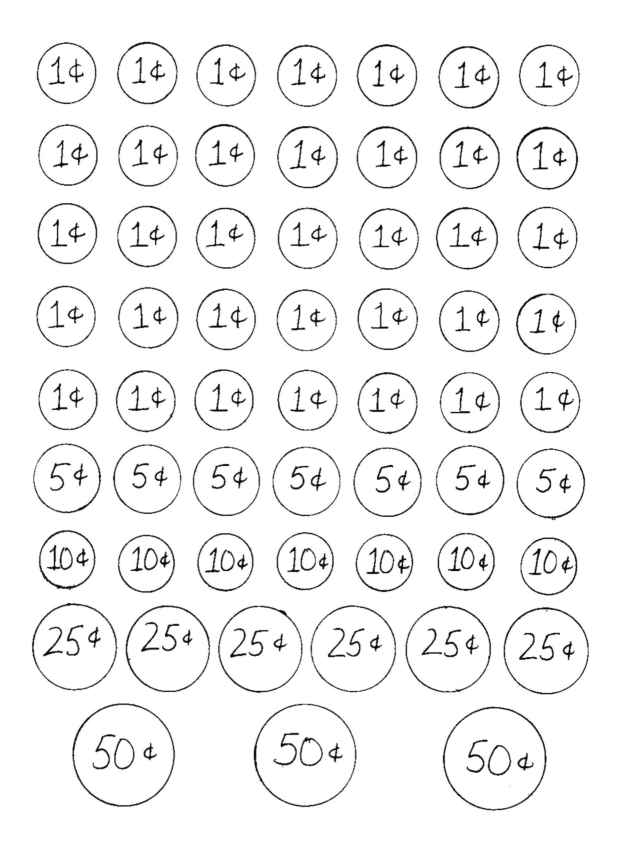

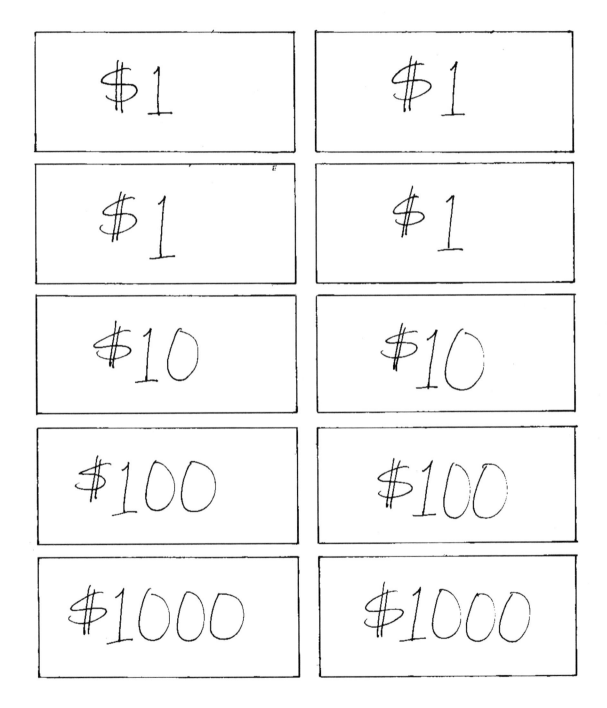

Date	Check Number	Written To	Amount	Deposit	Tax	Balance

Juan and Maria Torres   151

_____ 19 ____

PAY TO THE
ORDER OF _____ $ _____

_____ Dollars

Hometown Bank

For _____   _____

155: Map of United States

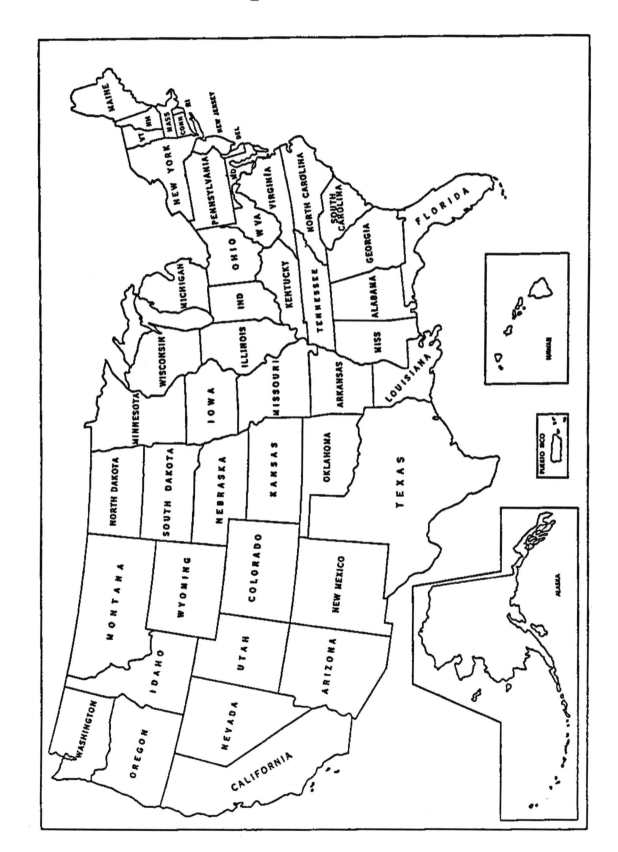

References

Ball, W. W. Rouse. *A Short Account of the History of Mathematics.* New York: Dover Publications, Inc., 1960.

Baroody, Arthur J. *Children's Mathematical Thinking.* New York: Teachers College, Columbia University, 1987.

Baum, Susan, Robert K. Gable, and Karen List. *Chi Square Pie Charts and Me.* Unionville, NY: Trillium Press, 1987.

Hatfield, Mary M., Nancy Tanner Edwards, and Gary G. Bitter. *Mathematics Methods for the Elementary and Middle School.* Boston: Allyn and Bacon, 1993.

Heddens, James W. and William R. Speer. *Today's Mathematics.* New York: Macmillan Publishing Company, 1992.

Helton, Sonia M. *Math Activities for Every Month of the School Year.* West Nyack, NY: The Center for Applied Research in Education, 1991.

Helton, Sonia M. *Ready-to-Use Math Activities for Primary Children.* West Nyack, NY: The Center for Applied Research in Education, 1993.

Jones, Roger S. *Physics for the Rest of Us.* Chicago, IL: Contemporary Books, 1992.

Kamii, Constance. *Young Children Continue to Reinvent Arithmetic—2nd Grade.* New York: Teachers College, Columbia University, 1989.

Krulik, Stephen and Jesse A. Rudnick. *Problem Solving: A Handbook for Elementary School Teachers.* Boston: Allyn and Bacon, 1988.

Krulik, Stephen and Jesse A. Rudnick. *Problem Solving: A Handbook for Teachers.* Boston: Allyn and Bacon, 1980.

Muschla, Judith A. and Gary Robert Muschla. *The Math Teacher's Book of Lists.* Englewood Cliffs, NJ: Prentice Hall, 1995.

Overholt, James L., Jane B. Rincon, and Constance A. Ryan. *Math Problem Solving for Grades 4 through 8.* Boston: Allyn and Bacon, 1984.

Piaget, Jean and Barbel Inhelder. *The Child's Conception of Space.* New York: W. W. Norton, 1948.

Post, Thomas R. ed. *Teaching Mathematics in Grades K-8: Research-Based Methods.* 2nd ed. Boston: Allyn and Bacon, 1992.

Riedesel, C. Alan, James E. Schwartz, and Douglas H. Clements. *Teaching Elementary School Mathematics.* Boston: Allyn and Bacon, 1996.

Shubnikov, A. V. and V. A. Koptsik. *Symmetry in Science and Art.* New York: Plenum Press, 1974.

Slater, Robert. *Portraits in Silicon.* Cambridge, MA: The MIT Press, 1987.

Smith, D. E. *History of Mathematics, Volume I.* New York: Dover Publications, Inc., 1951.

Smith, D. E. *History of Mathematics, Volume II.* New York: Dover Publications, Inc., 1951.

Thiessen, Diane and Margaret Wild. *The Elementary Math Teacher's Handbook of Activities for Teaching Elementary School Mathematics.* New York: John Wiley and Sons, 1982.

Troutman, Andria P. and Betty K. Lichtenberg. *Mathematics: A Good Beginning.* New York: Brooks/Cole Publishing Company, 1995.

Van De Walle, John A. *Elementary School Mathematics: Teaching Developmentally.* New York: Longman, 1994.

Answer Key

Section 1: Standards and Methodologies Worksheet

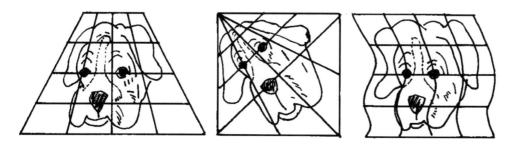

Section 2: Beginning Mathematics Worksheet

Section 3: Geometry Worksheet—The perimeter of the figure is approximately 50 units.

Section 4: Numeration and Counting Worksheet—Dots should be connected from numbers 1 to 46 and missing numbers should be filled in (6, 10, 13, 17, 21, 27, 31, 32, 33, 35, 38, 39, 40, 41, 45).

Section 5: Basic Operations Worksheet—The response depends on your class size. For example, if there are 20 students in your class, you would get the following answers: 22, 44, 352, 70 and remainder 2, 72 is not evenly divisible by 5.

Section 6: Number Theory—

$24 = 2 \times 2 \times 2 \times 3$

$72 = 2 \times 2 \times 2 \times 3 \times 3$

$7 = $ prime number or 1×7

$49 = 7 \times 7$

$35 = 7 \times 5$

Section 7: Fractions Worksheet—Drawings will vary with each child.

Section 8: Decimals Worksheet—

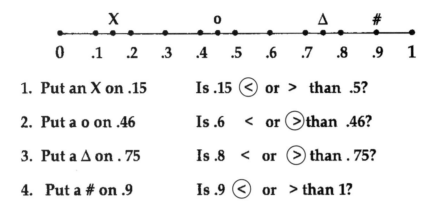

1. Put an X on .15   Is .15 ⓐ or > than .5?

2. Put a o on .46   Is .6   < or ⓑ than .46?

3. Put a Δ on . 75   Is .8 < or ⓒ than . 75?

4. Put a # on .9   Is .9 ⓐ or > than 1?

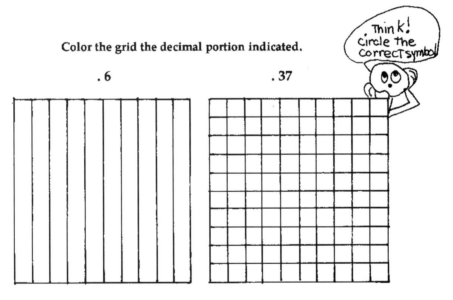

Color the grid the decimal portion indicated.

.6   . 37

Section 9: Measurement—20 cents, 1 dollar, 2 inches.

Section 10: Probability and Statistics Worksheet—The probability is 1 out of 64 or 1:64.

Section 11: Pre-Algebra Worksheet—Drawings should all be the same for each child.

Section 12: Problem Solving Worksheet—10, 8 (10–2), 12 (4 × 3)

Section 13: Technology Worksheet—1. Monitor, 2. Screen, 3. Disk Drive, 4. Hard Drive, 5. CD Drive, 6. Mouse, 7. Keyboard, 8. Speaker

Section 14: Patterns Worksheet—There are ____ shapes on this pattern. Drawings will vary from each child.

Notes

Notes